GLOBAL REGULATION OF FOREIGN DIRECT INVESTMENT

To Hirut, Hayat and Iman

Global Regulation of Foreign Direct Investment

SHERIF H. SEID
LLB (AAU, DISTINCTION); LLM, PHD (ANU)

Routledge
Taylor & Francis Group
LONDON AND NEW YORK

First published 2002 by Ashgate Publishing

Reissued 2018 by Routledge
2 Park Square, Milton Park, Abingdon, Oxon OX14 4RN
711 Third Avenue, New York, NY 10017, USA

Routledge is an imprint of the Taylor & Francis Group, an informa business

A Library of Congress record exists under LC control number: 2002100900

ISBN 13: 978-1-138-73867-6 (hbk)
ISBN 13: 978-1-138-73864-5 (pbk)
ISBN 13: 978-1-315-18463-0 (ebk)

Contents

PART III: EVALUATION: TOWARDS REGULATED OPENNESS

List of Figures

List of Tables

Preface

Foreign direct investment (FDI) can contribute positively to the economic development of the host country. Foreign investors usually bring capital into the host country, thereby influencing the quality and quantity of capital formation in the host country. The inflow of capital and reinvestment of profits increases the total savings of the country and the tax revenue of the Government. FDI can also increase the level of economic activity and social wellbeing in the host country. It can replace inferior production functions in developing countries with superior ones through the transfer of technology, managerial and marketing skills, market information, organisational experience, innovation in products and production techniques, and the training of workers. Moreover, FDI can increase competition in an industry with a likely improvement in productivity. FDI can also widen the market for host country producers by linking the host country industry more closely to world markets, leading to even greater competition and opportunities to technology.

However, if prudent regulatory mechanisms are not in place, FDI may not always be beneficial to the host country. It can, for example, cause considerable environmental damage. In some cases such environmental destruction has led to major social unrest, including calls for secession and civil war (e.g. Bougainville). Some foreign investors may even seek investment in a developing country to escape the burden and costs of stringent environmental regulations in their home countries. Multinational corporations (MNCs) may also involve themselves in transfer pricing, thereby negatively affecting the host government's tax revenue. Moreover, there have been instances where foreign MNCs were involved in internal political affairs of host countries, causing civil unrest and political instability in the host country (e.g. Chile).

After the failure of the Multilateral Agreement on Investment (MAI), the world does not have a global investment agreement that would regulate FDI. A global investment agreement dealing with FDI would clearly fill a large gap in the network of regulatory measures governing the world economy. Other attempts had been made prior to the MAI to address this problem, but all have failed so far. The main reason for such failures has always been the lack of compromise in the positions held by the major stakeholders. This book analyses the pros and cons of these opposing positions and uses them as a basis for forging a hybrid model called

"Regulated Openness". This hybridity is thus grounded in compromise and pragmatism. But it is a principled pragmatism in two ways. First, the book analyses the weaknesses and strengths of the positions of all the key players in the FDI debate in search of a marriage of these positions where the strengths of one might cover the weaknesses of the other. Second, the book defends a method motivated by the question: What is the best kind of FDI agreement from the starting point of the reality of the key players' present positions? This is seen as more productive method than crafting a model from purely analytic foundations that would not apply to any existing world because it would abstract from real positions of real players. In the method applied here, the role of analytic economics, for example, is still important, yet mostly limited to uncovering the weaknesses and strengths of extant economic postures in global politics.

The key players whose positions are described and diagnosed in this book are the OECD and its members, developing countries, public interest groups and representatives of the business community, and international organisations. The method used to collect these data were interviews, cyber observation, attendance of conferences, observation of negotiations and literature review.

Regulated openness is a compromise where the concerns of each major stakeholder would be addressed adequately. It has procedural and substantive dimensions. Procedurally, it is a process where all major stakeholders would have an input and role in the preparation and implementation of FDI laws. A binding international framework agreement on principles is a more pragmatic solution than comprehensive rules. Once the framework agreement of core principles has been formed, each country would have its own detailed rules consistent with the internationally agreed principles and the priorities of individual countries. Substantively, regulated openness means an investment regime where both regulation and openness co-exist in a balanced and pragmatic manner. This balance and co-existence could be achieved within a framework of internationally agreed core principles rather than detailed comprehensive rules. The core principles will be those principles which major stakeholders would regard as paramount, namely sustainable development, enhanced openness of markets, investment security, core labour standards, consumer protection and business ethics, good governance and effective dispute settlement. Moreover, host countries would commit themselves to continuously improve their openness policies as their domestic capability improves and as the guarantees they can secure under the other core principles strengthens.

Regulated openness aims at bringing development with justice. Development with justice requires both procedural justice and credible commitment to continuous improvement of the openness of investment policy, investment security, sustainable development, core labour standards, consumer protection, business ethics and good governance. A commitment to continuously improve these concerns is a path for development with justice. As such, it is a path to politically sustainable liberalisation, as distinct from the politically disastrous trajectory of the MAI. Through seeing why the MAI failed, as an exclusionary agreement that cloaked discrimination against domestic investors as non-discrimination against FDI, we might grasp how regulated openness could succeed. We also grasp how the seeds of the unsettling of the Millennium Round of the

World Trade Organisation (WTO) were sown by the NGO and developing country campaign against the MAI. What they ushered in was perhaps a new era when the powerless have some capacity to scuttle the plans of the powerful for the commanding heights of the world economy.

Sherif H. Seid
March 2002

Acknowledgments

I am indebted to a number of people who have contributed to the success of this book either directly or indirectly. First and foremost, I would like to Professor John Braithwaite for his advice, inspiration, comments, extraordinary support and commitment for the project. I would also like to thank Dr. Peter Drahos his very useful comments and extraordinary support. John and Peter have been cardinal for the successful completion of, first, my PhD course, and then this book. Some draft Chapters of the book have benefited from the useful comments of Professor Don Greig, for which I am grateful. I am also thankful to the various people who volunteered to be interviewed during my field research.

The support of the Law Program, Research School of Social Sciences was very important for the completion of my study and the book. I am particularly grateful to Professor Peter Cane, Head of the Program, and Ms Chris Treadwell for their administrative support. I would also like to thank Nathan Harris and Jennifer Balint for their companionship.

Finally, I am greatly indebted to my wife, Hirut Yigezu for giving me much needed support and encouragement throughout my course of study and the writing of the book, even in the most difficult times. Because of her, I shall always remember with pleasure the time I spent writing this book. My gratitude should also go to my beloved children, Hayat and Iman for giving me much of their leisure time as their contribution to my success.

List of Laws, Agreements and Conventions

Agreement between the Belgio-Luxemburg Economic Union and the Government of the Republic of Korea, Signed on December 20, 1974.

Agreement on Economic Cooperation between the Government of the Kingdom of the Netherlands and the Republic of Uganda.

APEC Non-Binding Investment Principles.

Broadcasting and Services Act 1992 (of Australia).

Compensation (Prohibition of Foreign Proceedings) Act 1995, of Papua New Guinea.

Convention on the Settlement of Investment Disputes between States and Nationals of Other States.

Defence Authorisation Act of 1993 (United States).

Foreign Investment Act 1990 (of Namibia).

Foreign Investment and Technology Act, 2038 (of Nepal).

General Agreement on Trade in Services (GATS).

Investment Code, 1991 (of Uganda).

Investment Incentives Council of Ministers Regulation No. 7/1996 (of Ethiopia).

Investment Law No. 230 for 1989 (of Egypt).

Law on Foreign Investment, 1987 (of Vietnam).

The American Pre-eminence Act of 1991.

The Commercial Fishing Industry Vessel Anti-reflagging Act of 1987 (United States).

The Convention Establishing the Multilateral Investment Guarantee Agency.

The Cuban Liberty and Democratic Solidarity Act of 1996 (United States).

The Defence Application Act of 1993 (United States).

The Federal Power Act (United States).

The Geothermal Steam Act (United States).

The National Cooperation Production Act of 1993 (United States).

The National Investment (Promotion and Protection) Act, 1990 (of Tanzania).

The North American Free Trade Agreement (NAFTA).

The Nuclear Energy Act (United States).

WTO Agreement on Trade Related Investment Measures (TRIMS).

Acronyms

ABC	Australian Broadcasting Corporation
ACA	Australian Consumers Association
ACCC	Australian Consumers and Competition Commission
ACP	Asia-Carribean-Pacific
APEC	Asia-Pacific Economic Cooperation
ASEAN	Association of East Asian Nations
BIAC	Business and Industry Advisory Council of the OECD
BIT	Bilateral Investment Treaty
CEO	Corporate Europe Observatory
CI	Consumers International
CIS	Commonwealth of Independent States
CNT	Conditional National Treatment
CUTS	Consumer and Unity Trust Organisation
EC	European Commission
ECOSOC	UN Economic and Social Council
EPZ	Export Processing Zone
FDI	Foreign Direct Investment
FIAS	Foreign Investment Advisory Service
G7	Group of Seven
GATS	General Agreement on Trade in Services
GDP	Gross Domestic Product
GNP	Gross National Product
GPS	Generalised System of Preferences
IBRD	International Bank for Reconstruction and Development
ICC	International Chamber of Commerce
ICFTU	International Confederation of Free Trade Unions
ICSID	The International Centre for the Settlement of Investment Disputes
ICSIR	Indian Council of Scientific and Industrial Research
IDA	International Development Association
ILM	International Legal Material
ILO	International Labour Organisation
IMCB	International Medical Commission on Bhopal

IMF	International Monetary Fund
IOCU	International Organisation for Consumer Union
ITO	International Trade Organisation
LIBERTAD	Cuban Liberty and Democratic Solidarity Act of 1996
M&A	Merger and Acquisition
MAI	Multilateral Agreement on Investment
MFN	Most-Favoured-Nation Treatment
MIC	Methyl Iso-Cyanate
MIGA	Multilateral Investment Guarantee Agency
MNCs	Multinational Corporations
MNE	Multinational Enterprise
NAFTA	North American Free Trade Agreement
NEP	New Economic Policy
NGO	Non-Governmental Organisation
NT	National Treatment
OECD	Organisation for Economic Cooperation and Development
OPEC	Organisation of Petroleum Exporting Countries
OTML	Ok Tedi Mining Limited
PCIJ	Permanent Court of International Justice
PNG	Papua New Guinea
R&D	Research and Development
RBP	Restrictive Business Practice
TNC	Trans-National Corporation
TRIMs	Trade-Related Investment Measures
TRIPS	Trade-Related Aspects of Intellectual Property Rights
TUAC	Trade Union Advisory Council of the OECD
UCC	Union Carbide Corporation
UK	United Kingdom
UN	United Nations
UNCITRAL	International Commission of International Trade Law
UNCTAD	United Nations Conference on Trade and Development
UNCTC	United Nations Centre for Transnational Corporations
UNEP	United Nations Environment Programme
UNICE	Union of Industrial and Employers' Confederations of Europe
UNIDO	United Nations Industrial Development Organisation
US	United States of America
USTR	United States Trade Representative
WGTI	Working Group on Trade and Investment
WTO	World Trade Organisation
WWF	World Wide Fund for Nature

Part I
The Theory of Foreign Direct Investment: The Law of FDI

Chapter 1

Introduction

Foreign Direct Investment (FDI) plays a significant role in the development process of most economies, and today it has become an integral part of higher living standards and economic prosperity. FDI is also a key determinant of trade since a large percentage of trade occurs between affiliated companies. According to the United Nations Conference on Trade and Development (UNCTAD), trade within MNCs and arms length trade associated with MNCs are estimated to account, together, for two-thirds of world trade, and intra-firm trade alone, for one-third (UNCTAD, 1999). A large number of countries around the world spend enormous resources and time in designing and implementing policies that would attract FDI to their respective territories.

Foreign investment enables investors to look beyond the constraints of their domestic investment environment and gain access to resources and bigger markets, and maximise investment returns. However, such transnational activities pose unique challenges to national governments (in addition to the opportunities they bring with them). Multinationally located and transnationally integrated company operations would give MNCs more independence from a national government's policy directions (particularly when the host country is a small, developing nation). During the 1960s and 1970s, several clashes arose between MNCs and host governments, and between host and home governments of these companies, over a range of regulatory issues affecting MNC operations.

This book analyses the regulation of FDI both nationally and internationally and the problems associated with it. It also proposes a pragmatic global regulatory framework that would solve the current stalemate on a multilateral investment agreement. The book is divided into three major parts.

Part One

The first part consists of three further chapters. Chapter Two discusses the theories that have had major influence in the past decades on national and international investment regulation. These theories are neo-classical economic theory, dependency theory and the theories of state intervention in economic activity. As the discussion in Part II will show, these theories, particularly neo-classical economics and theories of state intervention in economic development seem to have a major influence in the positions and strategies of the key international players. Therefore, each of these theories will be examined briefly in Chapter Two, and their impact on national and international rule making on FDI will be assessed. The benefits FDI brings to the host economy and its possible negativities will also be examined in light of these theories. The role of the State in addressing market failures and the pros and cons of state intervention will be analysed.

Chapter Three analyses the scope of coverage and weaknesses/strengths of the current rules on FDI. The current rules on FDI can be broadly categorised as national, bilateral and multilateral. The multilateral rules can be further classified as regional/sectoral and global. National laws set the rules for the establishment, operation and liquidation of business enterprises. Although broader in scope, national laws have geographical limits in their applicability. Whatever international arrangements we have at the moment, their scope is limited either geographically or in scope. Moreover, the diversity of national and international legal regimes governing FDI would introduce excessive distortions as between countries and sectors (Fatouros, 1996: 59). Chapter Two examines all of these issues in detail and puts a case for global investment rules/principles.

Chapter Four discusses the methodology used in this research. Multiple methods have been developed, and Chapter Four explains them all.

Part Two

The second part of the book consists of four chapters that examine the strategies of the key international players for global FDI regulation. The influence of the theories discussed in Chapter One will become more apparent throughout Part II. Chapter Five discusses the strategies of the Organisation for Economic Cooperation and Development (OECD) and OECD countries. Key players among the OECD countries are the US, the EC and Japan. The Chapter also examines the Multilateral Agreement on Investment (MAI) in detail, from its inception to its eventual burial.[1] The MAI was negotiated exclusively by OECD countries, and largely in secrecy. The intention was to invite other countries to sign once an Agreement has been reached among OECD states. Although OECD countries as a group hoped that the MAI would remove barriers to market access and enhance the liberalisation of investment rules, each of the three main players within the group had their own distinct priorities when they first decided to start negotiating the Agreement. This Chapter, therefore, examines the policies and strategies of the three major players. The contents of the MAI will be analysed in detail. The reasons for and the forces behind the MAI's failure to materialise will also be discussed.

Chapter Six discusses the strategies of developing countries for a global investment regime. The key players in developing countries do not have a common strategy for a global investment regime at this point in time. Their views are divided on whether to have such a regime in the first place, secondly on the appropriate forum for the negotiation and implementation of such a regime, and thirdly on the nature and emphasis of the regime, should a decision be made to have one. Their views were also divided on the extension of the MAI to non-OECD countries. Most developing countries generally accept that FDI could make big contributions to their development efforts. There is however concern that, when the major interests of MNCs and host States are in conflict, MNCs may use their muscle as well as the influence of their home countries to interfere in the domestic affairs of weaker host countries. Moreover, a global framework that would allow foreign investors to take the host country to international tribunals without the latter's consent is seen as a measure that would severely erode the sovereignty of host nations. It is therefore argued that FDI could only be beneficial to host economies if host countries can regulate and direct it according to their development objectives. The model of agreement proposed by the proponents of the MAI was opposed by many developing countries partly because it required host countries to give up their right to adopt a selective approach to foreign investment to promote their chosen development strategy. Moreover, any proposal that would give rights and protection to foreign investors, but not corresponding obligations would not be acceptable to these countries. The question of venue has also been as controversial as the substantive content of the future agreement itself. While there are some developing countries that want to negotiate the global agreement within the framework of the World Trade Organisation (WTO), others reject this and propose that the UNCTAD would be the appropriate forum. Chapter Six examines all of these issues in detail.

Chapter Seven discusses the strategies and positions of social movements (such as consumer, environmental and labour movements) and key international business associations (such as the International Chamber of Commerce and the Business and Industry Advisory Council of the OECD for global investment rules. International non-governmental organisations (NGOs) play key roles in shaping international rules and institutions (Braithwaite and Drahos, 2000). If the strategies they followed and the positions they took during the MAI debate are of any indication, consumer advocates, environmentalists and labour unions have commonality on most of the issues regarding FDI regulation, while business representatives stand on the opposite side. The first three groups formed a broad coalition in their stand against the MAI and unleashed a rigorous campaign to kill it. Business representatives largely gave strong backing to the MAI, to the extent of being accused of initiating and driving the negotiation process.

Despite the potentially positive contributions of FDI, consumer advocates, environmentalists and labour unions fear that because of their economic power and, in some instances, lack of accountability to host countries, MNCs have the potential to limit competition and force consumers to face less choice and higher prices. They also fear that MNCs could trigger the lowering of environmental, labour and other standards as host countries compete to attract foreign investors to their territories; or they may behave unethically by, for example, artificially avoiding taxes or indulging in corrupt practices. The business community largely supports an international investment regime because they believe that such a regime could be a tool for greater market access and better predictability of rules. Chapter Seven examines all of these issues in detail.

Chapter Eight discusses the roles of the major inter-governmental organisations in the process of making rules for FDI, since international organisations play significant roles in shaping the global regulatory regime. The organisations covered in the discussion are the United Nations, the WTO, the World Bank and the Asia-Pacific Economic Cooperation (APEC). The United Nations has played significant role in the debate about global investment rules. The UN was involved in facilitating the drafting of a Code of Conduct for MNCs until the early 1990s. Since then, it has also been active in the debate through UNCTAD. The WTO too is involved in the debate about global investment rules and, in fact, regulates FDI in a limited way. For examples, the Agreement on Trade-Related Investment Measures (TRIMS) deals with investment measures that have prohibitive effects upon trade in goods. One of the purposes of the World Bank as enshrined in its Article of Agreement is "to promote private foreign investment". Three other institutions created under the Bank's auspices complement its operations in support of the promotion of foreign investment. These institutions are the International Finance Corporation (IFC), the International Centre for the Settlement of Investment Disputes (ICSID), the Multilateral Investment Guarantee Agency (MIGA). In addition, in 1992, the World Bank adopted a set of non-binding Guidelines for the treatment of FDI. The regional organisation APEC, too, has adopted non-binding guidelines for the treatment of foreign investment in the Asia-Pacific region. Although some success has been seen at regional levels, none of the global organisations have so far succeeded in developing a comprehensive global investment regime acceptable to all countries. Several attempts to develop such a regime in the past have failed. The issues surrounding all of these activities will be discussed in detail in Chapter Eight.

Part Three

The third part consists of three chapters that evaluate the strategies of the key players and proposes a pragmatic regulatory framework. Developed countries, multilateral financial institutions like the IMF and World Bank, business groups and some developing countries advance the idea of having a more liberal regime at both global and national levels. Other developing countries and various NGOs, such as consumer organisations, environmental activists and the labour movement, on the other hand, see danger in an extensive liberalisation of investment rules and argue that what is needed is regulation. Chapter Nine evaluates these positions. It attempts to highlight the cons and pros of both excessive liberalisation and excessive regulation. Moreover, the implications of the Multilateral Agreement on Investment (MAI) will be discussed.

Chapter Ten explores an alternative approach in the regulation of FDI, called "regulated openness", which is a pragmatic and hedged model that seeks to preserve the strengths and cover the shortcomings uncovered in the regulatory models of the different players. It starts by asserting that the current approach in attempting to formulate an international regime for FDI has serious flaws, both in the manner negotiations are conducted and the substantive content of the rules. It then proposes a middle-ground position called "regulated openness", where the interests and concerns of all major international players could be accommodated in a balanced and pragmatic way, both regarding the manner in which the negotiations would be conducted and the substantive content of the rules. The Chapter consists of two major parts. The first discusses the structure of the principles/rules under "regulated openness", both at the international and national levels, and the content of the principles/rules at the international level. The second part covers the process of negotiating the international agreement, venue, and implementation of the rules.

Chapter Eleven summarises the entire book and draws conclusions about the contribution the ideas in this book could make in the debate on global investment rules.

Notes

1 The MAI is a draft investment agreement that had been negotiated by the OECD countries from April 1995 to May 1998 under the sponsorship of the OECD Secretariat. The negotiation was planned to be completed in April 1997 initially, but later the deadline was extended to April 1998. Because of the enormous controversy it generated both within the OECD grouping and around the world, the negotiation was suspended indefinitely in May 1998 and the Agreement has not been signed as of this date.

Chapter 2

FDI Theories and the Role of the State

Theories, economic or otherwise, play an important role in shaping legal attitudes. With regard to FDI, the theories discussed in this Chapter seem to have played a dominant role in shaping the legal regimes both nationally and internationally. These are neoclassical economic theory, dependency theory, and theories of state intervention in economic development

Neo-classical economic theory is the main driving force behind the global push for the liberalisation of trading and investment regimes. As such, it has played (and is playing) a significant role in the debate about global investment rules. Dependency theory, on the other hand, seems to be losing its influence in global rule making, but it has been a significant force in the rule making process so far, as the anti-book of neo-classical economics. However, the various theories on the benefits of State-intervention in the marketplace seem to be replacing dependency theory in the contemporary debate on global FDI rules. This Chapter will traverse a brief overview of all of these theories.

Neo-classical Economic Theory on FDI

The definition of neoclassical economics is not perfectly clear. It has meant different things to different writers. These different meanings include: the subjective marginal utility theory of the 1870s and beyond; the economics of Alfred Marshall (Marshall, 1879); the work of twentieth century writers in the tradition established by Marshall and some others; some combination of the foregoing; and the Samuelsonian synbook of price and resource allocation theory with Keynesian macroeconomics (Kennings and Samuels, 1999: 3).

Neoclassicism has also had a variety of technical meanings as to its central problem: "the mechanics of utility, price determination or operation of price mechanism, the working of free enterprise system, the operation of pure markets, the mechanics of the pure theory or logic of choice, constrained maximisation decision making, the allocation of resources, and so on" (Kennings and Samuels,

1999: 3). This study does not attempt to discuss the neoclassical school of economic thought in detail. Rather, the attempt will only be to discuss the position the school takes FDI.

Neoclassical economic theory propounds that FDI contributes positively to the economic development of the host country (Bergten et al, 1978: 355). There are several factors that are relied on to support this view. One such factor is that foreign investors usually bring capital into the host country, thereby influencing the quality and quantity of capital formation in the host country. The inflow of capital and reinvestment of profits increases the total savings of the country. Government revenue increases via tax and other payments (Bureau of Industry Economics, 1995: 7). The fact that foreign capital is brought into the host country also ensures that domestic capital available for use could be redirected to other uses (Sornarajah, 1994: 38). Moreover, the infusion of foreign capital into the host economy reduces the balance of payments constraints of the host country. In general, FDI increases the level of economic activity, and hence the level of social wellbeing.

The other principal argument in favour of the neoclassical theory is that FDI, particularly in developing countries, plays the role of a "tutor". It replaces the inferior production function in developing countries by a superior one from advanced industrialised countries through the transfer of technology, managerial and marketing skills, market information, organisational experience, innovation in products and production techniques, and the training of workers (Kojima, 1978: 152). Particularly multinational corporations (MNCs) are regarded as useful agents for the international transfer of technology and knowledge.

High technology MNCs generally prefer to service foreign markets through wholly owned subsidiaries to ensure that their patent and trademark rights are honoured and that the quality control associated with their well-established brand names is safeguarded (UNCTAD, 1996). Also, MNCs can have greater flexibility in minimising their global tax liabilities if they own their foreign affiliates. One of the most effective ways through which MNCs transfer knowhow and technology to other countries is therefore through their foreign affiliates (UNCTAD, 1993: 176). Moreover, although investors generally seek to protect their technology and knowhow in order to exploit their firm-specific advantage, over time it leaks to other firms through the movement of staff, formal and informal communication networks among professionals, input suppliers, and customers and joint venture partners (Bureau of Industry Economics, 1995: 9). The host country benefits from these transfers without directly compensating the investor.

While MNCs, through their foreign affiliates, can serve as the primary channel for the transfer of technology from industrially developed to developing countries, the welfare gains to the latter of adopting technologies depends largely upon the extent to which these innovations are diffused locally and prices are reduced. According to Antonelli, the cost of adoption is affected by the following five factors (Antonelli, 1991):

- the availability of information about the technology from other users;

- the availability of trained and skilled manpower;
- the availability of technical assistance and maintenance;
- the availability of complementary equipment and software;
- the availability of complementary innovations, both technological and organisational.

In developing countries all of these factors are likely to be relatively scarce and, hence, the cost of adopting a new technology could be high.

The proponents of neoclassical theory further argue that FDI increases competition in an industry with a likely improvement in productivity (Kojima, 1978: 153; Bureau of Industry Economics, 1995: 7). Increased competition can lead to reallocation of resources to more productive activity across the economy, reduction of overmanning, efficient utilisation of capital, and removal of poor management practices. FDI can also widen the market for host country producers by linking the host country industry more closely to world markets, leading to even greater competition and opportunities to technology transfer (Bureau of Industry Economics, 1995: 7).

Finally, it is said that FDI generates employment, influences favourably the distribution of income and power within the host country, and generates foreign exchange thereby easing the balance of payments constraints of the host country (Reuber et al, 1973: 22; Sornarajah, 1994: 38; Bergten 1978: 355). Infrastructure facilities would be built or upgraded by or for the foreign investor and these facilities would be to the general benefit of the economy (Sornarajah, 1994: 38-39). According to the important and controversial World Bank *East Asian Miracle* report, eight South East Asian countries have grown at the rate of three times that of Latin America and East Asia, and five times that of Sub-Saharan Africa (World Bank, 1993: 2). The proportion of people living in absolute poverty in these countries dropped, for example, from 58% in 1960 to 17% in 1990 in Indonesia, and from 37% to less than 5% in Malaysia during the same period (World Bank, 1993: 4-5). Life expectancy increased from 56 years in 1960 to 71 years in 1990 (World Bank, 1993: 4). Even though it is argued that private domestic investment and rapidly growing human capital, together with sound development policy, were the principal engines of the growth in these countries, FDI has also played a significant role. All of these economies flourished with the help of foreign technology and the majority of them welcomed FDI that came with technical and managerial skills (World Bank, 1993: 351). The benefits these countries derived from FDI was summarised by the former Prime Minister of Singapore, Lee Kwan Yew, as follows:

> ...when Singaporeans went into joint ventures with US, European and Japanese foreign entrepreneurs who provided the know-how, the experience, and the marketing, their casualty [failure] rate went down from 38 percent to 7 percent, just 1 percent higher than the 6 percent failure rate of the wholly foreign enterprises. When Singaporeans have less advanced partners from Hong Kong and Taiwan, their failure rate was 17 percent...For Singapore entrepreneurs to go into

> industry when their past experience has been in entrepot trading, the least hazardous way is to choose an experienced and expert guide.[1]

The neoclassical theory has played a major role in influencing the underlying principles of international law on foreign investment. Most bilateral investment treaties state the belief that foreign investment flows between the parties would encourage the development of their economies. They affirm that such investment would bring the economic prosperity of the contracting parties.[2] The documents sponsored by the World Bank also are based on the neoclassical economic theory. The Guidelines on the Treatment of Foreign Direct Investment, for example, incorporates the neoclassical theory when it recognises:

> ...that a greater flow of direct investment brings substantial benefits to bear on the world economy and on the economies of the developing countries in particular, in terms of improving the long term efficiency of the host country through greater competition, transfer of capital, technology and managerial skills and enhancement of market access and in terms of the expansion of international trade.[3]

Furthermore, the Convention establishing the International for the Settlement of Investment Disputes (ICSID) also states that provision for the settlement of investment disputes will increase flows of foreign investment which are beneficial to the economic development of the host country.[4] Furthermore, one of the objectives of the Multinational Investment Guarantee Agency (MIGA), an Organisation which devises a scheme for the insurance of non-commercial risks in respect of foreign investment, is "to encourage the flow of investment for productive purposes among member countries" (MIGA Convention, Article 2).

Neoclassical theory has also influenced the thinking of several arbitral tribunals. In Amco v Indonesia, for example, the Tribunal said that "...to protect investments is to protect the general interest of development and developing countries" (ICSID, 1984). The theory has influenced Economic Development Agreements (EDA) too. One of the arguments for the protection of EDAs through the use of international law is, for example, based on the neoclassical theory on FDI. In the dispute between Revere Jamaica Aluminium Ltd. (RJA) v Jamaica, the Tribunal stated:

> ...RJA brought to Jamaica technical assistance and training and assumed a real importance in the development of the country; roads, housing and other facilities were built; and the project became closely associated with the economic and social progress of Jamaica... (Revere Copper and Brass Inc. v. Overseas Private Investment Corporation).

The positive effects of FDI stated by the proponents of the neoclassical theory have been countered by opponents of the theory. It is said, for example, that the technology that is brought into the developing host country is usually outdated or capital intensive, thus not satisfying their needs. It is argued that one of the reasons for a company to invest in another country is that the product cycle for the goods it manufactured in its home country had been replaced by other goods incorporating newer technology (Vernon, 1966: 80). The older product with the older technology is then moved to the developing host country (Sornarajah, 1994: 40) because the developing country would have a comparative advantage in the older product line. Such older technologies sometimes have inferior safety standards that could endanger the lives of millions of people in the host country. As regards the building of infrastructure, it is said that usually the beneficiaries are "the elite who can afford to live according to the standards of the foreigners and pay sufficiently to enjoy the same educational and health facilities enjoyed by the foreign nationals working for multinational corporations" (Sornarajah, 1994: 40).[5] FDI is also accused of increasing unemployment or not generating significant employment by using capital-intensive techniques designed for developed economies, rather that Labour-intensive techniques believed to be more appropriate for developing countries (Bergten et al, 1978: 358).

Indeed, if the proper regulatory mechanisms are not in place, FDI may not be beneficial to the host country. It can, for example, cause considerable environmental damage that includes pollution of rivers and ground water, damage to fishing and farming, disruption of local population and damage to the health of workers and local population.[6] The US-Mexico border is an example of the potential environmental damage FDI can bring to a country with weak regulatory structures:

> Mexican border towns have become garbage dumps for millions of barrels of benzine solvents, pesticides, raw sewage and battery acid spewed out by foreign owned [companies]. The companies also dump toxins into land fills, rivers, populated canyons and storm drains...Along the Pacific costs near Tijuana and San Diego an estimated 1,000 gallons a second of poisoned water pours into the ocean (Atkinson, 1995: 80).

In some cases such environmental destructions have led to major social unrest, including calls for secession. The experience of Papua New Guinea in connection with the OK Tedi copper mines is a good example of this. Landowners and others in the mining areas long complained about the environmental impact of the mining operations: disposal of cyanide and other hazardous chemicals into the rivers; loss of fish, forests, and wildlife; unstable waste rock dumps and loss of farming land (Smith, 1992: 439). The environmental impact of the Bougainville copper mine was a major factor in the civil was that persisted over more than a decade on the island.

Environmental protection is costly and some multinational companies (as well as some domestic companies) may resist elaborate environmental protection requirements because of their impact on profit. Some may even seek investment in a developing country to escape the burden and costs of the stringent environmental regulations in their home countries (Porter, 1990). In considering its own options for investment, comparative environmental costs or the tightness of environmental regulations between a number of developing countries could well be a factor for a multinational company (Smith, 1992: 439). Some governments, too, that are very keen to attract FDI, are sometimes reluctant to put in place the proper regulatory mechanisms which might deter foreign investors from investing in their countries. But there is a trade-off, in terms of higher incomes. The real question is, therefore, what would be the optimal trade-off between environmental quality and anticipated income. This would, in general, differ across countries.

There are also practices associated with technology transfer that may prevent the host country from fully benefiting from FDI. The technology that is brought in may not be the best, from the particular host country's point of view, for the economic conditions of the host country in question. For example, the use of labour-intensive technology, rather than capital-intensive technology, in a country where unemployment and underemployment are major problems may be more beneficial for the host country. Sometimes foreign investors (as well as some domestic investors) apply hazardous technology with disastrous consequences. The Bhopal disaster in India, caused by a gas leakage in a plant set up by the US company Union Carbide, resulted in enormous damage to life and property (Sornarajah, 1994: 49). There are also instances where restrictive clauses introduced in technology transfer agreements were intended to maximise the benefits to the foreign investor, indirectly hurting the host economy. Some examples of such instances include restrictions on the export of goods manufactured with the technology, requirement that new inventions or adaptations be given over to the transferor, requirements to purchase associated products only from the transferor, and other similar provisions controlling the use of the technology.

MNCs are also sometimes accused of involvement in transfer pricing. The practice involves fixing an artificially high price for an item bought at concessional rates from the parent company. Tax credit would then be claimed on the basis of the artificial price. The effect would be loss of tax revenue for the host government and increased flows of funds out of the host country.[7] This problem could be addressed, at least partly, through tax treaties.

The post-war period was the period where FDI was regarded most favourably in the developed as well as the developing world alike. Both in the newly emerging developing countries as well as war-ravaged Western Europe, the capital, technology, organisational capability, managerial skill and entrepreunership FDI brings with it was highly sought (Kennedy, 1992: 67). Most of those countries believed that FDI could bring substantial benefits to their economies and improve the living standards of their peoples. Accordingly, they accepted FDI with open arms and gave it favourable treatment. At the same time, foreign-owned corporations, particularly American corporations, were seeking to supplement their indigenous supplies (Kennedy, 1992: 67). It seemed, therefore, a perfect partnership between the foreign investors and the host countries throughout the 1950s and early 1960s. By the end of the 1960s, however, the first signs of discontent have began to surface. Figure 2:1, which is about the history of nationalisations, shows these fairly distinct periods.

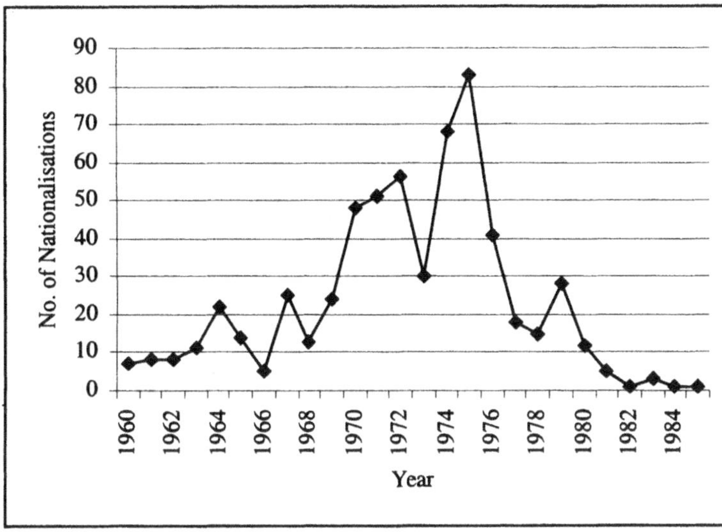

Figure 2:1 Nationalisation by Year

Source The data are taken, with modification in presentation, from C.R. Kennedy, "Relations between Transnational Corporations and Governments of Host countries: a Look to the Future", Transnational Corporations, Vol. 1, No. 1, (1992), p.69.

While in the 1960s and 1970s attitudes towards FDI in most host countries, particularly developing countries, were hostile or sceptical, these attitudes have changed since then and countries are becoming increasingly appreciative of the benefits that can be gained from FDI. Host countries now seem to have learnt from the experiences of the previous period as to how to refine, modify and extend their policies to better harness the contribution of FDI. Among countries that had the fastest economic growth in the past decade, most of them were favourably disposed towards FDI (Dunning, 1993: 558). In fact, it now appears that there is an emerging broad consensus among both developing and developed countries that FDI can hasten economic growth and that any possible adverse effects can be controlled (Shihata, 1991: 488).

Table 2:1 Countries that Conducted Mass Nationalisation

COUNTRY	YEARS	NO. OF FIRMS
Algeria	1965-1978	107
Angola	1975-1978	128
Benin	1974	10
Burma	1962-1983	24
Chile	1970-1973	46
Congo	1970-1977	31
Egypt	1956-1967	70
Ethiopia	1975-1978	105
Guinea	1959-1979	7
India	1967-1975	48
Indonesia	1957-1965	24
Iran	1979-1980	58
Iraq	1968-1977	8
Jamaica	1972-1977	12
Libya	1969-1974	33
Madagascar	1975-1978	50
Morocco	1965-1975	30
Mozambique	1975-1980	43
Nigeria	1967-1974	35
Peru	1968-1975	47
Somalia	1970	10
Sri Lanka	1971-1976	254
Sudan	1970-1978	25
Trinidad & Tobago	1969-1981	10
Uganda	1970	9
Tanzania	1963-1978	27
Yemen	1969-1978	30
Zambia	1964-1980	21
Total		**1404**

Source The data are taken, with slight modification in presentation, from C.R. Kennedy, supra note 4, p.73.

A number of reasons have been suggested for the shift in the attitude of host countries from confrontation to compromise. First, as the administrative, technical and managerial capabilities of host countries increased, they became more confident and sophisticated in their abilities to gain greater economic benefits from FDI without resorting to nationalisation (Kennedy, 1992: 69). Second, the drop in commodity prices in the international market that followed the oil shocks and the rising debt burden placed constraints on developing countries, making regulatory control of FDI a necessary alternative (Kennedy, 1992: 79). Third, as time passed, colonial history became less of an issue and attitudes towards FDI became more pragmatic in the former colonies (Kennedy, 1992: 79). Fourth, MNCs themselves appear to have started to realise that their long-term global strategy can be better achieved by giving emphasis to promoting a more mutually rewarding relationship between host countries and themselves, and not by trying to extract the most economic rent in the short term from their investments (Dunning, 1993: 557).

The success of the Newly Industrialised Economies of South Korea, Taiwan, Hong Kong and Singapore has generally been seen as a model for many developing countries. The experience of these countries (except Hong Kong, which to a large extent has been an open economy) shows that a mix of regulation and openness to FDI may be more beneficial to the host country (Chu, 1989: 647). This seems to be the position being adopted by most developing countries (Lall, 1984: 2-16).

Dependency Theory

We have seen that around the end of the 1960s, the number of nationalisations began to rise, but that activity was most pronounced in the 1970-1979 period (see Figure 2:1 and Table 2:1). The extensive nationalisations of this period were undertaken mainly by a small group of Governments that accounted for nearly two-third of all the acts of nationalisation (Kennedy, 1992: 71). The nationalisations were in all sectors of the economy including banking, natural resources, services and manufacturing (Kennedy, 1992: 71). Dependency theory seems to have played an important role in shaping the attitudes of most of these governments during that period.

Dependency theory is a result of the convergence of two major intellectual trends: one with its background in the Marxist tradition, which in turn contained several theoretical orientations, and the other rooted in the Latin American structuralist discussion on development (Hettne, 1990: 82).[8] Marxism in its classical form was focused on the concept of development and took a basically Eurocentric view (Hettne, 1990: 82). Marx and Engels thought that capitalist development is a process that takes place in a similar fashion in one country after another. Lenin too at first held this view. Later on as it became clear that there was no capitalist development happening in the colonies, he modified the classical view and argued that capitalist transformation was not possible in the Third World under imperialism (Hettne, 1990: 82). The focus of the neo-classical form of Marxism, therefore, shifted from the concept of development to underdevelopment, and from Europe to the Third World.

The other background of dependency theory is, as mentioned above, the indigenous discussion on underdevelopment in various Latin American countries, particularly during the economic crisis of the 1930s. One of the prominent Latin American structuralists, Raul Prebisch, argued that continued reliance on the export of primary products would only consolidate the "peripheral position of the developing country in the world economy" (Hettne, 1990: 85). Even though he supported the promotion of exports, he also argued that a necessary pre-condition for that was a developed industrial base which could only be created through a temporary seclusion (Hettne, 1990: 85).

Some say that dependency ideas have only one origin, that is Marxism. It is said that Marxism had a long tradition in Latin American thought and that the dependency perspective restates Marxist ideas, supplemented by the works of Lenin and others on imperialism, about Latin American developments. Fernando Henrique Cardoso, one of the prominent Latin American dependency theorists, comments on the origin of dependency ideas as follows:

> The analysis of the dependency situation in Latin America done in the second half of the sixties did not represent new methodological propositions. What happened was that a current which was already old in Latin American thought managed to make itself heard in the discussions that were taking place in institutions normally closed to it: ECLA (Economic Commission for Latin America), the universities, some government planning agencies, and the North American academic community... A study of the history of ideas in the twentieth century would show that each generation of critical intellectuals seeks to revive Marxism with a new breadth of life... Studies of dependency, then constitutes part of this constantly renewed effort to reestablish a tradition of analysis of economic structures of domination (Cardoso, 1997: 9-10,17).

The Marxist literature that emerged after World War II advocates that underdevelopment is a continuous process and its principal cause is capitalist penetration (Hettne, 1990: 84). It argues that the development and expansion of the capital exporting countries is (a) necessarily conditioned on the underdevelopment of the capital receiving countries (the periphery), for the periphery is deprived of its economic surplus through mechanisms of imperialist exploitation (Hettne, 1990: 84).

Latin American structuralists, on the other hand, define dependence as a conditioning situation in which the economies of one group of countries are conditioned by the development and expansion of others. Hence, a relationship of interdependence between two or more economies or between such economies and the world trading system becomes a dependent relationship when some countries can expand only as a reflection of the expansion of the dominant countries (Evans, 1979). It is, therefore, argued that any form of development in the dependent country requires the continued acceptance of its products in the centre. Hence, "economic fluctuations in the centre may have severe negative consequences for the periphery, whereas an economic crisis in the periphery offers no real threat to accumulation in the" (Evans, 1979: 26).

Probably the chief feature of the dependency school is its insistence that the most important variable to be studied in order to understand development and underdevelopment of countries is not the internal characteristics of particular countries but the structure of the international system - particularly in its economic aspect. It emphasises that contemporary Southern development or any political or economic change in the South must be understood as aspects of imperialism today and yesterday (Evans, 1979).

Many writers of this school argue that the international system (the whole) is greater than individual states (the part), and the parts operate simply in functionally specific manners having no significant existence separately from the whole. Samir Amin, one of the leading dependency theorists, writes:

> Apart from a few "ethnographic reserves", all contemporary societies are integrated into a world system. Not a single concrete socio-economic formation of our time can be understood except as part of this world system (Amin, 1974: 3).

As a result, underdevelopment was believed to be generated by the very same historical process which also generated economic development: the development of capitalism itself. Neoclassical economists deny this.

Another dependency theorist, Wallerstein, declares that "the only kind of social system is a world-system, which we define quite simply as a unit with a single division of Labor and multiple cultural systems...But if there is no such thing as 'national development'...the proper entity of comparison is the world system... And the only totalities that exist or have existed historically are mini-systems ['simple agricultural or hunting and gathering societies'] and world systems, and in the nineteenth and twentieth centuries there has been only one world-system in existence, the capitalist world economy" (Wallerstein, 1974: 390). In contrast, neoclassical economics begins with individual choice, and studies the consequences of the choices made by individuals, tracing these through the national and global levels.

In explaining the supremacy of the whole over the part, Paul Baran, another prominent dependency theorist, takes India under the British colonial rule as an example and says:

> ...the British administration of India systematically destroyed all the fibers and foundations of Indian society. Its land and taxation policy ruined India's village economy and substituted for it the parasitic landowner and moneylender. Its commercial policy destroyed the Indian artisan and created the infamous slums of the Indian cities filled with millions of starved and diseased paupers. Its economic policy broke down whatever beginnings there were of an indigenous industrial development and promoted the proliferation of speculators, petty businessmen, agents, and sharks of all description...India, if left to herself, might have found in the course of time a shorter and surely less tortuous road toward a better and richer society (Baran, 1962: 149).

When explaining the reasons for the success of Japanese industrialisation, Baran argues that it was because "Japan is the only country in Asia (and in Africa or in Latin America) that escaped being turned into a colony or dependency of Western European or American capitalism, that had a chance of independent national development" (Baran, 1962: 149). But Thailand in Asia and Ethiopia in Africa also escaped colonialism, but have not been successfully industrialised. Moreover, the fact that Japan has initiated a successful attempt to industrialise outside of North America and Europe in the nineteenth century for reasons having to do with forces internal to the country runs counter to Amin's or Wallerstein's argument that independent national development is impossible.

Owing to the different intellectual origins of the notion of dependency, there are several conceptualisations that differ in style, emphasis, disciplinary and ideological preferences. Nevertheless, they all share the basic idea about the interrelated process of development and underdevelopment (Hettne, 1990: 87). The dependency theory concerning development and underdevelopment can, therefore, be summarised as follows (Hettne, 1990: 91):

- the most important obstacles to development are not lack of capital or entrepreneurial skills, but external to the underdeveloped economy;
- a transfer of surplus takes place from the periphery to the centre;
- due to the fact that the periphery is deprived of its surplus, which instead can utilise for development purposes, development in the centre somehow implies underdevelopment in the periphery. Thus development and underdevelopment can be described as two aspects of a single global process;
- since the periphery is doomed to underdevelopment because of its linkage to the centre, it is necessary for a country to "disassociate itself from the world market, to break the chains of surplus extraction, and to strive for national self reliance". The removal of such "external obstacles" facilitates a more or less automatic and endogenous development.

Dependency theory is diametrically opposite to neoclassical theory and takes the view that foreign investment does not produce any meaningful economic development to the host country. It argues that foreign investment suppresses economic growth and increases income inequality in the host country (Rothbeb, 1995: 189). Growth is supposedly slowed for several reasons. One is that FDI is mostly made by MNCs and that MNCs normally devise global policies in the interest of developed countries in which they have their headquarters and shareholders in the home countries. As a result, the home countries of the foreign investor become the central economies and the host countries become peripheral economies serving the interests of the central economies (Sornarajah, 1994: 43; Bennett and Sharpe, 1985). Second, as much as there is an initial inflow of capital, there is subsequent repatriation of capital and profits from the host country. According to some studies, foreign investors in developing countries repatriate twice as much capital and profit as the capital they brought in (Cunningham, 1986: 46). Third, it is alleged that foreign investors use local resources without concern for local needs, leading to lost jobs and commercial bankruptcies (Rothgeb, 1995: 189).

FDI is also seen as producing unequal income distribution, which in turn may result in less growth. It is said that FDI creates a foreign dominated local high income-group or elite who formulate policies and enact laws that protect foreign interests and ignore the needs of the people (Rothgeb, 1995: 189). The result is smaller income shares and lower standard of living for the majority of the people in the host country. Furthermore, FDI is accused of creating new consumer tastes that may not be beneficial to the local consumer in the developing host country (Sornarajah, 1994: 40; Bergten et al, 1978: 358); of transfer pricing practices followed within companies (Reuber et al, 1970: 20); of failure to coordinate investment and production policies with development priorities of the host country (Reuber et al, 1970: 20); and of failure to make purchases locally (Reuber et al, 1970: 21).

FDI is seen as a threat to the sovereignty of the host country and to the independent development of its social and cultural life (Reuber et al, 1970: 16). It is argued that foreign investors are to some extent within the jurisdiction and influence of a comparatively powerful foreign government, and are less firmly under the jurisdiction of the host government. In case of disputes, the power and influence of the investor's country would be exercised on behalf of the foreign investor against the host country or, alternatively, the investor's country may use the economic power of its foreign investors to further its political ends (Reuber et al, 1970: 16). At the social level, it is argued FDI would result in redistribution of income from locals to foreigners; that alien personnel and practices would be introduced into the local scheme; and that local arrangements and interests would be challenged and traditional beliefs would be threatened (Reuber et al, 1970: 16).

Dependency theory has been the moving force behind several pieces of legislation in developing countries that are related to the regulation of foreign investment. The Nepalese Foreign Investment and Technology Act, 2038 (Article 5), for example, requires that the authorities consider the following before granting foreign investors permission to invest in the country:[9]

- whether the particular investment is desirable for the country;
- whether the investment contributes to import substitution or export promotion;
- whether the investment makes available employment opportunities, management, skill and technical training to the Nepali citizens.

Some countries impose ownership restrictions on foreign investors and give priority to domestic investors having the necessary investment capital and knowhow with a view to increasing national participation. A policy statement of the Government of Zimbabwe, for example, states:

> ...[T]he Government prefers majority Zimbabwean participation in new foreign investment projects. The extent of Zimbabwean ownership, management and control following implementation of projects will thus be one criterion used for assessing applications by foreign investors...Whilst the Government is prepared to allow majority foreign ownership in high priority projects, and in

> some cases even 100% ownership, it will encourage arrangements to be negotiated for the eventual transfer of majority ownership to Zimbabwean entities; ideally these arrangements would be negotiated at the outset or after a stipulated period (Government of the Republic of Zimbabwe, 1991: 11).

In other cases, foreign investment is prohibited or discouraged from areas or activities where the host country believes domestic entrepreneurship and capability is adequate or can be developed, either because such activities do not require much capital investment or because they are relatively less complex.[10]

Dependency theory has been attacked for having limited explanatory value. It is said that almost all countries do import technology, are dependent on exports, have a tendency to emulate consumption patterns in other countries, contain marginalised groups and regions within their territory, and so on, rendering the attempt to make a distinction between "dependence" and "non-dependence" unworkable (Hettne, 1990: 94). Moreover, as became clear since the 1970s, a number of developing countries have been industrialising (such as Korea, Taiwan, Singapore and Hong Kong) at a relatively high speed. Dependency theory fails to adequately explain these phenomena (Hettne, 1990: 94).

Opponents of the dependency school argue that the chief methodological error of the school is its deprivation of local histories of their integrity and specificity, thereby making local actors little more than the pawns of outside forces:

> Because this approach is formalistic and reductionist, it is bad historiography. It is formalistic in the sense that it seeks to specify universal laws or processes in blatant disregard of the singular or the idiosyncratic. By the same token it is reductionist, since it forces the particular case to express its identity solely in the terms provided by the general category. The error of this approach is not that it draws attention to the interconnectedness of economic and political processes and events in a global manner, but that it refuses to grant the part any autonomy, any specificity, any particularity independent of its membership in the whole (Baran, 1962: xxxvi).

The relationship of the whole to the part is, of course, a recurrent one in the social sciences. However, part and whole must be comprehended at the same time as an aspect of each other and as independent entities. Hence, systems composed of complex parts may change not only because of the evolution of the whole, or because of outside influence from other systems, but also from developments within the parts whose movements are endogenously determined. In connection with this, Smith writes:

> In studying the changing configurations of power in North-South relations over the past several decades, we must be aware not only of the way the system is changing overall (for

> example, in terms of the growing role of MNCs), or of the way the system is being challenged from outside itself (such as in the arms race with the Soviet Union), but also of the manner in which the units within it (both North and South) are evolving in response to locally determined forces whose ultimate development may have profound effects on the greater system outside (Smith, 1986: 37).

It may therefore be proper to say that an aspect of the growing international strength of some developing countries is their ability to grow strong internally. As their economies become more diversified and their societies are better organised politically, the probability is that they would gain international strength. Nevertheless, one must be careful not to push this point too far and thereby fail to recognise the substantial power that the North still retains over the South. Dependency theory may be correct when it maintains that the North significantly influences the course of economic, social, and political development in the Southern countries. But it is essential not to assume that the North moulds single-handedly all aspects of social life in the South. The strength and independence of local factors should not be underestimated.

State/Government Intervention

Over the last century, the size of governments and the scope of their activities have expanded enormously, both in developed and developing countries. Developed countries expanded the welfare state, and much of the developing world embraced state-dominated development strategies. The result was a tremendous expansion in the size and reach of government worldwide (World Bank, 1997).

The role of the State in economic development is one of the oldest topics in economics. Scholars from Latin America, Africa, and Asia have examined the roles of states in instituting comprehensive political reforms and shaping national economic development. In the advanced industrial countries, too, people have invested a lot of energy and resource in studying social programs and the role of governments in managing domestic and international economic problems.

States may formulate and pursue goals that are not simply reflective of the demands or interests of social groups, classes, or society within their territories. This is what is usually called "state autonomy". Several lines of reasoning have been used to explain why and how states formulate and pursue their own goals. The extranational orientations of states, the challenges they may face in maintaining domestic order, and the organisational resources that collectivities of state officials may be able to draw on and deploy – all of these features of the state are believed to explain autonomous state action (Evans, 1985: 9). The linkage of states into transnational structures and into international flows of communication may encourage leading state officials to pursue transformative strategies even in the face of indifference or resistance from politically weighty social forces. Similarly, the basic need of States to maintain control and order may spur state-initiated reforms (as well as repression). Organisationally coherent collectivities of state officials, especially collectivities of career officials relatively insulated from ties to currently dominant socioeconomic interests, are likely to launch distinctive new state strategies in times of crisis (Evans, 1985: 9).

Ellen K. Timberger writes that dynamically autonomous bureaucrats, including military officials – in Japan's Meiji restoration, Turkey's Ataturk revolution, Egypt's Nasser revolution, and Peru's 1968 coup – seized and reorganised State power, and then they used the State to destroy an existing dominant class, a landed upper class or aristocracy, and to reorient national economic development (Timberger, 1978: 3). She stresses that a coherent official elite with a statist and nationalist ideological orientation can be formed through prior career interests and socialisation. She also states that "a bureaucratic state apparatus, or a segment of it, can be said to be relatively autonomous when those who hold high civil and/or military posts satisfy two conditions: (1) they are not recruited from the dominant landed, commercial, or industrial classes; and (2) they do not form close personal and economic ties with those classes after their elevation to high office" (Timberger, 1978: 4). She also argues that state-initiated authoritarian reforms may occur when bureaucratic elites retain ties to existing dominant classes, as, for example, in Prussia in 1806-1814, Russia in the 1860s, and Brazil after 1964. But more sweeping structural changes that Timberger labels "revolution from above", including the actual dispossession of a dominant class, occur in crisis situations only when bureaucratic state elites are free of ties or alliances with dominant classes (Timberger, 1978: 5).

Timberger's work deals with instances in which non-constitutionally ruling officials attempt to use the state as a whole to direct and restructure society and politics. Meanwhile, other scholars have studied more instances of state autonomy in the histories of public policy-making in liberal democratic, constitutional polities, such as Britain, Sweden, and the United States (see for instance Greenberg, 1980; Katznelson, 1981; Skowronkel, 1982). The same basic analytical factors – the international orientation of States, their domestic order-keeping functions, and the organisational possibilities for official collectivities to formulate and pursue their own policies also enter into these analyses in different forms.

On the other hand, some scholars agree that there is less structural basis for such state autonomy in the United States than in any other modern liberal capitalist regime. According to these scholars, some of the reasons are "the United States did not inherit a centralised bureaucratic state from pre-industrial and pre-democratic times, and that the dispersion of authority through the federal system, the division of sovereignty among branches of the national government, and the close symbiosis between segments of the federal administration and Congressional committees all help to ensure that state power in the twentieth-century United States is fragmented, dispersed, and everywhere permeated by organised societal interests" (Evans et al, 1985: 12). They also say that "the national government lacks such possible underpinnings of strong state power as a prestigious and status-conscious civil career service with predictable access to key executive posts; authoritative planning agencies; direct executive control over a national central bank; and public ownership of strategic parts of the economy" (Evans et al, 1985: 12).

Effective state intervention is now assumed by many to be an integral part of a successful economic intervention. There are a number of theoretical arguments as to why state intervention is necessary for economic transformation. One argument is that state intervention is required to rectify market failures, that is, the inability of a market economy to reach certain desired outcomes in resource use (Rueschemeyer and Putterman, 1992: 243). The market accomplishes a number of things at once, many of them critical for economic efficiency: it coordinates the activities of a multitude of economic units and uses their varied knowledge and energy in ways that elude any form of administrative coordination; it signals supply conditions - shortage and abundance - as well as variable needs and wants; it provides incentives for responding to changing demand and supply situations; and it channels resources required for such responses. At the same time, however, it also allocates income in disregard of prevalent notions of equity, leaving some needs unmet, and it creates concentration of economic power or monopolies (Rueschemeyer and Putterman, 1992: 243). It is argued that without state intervention, "collective goods will be inadequately provided, negative externalities will not be controlled, and the rate of accumulation will suffer correspondingly" (Ruschemeyer and Evans, 1992: 45). The state should therefore undertake activities that would compensate these and other market failures.

State intervention may also be needed when markets fail to instigate industrial or economic development. At times, the private sector may not initiate industrialisation because it may be undercapitalised and hence unable to take short-term losses due to the underdevelopment and inefficiency of capital markets. Or future profits may not compensate for current losses, or investing in manufacturing may be less profitable than, say, speculating in land or importing foreign products. In all of these instances, state intervention of one form or another may be needed (Amsden, 1992: 59).

Another argument that may apply mainly to developing countries is that late industrialisation would not be possible without effective state intervention (Amsden, 1992: 53). Late industrialisers can grow only by borrowing technology from industrialised countries (Amsden, 1992: 53). This denies them a competitive advantage from new products and processes. Governments must therefore protect and subsidise their domestic industries for them to develop in a far more pervasive fashion and become competitive in the world market (Amsden, 1992: 53).

Proponents of State intervention further argue that protection of infant industries in developing countries from the competition of industries in already developed countries is essential for national development (Grabowski, 1994: 416). In the past, this protection was made mainly through the application of higher tariffs on imported goods and services. More recently, quotas, domestic content requirements and the allocation of concessional credits to favoured industries are used. This view is opposed by neoclassical economists on the ground that resources should be allocated according to comparative or relative advantage. Thus long-term growth is seen to be the result of effectively allocating resources in the short-term (Grabowski, 1994: 416). Proponents of infant industry protection, on the other hand, argue that resources should be allocated inefficiently in the short-term in order to achieve more rapid long-term growth (Grabowski, 1994: 416). However, many economists argue that if such protection is ever appropriate, it is only so during the interim period of technology transfer.

> After a firm introduces a globally efficient technology, its total factor productivity is assumed to be the same as that of firms in other countries, and it follows that the lowest-wage countries can dominate international markets for the most labor-intensive goods (Amsden, 1992: 54).

State-intervention has long been credited by many for the sustained high growth of some Asian countries. When most of these countries were hit by the financial crisis of 1997-98, there were many who spoke loudly, including the Deputy Managing-Director the IMF, Stanley Fisher, that the crisis lay in the economic policies of the affected countries. Dieter, however, argues that the main cause of the crisis was the loosening of State-intervention. Among the main factors that contributed to the outbreak and the deepening of the crisis in those countries were (Dieter, 1999: 32-35):

- the dismantling of capital controls in the process of the deregulation of their economies;
- the use of open financial systems that were not properly prepared for international competition; and
- the new, increased power of international speculators, who first brought down the Thai baht and then other currencies.

Governments have been taking, in various degrees, a leading role in the allocation of investment, controlling the "commanding heights" of the economy, and otherwise intervening to compensate for market failures. Such interventions have brought mixed results. Industrial success stories like Japan, South Korea and Taiwan grew through effective state intervention. South East Asia is another example. By contrast, the outcomes were different in many other countries. Governments in most of the countries where intervention failed embarked on fanciful schemes, such as high-cost public sector enterprises and a variety of manufacturing and other economic activities not traditionally associated with the public sector. Notable among them were: State marketing enterprises, which often served as a monopoly distribution network; State ownership of retail shops for the distribution of foods and other items deemed essential; state operation of mines and manufacturing activities; State enterprises accorded monopoly rights for importing a variety of commodities; nationalised banking and insurance operations (Krueger, 1990: 10).

As by-products of these failures, large-scale and visible corruption often emerged. Private investment, lacking confidence in public policies or in the steadfastness of leaders, held back. Many of the programs and policies that had been adopted with the stated objective of helping the poor had in fact disproportionately benefited the more affluent members of the society. Powerful leaders acted arbitrarily. Development faltered, and poverty endured. All of these phenomena took place in the context of pervasive State involvement in, and control over, economic activity (Krueger, 1990: 10).

As discussed above, state intervention can bring both positive as well as negative results. One should therefore ask what factors determine the effectiveness of State intervention. A distinction is often made between "hard" and "soft" States. Soft States are generally thought to be responsive to a variety of interest groups, with the latter playing an important role in defining government policies. Hard States are able to resist these influences so as to define autonomous goals and policies (Myrdal, 1968). It is therefore argued that an autonomous State is a necessary pre-requisite for State-driven economic development. The success of East Asia (with the exception of Hong Kong) is often attributed to the existence of such hard States in those countries.

What makes for effective state intervention may differ across countries at different stages of development. What works for Malaysia or Taiwan may not work for Germany or the US. Every State has its unique features. Despite these differences, however, a study by the World Bank provides a broad framework for addressing the issue of effective State intervention (World Bank, 1997).

According to this study, the path to an effective State is a two-stage process. The first is matching the State's role to its capacity. The state must focus its capability on those tasks it can and should undertake.[11]

> Where state capability is weak, how the State intervenes - and where - should be carefully assessed. Many States try to do too much with few resources and little capability, and often do more harm than good. A sharper focus on the fundamentals would improve effectiveness (World Bank, 1997: 3).

Matching the State's role to its capability may not be a simple matter. Choosing what to do and what not to do is critical. This also involves deciding how to do things – how to deliver basic services, provide infrastructure, regulate the economy – and not just whether to do them at all. The choices here are many and must be tailored to the circumstances of each country. The World Bank study, however, suggests that getting the fundamentals right should be the first job of every State. The study singles out five fundamental tasks as the core of every government's mission (World Bank, 1997: 4):

- Establishing a foundation of law;
- Maintaining a non-distortionary policy environment, including macro-economic stability;
- Investing in basic social services and infrastructure;
- Protecting the vulnerable; and
- Protecting the environment.

To make development stable and sustainable, the State has to keep its eye on these fundamentals. Since lawlessness is often related to a sense of marginalisation, public policies can ensure that growth is shared and that it contributes to reducing poverty and inequality. They must aim not merely to deliver growth but to ensure that the benefits of market-led growth are shared, particularly through investments in basic education and health. They must also ensure that people are protected against material and personal insecurity. Where poverty and economic marginalisation stem from ethnic and social differences, policies must be carefully crafted to manage these differences (World Bank, 1997: 6). Moreover, when markets are underdeveloped, the State can encourage market development.

> Many of today's oldest industrial economies used various mechanisms to spur the growth of markets in their early stages of development. More recently, Japan, the Republic of Korea, and other countries in East Asia used a variety of mechanisms for market enhancement, in addition to securing the economic, social, and institutional fundamentals. Sometimes these interventions were quite elaborate...Other times they were less intrusive... (World Bank, 1997: 6-7).

The second stage of the path to effective State intervention is raising the State's capability by reinvigorating public institutions. This is done through designing effective rules and restraints, to check arbitrary State actions and combat entrenched corruption, subjecting State institutions to greater competition to increase their efficiency, increasing the performance of State institutions, improving pay and incentives, making the State more responsive to people's needs, bringing government closer to the people through broader participation and decentralisation (World Bank, 1997: 3).

To sum up, the last five decades have shown clearly both the benefits and the limitations of State intervention, especially in the promotion of development. States have helped to deliver substantial improvements in the lives of their people. They have also led to some very poor outcomes. The World Bank study has postulated the key features and challenges of the effectiveness of States in various regions as follows (World Bank, 1997: 16-17):

- Many countries in *Sub-Saharan Africa* are suffering from a crisis of statehood – a crisis of capability. An urgent priority is to rebuild State effectiveness through an overhaul of public institutions, reassertion of the rule of law, and credible checks on abuse of State power.
- The capability of the State in most *East Asian* countries cannot be considered a problem. But States' ability to change in response to the new challenge facing the region will play a critical role in their continued economic success.
- The main issue in *South Asia* is "over-regulation", both a cause and an effect of bloated public employment and a route to corruption.
- The job of reorienting the State toward the task of "steering, not rowing" is far from complete in *Central and Eastern Europe*. But most countries have made progress and are on the way to improving capability and accountability.

- Low State capability in many countries of the *Commonwealth of Independent States* is a serious and mounting obstacle to further progress in most areas of economic and social policy. Reorientation of the State is still at an early stage, and a host of severe problems have emerged from a general lack of accountability and transparency.
- In *Latin America*, decentralisation of power and of spending, coupled with democratisation, has dramatically transformed the local political landscape, in what some have called a "quiet revolution". A new model of government is emerging in the region. But greater emphasis is also needed on reforming of the legal system, the civil service, and social policies.
- In the *Middle East and North Africa*, unemployment is by far the greatest economic and social problem and makes government downsizing especially difficult. Because the political and social difficulties of reform are considerable, a promising approach might be to begin decentralising selected services, and focus on reforming state enterprises, while preparing the ground for wider-ranging reforms.

Conclusion

As the above discussion shows, neo-classical economics gives strong emphasis on the benefits of FDI and market liberalisation. While it may be true that FDI brings lots of benefits to the host country, it also has some negativities. Moreover, the flows of FDI and market liberalisation are not necessarily inseparable.

Host countries may benefit from FDI through the transfer of technology and technological spill-over, increased productive efficiency, production of exportable goods and services which generate foreign exchange, increases in savings and investment, and faster growth of output and employment. FDI can also perform an indirect beneficial role by producing such goods and services, which may help in producing other exportable goods or services or in replacing imported goods and services. An indirect role can also include developing infrastructure facilities, which may encourage further FDI flows.

Among the costs of FDI are the possible negative effects on the balance of payment of the host country due, for example, to an increase in imports and repatriation of profits and earnings. If FDI targets the domestic market, it can still generate profit for the investor, but such profit may leave the country in foreign exchange. As most developing countries have constraints in the balance of payments especially during their earlier phases of development, these foreign exchange outflows could easily raise problematic policy questions. Whether or not any particular FDI project or FDI collectively generates sufficient foreign exchange to cover foreign exchange costs associated with it is, therefore, a relevant question to be considered when a country forms its FDI policies.

The fact that FDI has costs associated with it does not necessarily strengthen dependency theory's claim that FDI is bad for the host country. The reality is that, in the world of today where official development assistance flows are steadily diminishing, FDI has become a major source of funding development projects in many developing countries. Moreover, it is very doubtful if dependency theory's position on FDI is tenable in the era of globalisation.

However, a regime of unrestricted FDI entry may not necessarily be beneficial to the host economy, as it will not allow the host country to determine the optimum level and type of FDI suitable for the country concerned. Governments may not see advantage in the liberalisation of FDI regimes unless the latter result in more inflows of FDI in the sectors they would like it to be. Experience shows that liberalisation may not necessarily result in increased inflows of FDI. For example, China has been the largest recipient of FDI in the developing world since 1992 (UNCTAD, 1997:92) despite its restrictive investment regime, whereas many African countries receive little or no FDI (UNCTAD, 1997: 56-64) even though their investment regimes are far more liberal than that of China. Countries like Malaysia and Thailand have more strict regulations towards FDI than Latin American countries, and yet they receive more FDI than the latter (UNCTAD, 1997: 71-74, 90-92).

Therefore, in order to realise the full potential of FDI, it may be necessary for any government to have an interventionist role and adopt a policy that is selective with respect to projects and the volume and timing of FDI inflows. There is ample scope for government intervention: the identification of sectors in which a country can reasonably expect to acquire comparative advantage and the promotion of production in such sectors; the promotion of sectors with large externalities for the rest of the economy; channelling FDI so as to bring balanced regional development; and so on. The challenge, however, is how to identify the best methods of selective intervention in the economy and deciding where the limit is for such intervention. Regulated openness is developed in this book not as a cookbook with instructions on how to do such selective intervention, but as a framework within which the systemic wisdom for choosing the best methods might flourish.

Liberalisation should also be seen as a continuous movement, rather than a one-off radical measure. The pace of the movement could vary from country to country. Governments should be able to examine their policies and laws on FDI on a regular basis in order to decide if new circumstances would necessitate change in their current policies and laws. As a result of such evaluations, the number of restrictions on FDI could be reduced, or new restrictions may be introduced if aspects of liberalisation proved counter-productive.

Notes

1 Quoted from Yue (1986: 102).

2 See, for example, the Preamble of the Agreement between the Belgio-Luxemburg Economic Union and the Government of the Republic of Korea, Signed on December 20, 1974, reproduced in ICSID (1993).

3 The World Bank Guidelines on the Treatment of FDI are reproduced in ICSID (1992: 297-306).

4 The Convention is reproduced in ICSID, Investment Laws of the World, Vol. I.

5 There has been considerable literature on the alliance between elites of developing countries and foreign investors resulting in repressive regimes. For a review of literature on the subject, see Rothgeb (Jr) (1996).

6 For a detailed description of environmental damages caused by FDI, see Smith (1992).

7 For further reading on transfer pricing, see Picciotto (1992: 171-228).

8 For a review of the theory, see also Peet (1991); Evans (1979); Biersteker (1987); Amin (1976).

9 Foreign Investment and Technology Act, 2038 (of Nepal), Article 5, reproduced in ICSID, Investment Laws of the World, Vol. VI.

10 See, for example, The National Investment (Promotion and Protection) Act, 1990 (of Tanzania), Schedule C.

11 Capability, as applied to states, is the ability to undertake and promote collective efficiency – such as law and order, public health, and basic infrastructure; effectiveness is a result of using that capability to meet society's demand for those goods. A state may be capable but not effective if its capability is not used in society's interest.

Chapter 3

The Current Regulatory Framework for FDI

The previous Chapter discussed some of the theories that have played significant roles in shaping the content and form of FDI policies and laws, both nationally and internationally. The strengths and weaknesses of these theories have also been examined briefly. This Chapter examines the current national and international regulatory framework on FDI.

The current rules on FDI can be broadly categorised as national, bilateral and multilateral. The multilateral rules can be further classified as regional/sectoral and global. Accordingly, the following part of the Chapter will examine each category separately, starting with national norms.

National Laws and Policies

National laws and policies on FDI have varied widely from time to time and from place to place. This variation could be attributed partly to the influence on national law/policy-makers of the theories discussed in Chapter Two, and partly to other factors. Investment laws and policies, however, have a common aspiration: the desire to make the most of foreign investment. As a result, policy-makers are obliged to confront at least the following three common problems (Solomon and Mirsky, 1990-91: 257, 259):

- how to attract foreign investment without incurring a damaging drain on domestic foreign exchange savings and other resources;
- how to preserve the foreign investor's legal rights and give it adequate protection while, at the same time, keeping its domination and negative effects to a minimum; and

- how to design their laws and tax systems in such a way as to simultaneously foster economic growth and attract foreign investment while concurrently raising enough revenue to meet the budgetary requirements of the government.

Investment laws could, therefore, be seen as a means as well as a consequence of state intervention in the economic process, designed to keep the balance between the above three problems. Sometimes, the concerns of home and host states behind their national laws and policies could be different. According to Muchlinski, for example, the concerns of home states centre on, *inter alia*, the protection of domestic labour against the export of jobs abroad, adequate revenue from the repatriation of dividends earned by overseas subsidiaries of home-based parent companies, the promotion and protection of technological leads enjoyed by home based MNEs, access to raw materials in short supply in the home state, or the need for the equal and reciprocal treatment of inward and outward investment (Muchlinski, 1995: 103). With regard to host states, FDI that comes with new capital, technology, goods or services not normally found locally at equivalent or lower cost is generally encouraged. However, conditions may be imposed relating to level of investment and local ownership, performance requirements, import levels, technology and skills transfer, job levels, export levels or long-term investment strategy (Muchlinski, 1995: 104).

Increasingly, the laws of host countries on FDI are taking the form of a code or a single piece of legislation that states the pertinent rules relating to FDI in the country.[1] They specify the authority responsible for supervising investment, conditions of entry and the sectors open to FDI, the controls FDI is subjected to, remissibility of funds, performance requirements, incentives granted to investors, and the circumstances of the termination of foreign investment and other similar matters. Such codes typically apply to FDI alone, while foreign investors in other sectors must generally obey all relevant laws. The existence of a single code enables the foreign investor to acquaint itself with the laws on foreign investment of a country more easily. It is part of an attempt to communicate the certainty in the rule of law that was discussed as part of the arguments for "good governance" in state intervention discussed in the last Chapter.

Many countries now have laws controlling FDI. Even countries which traditionally maintain an open policy towards FDI now impose restrictions on the flow and activities of FDI. Until recently, the US policy on FDI, for example, was driven by "the principle of neutrality", that is, trying not to be biased either in favour of or against FDI (Graham and Krugman, 1991: 119). Accordingly, foreign firms had identical rights of establishment as domestic firms and, once established, foreign firms did not face greater burdens as a result of government action or policy than domestic firms, nor did they receive special privileges that domestic firms did not (national treatment) (Graham and Krugman, 1991: 120). There were, of course, some exceptions to the "principle of neutrality" which applied essentially to those industries subject to federal regulation (Graham and Krugman, 1991: 120).[2] Since 1988, however, there has been a tendency to extend the Federal Government's ability to restrict FDI in areas beyond the federally regulated industries. The Exon-Florio Amendment,[3] for example, gave the President power to prevent the entry of foreign investment that threatens "national security" or terminate such existing foreign investment (Graham and Krugman, 1991: 121). The European Union, too, uses competition laws and merger controls to prevent large multinationals from entering the European market and to protect smaller European firms from being squashed by them (Sornarajah, 1994: 88).

One of the reasons for such increase in laws controlling FDI could be attributed to the rapid change in the flow of FDI around the world. Those countries which used to be the traditional exporters of FDI are increasingly becoming the major importers of capital themselves. If we take the US, for example, the volume of FDI stock in that country in 1980 was $US80 billion while US investment abroad amounted to $US220 billion; the ratio of inward to outward investment during that time was 0.36. In 1998, FDI stock in the US rose to $US875 billion while outward investment rose to 993.5 billion, the ratio of inward to outward investment becoming 0.88 (UNCTAD, 1999: 477, 495). This shift in the pattern of investment flows may have caused concern among the traditional exporters of capital and made them realise that there was a need to take measures to prevent the threat to their national and business interests (Sornarajah, 1994: 87-88).

Codes and laws of host countries on FDI broadly fall into three categories: entry and performance requirements, incentives, and treatment and protection of investments/investors. In the following section we will discuss briefly each of these categories of regulation.

Entry and Performance Requirements

An investor contemplating investment in a foreign country is normally subject to screening and approval procedures by the state agency responsible for the administration of investments. In some countries the screening and approval procedure is accomplished in one place, popularly known as a "one-stop" or "single window" centre - a focal point which is used to solve all problems associated with investment administration.[4] In others there are no such centralised bodies which receive, screen and decide on applications, so that different government agencies might be responsible for the screening and approval of different types of investments. This is particularly so in countries with a federal form of government.

Centralised structures for the administration of investment have various advantages over fragmented administrative frameworks. The first is that, in the absence of the centralised structure, the investor's application has to go around several government agencies and comply with the numerous formalities and to press constantly for decisions (sometimes against demands for corrupt payments). This could be time consuming, costly and at times frustrating. In some cases, it may even dissuade the investor from investing in the country. The second is that fragmented administrative frameworks may give foreign investors conflicting signals as to what is expected of them. The Ministry of Labour, for example, may be primarily interested in attracting the kind of FDI that reduces unemployment. However, this goal may not always be consistent with the objectives of the Ministry of Science and Technology whose main interest could be to upgrade domestic innovative capacity, or that of the Ministry of Trade whose main preoccupation could be to improve the balance of payments. Third, fragmented approaches could, at best, be less cost effective and, at worst, reinforce structural distortions as one government department seeks to offset any adverse effects of another department's actions on its own policies (Dunning, 1993: 567).

Conditions of entry Conditions that restrict the entry of FDI can be categorised into three groups: capitalisation requirements, carve-outs/exclusions, and ownership restrictions. Some countries insist that the foreign investor should bring in all or a certain percentage of its capital from overseas.[5] One reason for this is the country's wish to overcome its shortage of foreign currency through FDI (Dunning, 1993: 559). Another is its interest in preventing the foreign investor from raising capital locally so that local savings that could be utilised for other projects of benefit to the country should not be absorbed in serving the interests of the foreign investor (Sornarajah, 1994: 106). The attraction of local investors to invest in shares in a project with a large corporation can indeed divert investment funds that could have gone to finance local entrepreneurs or local projects.

Where a capitalisation requirement is a condition of entry, a foreign investor who does not satisfy this requirement would not be given permission to invest in the country. Where the foreign investor agrees to capitalisation requirements and later fails to comply, either fully or in part, the host state may terminate the permission or otherwise interfere with the FDI. Such an action by the State does not amount to a violation of international law, provided due process standards have been met (Sornarajah, 1994: 106).

In some countries, the investment code carves out certain areas into which FDI cannot enter.[6] There are economic reasons given to justify such exclusions. One is that, because the particular industries may not require large capital investment or are less complex, they could easily be undertaken by domestic entrepreneurship. Another reason is that it would be better if such industries were run by local investors as otherwise the state may be left stranded by a foreign investor which might relocate any time. A third reason is the fear that the entry of a big foreign multinational may squash the emergence of a domestic entrepreneurial class. Negative public perception is the other reason.[7]

Foreign investment may also be kept out of certain industries for reasons of "national security". In the United States, for example, FDI in the areas of communication and transport systems, the exploration of natural and energy resources, and the ownership of land are subject to stringent regulations.[8] In addition, the President has the power to block any mergers, acquisitions, or takeovers of US companies by foreign interests when such actions are deemed a threat to national security. The power of the President includes termination of existing investments (Graham and Krugman, 1991: 121).

Some countries put a cap on foreign ownership of certain industries. In Australia, for example, foreign ownership in commercial television broadcasting services is limited to 15% for individuals and 20% in aggregate (Broadcasting and Services Act 1992). In other countries, FDI is allowed, especially in some select areas, only in joint ventures with a state entity of the host country or with local investors. This had been a widespread pattern in the states of Eastern Europe, both prior to and after the fall of communism, and in many developing countries (Sornarajah, 1994: 104,111).[9] In some countries like Malaysia, this has been mandated by policies which require that the disadvantaged indigenous people should be given some priority in the ownership of the means of production. In its New Economic Policy which was to be implemented over a period of twenty years, Malaysia announced in 1970 that it wanted to restructure the economy to ensure that foreign nationals participate in the economy only as minority shareholders (Government of Malaysian, 1976). In China and Vietnam, joint ventures were the principal mode of foreign investment for a long time. But more recently, wholly owned subsidiaries have been permitted, subject to certain conditions. In the developed countries, on the other hand, joint venture associations between foreign and local investors is not coerced, as is the case in some developing countries.

Joint venture association between foreign and local investors has various advantages to the foreign investor: diversification of risks, providing a local partner who could be an effective mediator with the local government, and its ability to pool larger resources and technology. It also has advantages to the host country. Less profit would be repatriated abroad, the government can have direct or indirect control over the venture, and a local entrepreneurial class will emerge through the acquisition of managerial and business skills from the foreign investor.

It is widely accepted in the contemporary world that a country may impose conditions of entry upon foreign investors.[10] Discrimination between nationals and foreigners is said to be lawful under international law if it is based on rational economic grounds. The discrimination will, however, become unlawful if it is based on racial grounds or if it is in breach of bilateral agreements made between the host country and the investor's home country (when these stipulate national treatment).[11]

Questions arise when a country fears economic domination by nationals of a particular country who are of a particular racial group and limits their entry. To give a concrete example, Indians were expelled from Uganda during the administration of Idi Amin and new Indian investors were denied entry on the ground that they had dominated the country's economy. In such circumstances, is it possible for a state to prevent entry by foreign investors of a particular race? Some say that a state should be able to secure its economic independence by ensuring that its foreign investors come from a diversity of nations (Sornarajah, 1994: 136).

There are also instances where discrimination may be made between nationals of different countries, without reference to a particular race. In Nigeria, for example, nationals of members of the Organisation of African Unity are exempt from screening procedures (Sornarajah, 1994: 136). The free movement of persons and goods within regional groupings like the EC also depends on nationality and the exclusion of nationals of other countries. It has been held that discrimination of this type between categories of persons is lawful when the categorisation is not based on race (Sornarajah, 1994: 136).

Performance requirements Performance requirements are the operating expectations demanded of foreign-owned enterprises. They are often applied to foreign investors only. They may also be a condition of entry, but we shall consider them separately as they concern the day-to-day operations of the foreign enterprise.

Performance requirements may embrace the whole spectrum of operating practices, such as requirements for local purchase of capital goods, raw materials, intermediate goods and services; recruitment, employment and training practices; the proportion of output exported; trade balancing requirements; technology transfer; information provided on intra-firm pricing practices; and types of production methods utilised (Bale (Jr), 1990: 62; UNCTC, 1992: 70-71; Fisher and Turner, 1983: 75). Performance requirements tend to cause investors to pursue practices they would not otherwise adopt in the open market. For example, local content requirements could force or encourage firms to use local inputs in the production process, although one of the central considerations in determining where to get inputs from, in an open market setting, is cost competitiveness.

Strong economic and political arguments have been raised both for and against performance requirements. One of the arguments for their use is that a performance requirement serves as an appropriate means to promote and protect a local industry during its infancy and until it will be able to compete by itself in the world market (Fisher and Turner, 1983: 78; Bale (Jr), 1990; 68). It is also argued that performance requirements, especially the requirement to provide information on intra-firm practices and a local content requirement, can be used as tools for preventing pricing abuses and tax evasion (Fisher and Turner, 1983: 78). Furthermore it is said that performance requirements foster the transfer of technology and help the host country develop a comparative advantage in a particular sector of its economy in a relatively faster span of time. Performance requirements, particularly export requirements, also have a balance of payments justification (Bale (Jr), 1990: 70). Finally, performance requirements are viewed by the host countries as a means of requiring foreign investors to serve national goals. It is said that key strategic decisions by the most common foreign investors, multinational corporations, are made outside the host country's borders and these decisions are usually influenced predominantly by factors such as global marketing objectives assigned to various divisions in the multinational corporation and/or as international tax and other regulatory policies (Bale (Jr), 1990: 79). Therefore, the use of performance requirements is seen as essential to assert the host country's control over the national economy and its development and channel foreign investment into areas of priority for the host country (Fisher and Turner, 1983: 80).

These arguments for performance requirements are matched by counter arguments. It is said that the protection of infant industries through performance requirements tends to create inefficient indigenous firms which may adversely affect the host economy. Higher prices and subsidisation costs are incurred in order to accelerate development in a sector that may have little chance of achieving a true competitive advantage (Fisher and Turner, 1983: 77). Consumers too may not get better and cheaper products (Fisher and Turner, 1983: 77). Transfer pricing practices also can be regulated by other means, such as the use of world market prices or other commercial standards to determine arm's-length transactions between parent companies and their subsidiaries, rather than using performance requirements for such purposes (Fisher and Turner, 1983: 79). Moreover, since performance requirements protect the local industry, and foreign investors are forced to purchase inputs locally, local manufacturers would not have the incentive to acquire new technology and become competitive (Fisher and Turner, 1983: 79). Finally, it is argued that performance requirements are not the best way to solve balance of payments problems since these problems can best be resolved by deflationary monetary or fiscal policies or exchange rate depreciation (Fisher and Turner, 1983: 79).

Many countries impose some form of performance requirement on FDI.[12] In Australia, for example, the Partnership for Development Scheme requires foreign investors in the information technology industry making sales to government over a certain threshold to enter into agreements to achieve, within seven years, exports equal to at least 50% of annual imports, Research and Development expenditure equal to at least 5% of local turnover, and an average of 70% of local value added across all exports (Industry Commission, 1992: Appendix B). In China, local content is required on a case-by-case basis and depends on the level of technology and the export to output ratio. Foreign exchange balancing is also required (Bureau of Industry Economics, 1995: 41). In Malaysia, export requirements apply to almost all sectors. There are technology transfer requirements for FDI too. Restrictions also exist on the employment of foreign personnel, and local content is required in certain sectors (Bureau of Industry Economics, 1995: 41).

Investment Incentives

The realisation that FDI can play an important role in the development of a country has spurred competition between host countries for such investment. The competition in turn has led a number of countries to provide more and more incentives of one kind or another in their attempt to increase their attractiveness for FDI.[13]

As industrialisation is a priority in many countries, under the implicit assumption that it will speed up the country's economic development, incentives are regarded as a useful tool to attract the capital and technology required for that purpose. Incentives may also be used to spur industrial growth in particular geographical locations with the purpose of regional development and diversifying development projects (Kofele-Kale, 1990: 394). In places where there is little or no infrastructure, or where the risk of losing investment capital is reasonably high, incentives in fact might play a role in influencing the decision of investors to invest in that particular location.

Incentives may be used to protect infant industries. They may also be given to industries for a specific purpose, such as developing human resources, the creation of additional employment, the development of infrastructure, or improving the balance of payments.

Appropriately designed incentives can induce the investor to undertake the investment, provided the general investment climate is conducive. However, the use of incentives can also be a loss for the host country. They undoubtedly impose both financial as well as administrative burdens on the government. They can even lead to a distortion of the country's productive structure, rendering it less efficient. For example, maintaining high prices for industrial products as an incentive to investment in industry may result in disincentives to agricultural production, thus reducing agricultural incomes, increasing rural-urban migration, and exacerbate problems of unemployment. Therefore, any incentive has to balance its costs against its expected benefits.

The definition of incentive measures has always been controversial. The OECD defines them as "any government measures designed to influence an investment decision or having the effect of increasing the profit accruing to the potential investment or altering the risk attached to it" (OECD, 1989: 9). This, of course, is a very broad definition and a wide range of measures, such as business taxation arrangements, infrastructure-related measures, labour market reforms, competition policy measures, investment promotion and support services, regulations and controls on FDI may all be consistent with the definition.

Some studies define incentive measures more narrowly and draw distinctions between factor-based incentives (that is, cash grants and tax holidays) which impact directly on the factor costs of a project, and product based incentives (e.g. tariffs and import quotas) which impact directly on returns from the sale of a project's products (Wells, 1986: 58).

Whatever the proper definition of incentives, once the decision is made to use incentives, a wide choice of instruments is available. The commonly used incentives are tariff and fiscal concessions to firms that meet certain conditions, various kinds of subsidies, building and maintaining infrastructure and services, and protection from competition.

Tariff concessions are an integral part of many investment incentive packages. Capital goods and equipment, raw materials, and spare parts are usually exempt from import duties for a certain period of time.[14] In most cases, the concessions apply only to items that are not available in the country in comparable quality, quantity and price. Since most countries wish to avoid reliance on foreign raw materials or semi-finished goods, tariff concessions on raw materials raise particularly difficult policy issues. As a result, governments normally impose higher conditions and qualifications on concessions to imported raw materials than they do on capital goods and components.

Tax holidays are one of the most frequently used incentives to attract FDI. The usual form of the holiday is to allow an enterprise operating in a designated investment activity to be fully or partially exempted from income or corporate taxation for a certain period of time, with full taxation applying after the holiday period.[15]

Tax holidays allow firms to recover their capital more quickly and maintain greater liquidity in their early years, thus reducing risk. However, a tax exemption is worthless if there is no tax liability. If the holiday period runs from the date of commencement of production or operation, and if the firm, as in the case of infant industries, earns no or little profit in its early years, the firm hardly benefits from tax holidays.

A lengthy period of exemption from taxes can be very costly to the host country. The more extended the tax exemption period, the greater its cost will be for the government. One way of protecting against excessive revenue loss from firms that become profitable quickly is to set a ceiling on tax benefits, that is, by restricting exempt earnings to a certain percentage of the invested capital. Another way is suspending the exemption if annual earnings exceed a certain percentage of the invested capital.

Some countries designate certain areas as Export Processing Zones (EPZ) and supply them with improved infrastructure facilities.[16] Enterprises wishing to invest in such areas can be offered special incentive packages as well. For example, in the Korean EPZ, enterprises received a range of incentives, including the right to import raw and semi-finished materials duty free, and support and service facilities from the government including electricity, telecommunications, packing, and machine repair and maintenance. They also received tax exemptions and special depreciation allowances. In return, the enterprises were required to manufacture, process and assemble goods for export (Industry Commission, 1992: 51). Similarly in Australia, enterprises located in the Trade Development Zone (another name for EPZ), centred in Darwin, receive tax and other concessions as well as the right to import components and raw materials duty free, provided the final product was exported (Bureau of Industry Economics, 1993: 161). Lacking the capacity to build an industrial infrastructure nationwide, many developing countries choose to establish an EPZ enclave. Some even see it as a necessary transitional stage in their development that will rapidly promote industrial export manufacturing (Basil and Germidis, 1992: 5).

It is clear that countries devote considerable effort to designing, implementing, and modifying strategies to influence the location and operation of foreign investment projects through the provision of incentives. Do the strategies work?

The location decision of foreign investors is influenced by many factors, but they can be classified into two broad categories: factors other than incentives and incentive policies (Guisinger and Associates, 1985: 39). The first category refers to all considerations other than government incentive policies that an investor would apply to a location decision, including all advantages of production, marketing, transportation, exchange rate and price stability, quality of public management of monetary, fiscal, and social policy, and political and social stability (Guisinger and Associates, 1985: 40). The second category comprises all government incentives and disincentives that affect foreign investment, whether applied to foreign investments or to investments in general (Guisinger and Associates, 1985: 40-41). These include tax holidays, customs duty exemption, various types of allowance, externalisation of fund, and so on.

Of all the incentives provided by governments to investors, however, the issue of tax incentives has been the subject of a heated debate for decades among theoreticians, labour unions, policy-makers makers, and others interested in the foreign investment process. The basic question raised in the debate is whether tax incentives should be provided as instruments for inducing the flow of or attracting foreign investment (OECD, 1989; UNCTAD, 1992). At one extreme are those who argue that tax incentives have a moderate to significant impact on investment. According to a study conducted by the IMF, for example, in two-thirds of the cases analysed, the choice of country for investment was influenced by incentives provided, in the sense that the investment would have been located elsewhere without those incentives (IMF, 1985: 17; Ghandi, 1986: 28). At the other extreme are those who charge that tax incentives constitute unnecessary costs to incentive granting countries because their impact on private investment flows is "somewhere between ineffective and inefficient" (Billerback and Yasugi, 1979: 17). They are ineffective because many countries have similar and competing schemes and, as a result, they have little impact on the distribution of FDI (Billerback and Yasugi, 1979: 17). It is said that with better general economic policies and a better entry system, the same amount of investment could be attracted at a lower cost (Billerback and Yasugi, 1979: 17).

Central to the controversy over the desirability of tax incentives to attract foreign investment is the multinational enterprise (MNE), because MNEs account for a significant portion of foreign investment in the world.[17] Since the primary motivation for MNEs is profit maximisation, minimising all variables that would act to decrease profits in their gross or net form would induce the inward flow of FDI. Tax exemptions, therefore, would contribute to inducing the inflow of FDI.

Critics of this theory, on the other hand, say that since MNEs constitute a system of interconnected operations, all responding to a general global strategy, an operating loss in any particular country or region may have little or no effect on the overall strategy and profit picture (Horst, 1974: 31-32). For example, it is not uncommon for MNEs to extract raw materials in one country, as inputs in sourcing investment in another, in turn to be used as inputs in the final production process in a third country. Under these circumstances, the rate of return in any one of these countries might be completely irrelevant in the location decision process (Yelpaala, 1985: 381).

Another argument put forward against the efficacy of tax incentives is that for many economically less developed countries the tax system is relatively unimportant, compared to other factors impeding investment. It is said that the more important obstacles to investment in most of these countries are either the underdeveloped state of the economy itself or a fundamental lack of natural resources, or both (Heller and Kauffman, 1963: 60). Hence, limited market size or restricted potential demand in the case of inward oriented industries, the unavailability of a skilled or industrially disciplined work force, and inadequacies in the country's infrastructure would discourage the inflow of foreign investment even if taxes were non-existent (Heller and Kauffman, 1963: 60). Administrative corruption, arbitrariness, or ineptitude in the implementation of the tax or other laws pertaining to industrial activity are also presumed to be other factors which discourage foreign investment. Tax incentives cannot compensate for such negative factors (Heller and Kauffman, 1963: 63).

Taxes in the foreign investor's home country also bear directly on the operation of tax incentives in the host country. Many capital exporting countries extend their income tax jurisdiction to the worldwide income of their taxpayers.[18] In addition to taxes in the capital-importing country, therefore, the foreign investor may also be required to pay income tax in its home country on foreign sourced income. In some instances this double taxation may result in the elimination of any money saved from the incentives in the capital importing countries. This is a disincentive for foreign investment. Hence, measures utilised for eliminating international double taxation in capital-exporting countries could be of far more significance to investors from such countries than tax incentive in the capital-importing countries. The relative importance of these incentives as a reason for investment decisions is reflected in a number of studies that show that such decisions are more likely to be influenced by generally favourable economic conditions, rather than by incentives:

> The level and pattern of economic activity is affected much more by the general economic policy of the government than by any set of measures labelled 'incentives'. Government decisions about public expenditure, the overall level of taxation, money supply, interest rates, the pricing policies of state-sponsored bodies, income policy and the exchange rate have more fundamental effects on economic growth than any tax or other incentives which may be provided. If general economic policies create a climate that is unfavourable to economic expansion, incentives to compensate cannot provide a long-term solution. The double distortion created merely delays efforts to solve the underlying problems (Irish Commission on Taxation, 1984: 17).

The problem of inducing business enterprises to commit their capital to overseas investment is multidimensional, complex and elusive. Incentive laws do not operate in isolation, but they function in relation to a given economic and political framework, and an existing underlying tax system. An attractive investment opportunity and an acceptable investment climate represent the optimum mix of high financial returns and low non-commercial risks. Hence,

> A stable and more favourable economic regime, including a good tax system with overall reasonable tax rates, is more attractive to investors than a hostile general environment 'mitigated by numerous incentives'. Most important of all, therefore, is a national socio-economic and stable political regime that is conducive to private business, a developed infrastructure, and general financial and investment related services (Irish Commission on Taxation, 1984: 17).

To sum up, the role of investment incentive measures in influencing the location decision of investors is subject to considerable debate. The problem is aggravated by the absence of an agreed definition of incentive measures, the differing effects of incentives on different types of investment activities, the interaction between incentives and other government policies in shaping location decisions, and so on. Whatever the role of incentives, governments have continued to compete for FDI by providing incentives or seeking to match those of other governments. This, however, has a number of problems. First, the provision of competitive incentives can give rise to a situation where nations collectively are worse off than if each of them had offered no incentives at all. On the other hand, an unmatched decision not to become involved in a bidding process in this environment could impair a country's attractiveness and thereby direct potentially beneficial investments to other locations. Secondly, countries differ in their attractiveness to FDI. Accordingly, countries with fewer inherent advantages might need to provide larger incentives to offset their location disadvantages. As a result, the cost of incentives may well exceed the benefits the host country anticipates from the FDI. Thirdly, if the investor's investment decision is driven largely by non-incentive related considerations, the provision of incentives may simply transfer wealth from the host country to the investor without its intended effect.

Treatment and Protection of Investors/Investments

Among the most important factors an investor considers before deciding to invest in a foreign country are the host country's treatment of foreign investors and their investments, the degree of protection the host country provides to the investor and its property, and the right to repatriate earnings. No investor is willing to invest in a country where there is a danger of losing its property through "taking"[19] by the government and in a climate of uncertainty about repatriating profits and capital. Therefore, any country that seeks to encourage the flow of foreign capital to its territory should try to provide foreign investors with the necessary assurances in respect of their investment.

The treatment of investments and investors Many countries accord foreign controlled enterprises either national treatment or "fair and equitable treatment" (OECD, 1993). National treatment requires that foreign controlled enterprises be treated by the host country no less favourably than domestic enterprises (OECD, 1976: Article II).

In many countries, including the OECD members, national treatment is accorded post entry and establishment, that is, countries may regulate discriminatorily the entry of foreign investment or the condition of establishment of foreign enterprises into their territories (OECD, 1993: 14). There are always exceptions to the application of national treatment that may differ from country to country. In Australia, for example, the national treatment principle does not apply to foreign investments in rural properties, agriculture, fishing, forestry, resource processing, oil and gas, air transport, newspaper circulation, real estate, radio and television (OECD, 1993: 62-64).

The principle of national treatment is aimed at eliminating discrimination vis-à-vis foreign investment, the comparison usually being between firms in the same sector (OECD, 1993: 22). However, some argue that more than national treatment may be needed when national treatment is below the international minimum standard. Schwarzenberger, for instance, has pointed out that where there is a conflict between national treatment and the minimum standard of international law, "equality of treatment is not enough" (Schwarzenberger, 1948: 412). Brierly has also observed that:

> If a state has a low standard of justice towards its own nationals, an alien's position is in a sense a privileged one, for the standard of treatment for which international law entitles him is an objective one, and he need not, even though nationals must, submit to unjust treatment (Brierly, 1955: 22).

To sum up, the principle of national treatment has no uniform application at the moment. Even though the great majority of countries apply it on already established investments, others would like to see it applied at pre-establishment phase as well. Its current application is also qualified by numerous exceptions the selection of which is left entirely to the host country. Moreover, it is arguable whether national treatment brings its intended effect, at least in countries where the nationals themselves are subjected to a lower standard of treatment. Finally, the international minimum standard itself to which national treatment may be compared in countries where there is no or little "justice" has no agreed upon set of rules of standard.

Some countries accord foreign investment "fair and equitable treatment". What is fair and equitable may largely be a matter of interpretation in each individual case. However, non-discrimination, the international minimum standard, and the duty to protect foreign property by the host state are normally considered by classical international law as the firm ingredients of "fair and equitable treatment" (UNCTC, 1988: 42).

Non-discrimination is generally considered to mean that the host country should abstain from discriminatory actions towards foreigners in general or towards the nationals of a particular country (UNCTC, 1988: 42).[20] In the Oscar Chin Case, for example, the Permanent Court of International Justice made the following remarks regarding the form of discrimination forbidden by international law:

> The form of discrimination which is forbidden is therefore discrimination based upon nationality and involving differential treatment by reason of their nationality as between persons belonging to different national groups.[21]

There is however considerable controversy as to the extent of the application of this principle and its exceptions. It is said that absolute non-discrimination is not a principle of either municipal law or international law (Sornarajah, 1986: 185). Non-discrimination is a principle which can only be applied in a general way, taking into account all the circumstances of the case (Amerasinghe, 1967: 141). It is also argued that the non-discrimination principle applies when there is discrimination between foreigners, and not when the discrimination is between nationals and foreigners (Sornarajah, 1986: 185). It is further said that discriminatory measures aimed at ending the domination of the economy by foreigners from a particular country are not unlawful under international law (White, 1961: 119; Friedman, 1953: 189). Such types of actions are sometimes called "reverse discrimination" (Friedman, 1953: 189).

Investment protection The issue of investment protection is one of the most important subjects in the area of FDI regulation. Host countries generally provide foreign investors with guarantees of one form or another in respect of their property. The main contentions regarding investment protection lie, however, in issues such as the definition of expropriation, its legal preconditions, the amount of compensation to be paid, and the standard of compensation.

Expropriation

The term "expropriation" may not, however, be confined to the compulsory transfer of private property to state ownership. Property may, for example, be taken from foreign owners, not to put it in the hands of the state (or state-owned enterprises), but to transfer ownership to local private nationals (that is, expropriation for the purpose of achieving national control). The Mexican agrarian reform of the 1930s and the Ugandan nationalisation of Asian-owned businesses in the 1970s may be cited as examples of this.[22] Another instance is that instead of transferring the privately owned property to state ownership or to the ownership of third parties (direct expropriation), the state may "unreasonably" interfere with property rights or take measures or enact laws the practical effect of which would be equivalent to expropriation. [23] Such acts are normally called "creeping" or "disguised" or "indirect" expropriation. Exactly what acts or measures constitute indirect expropriation, and the point where the different acts or measures reach the stage of being considered an expropriation, even though the individual owner retains title, are not clearly demarcated. The Harvard Draft Convention of 1961 explains "indirect expropriation" as follows:

> A State may make it impossible for an alien to operate a factory which he owns by blocking the entrances on the professed ground of maintaining order. It may, through its labour legislation and labour courts, designedly set the wages of local employees of the enterprise at a prohibitively high level. If technical personnel are needed from outside the country, entry visas may be denied them. Essential replacement parts or machinery may be refused entrance, or allocations of foreign exchange may deliberately be denied with the purpose of making it impossible to import the requisite machinery. Any one of these measures...could make it impossible for the alien owner to use or enjoy his property. More direct interference may also be imagined. The alien may simply be forbidden to employ a certain portion of a building which he occupies, either on a wholly arbitrary basis or on the authority of some asserted requirement of the local law. A government, while leaving ownership of an enterprise in the alien owner, might appoint conservators, managers, or inspectors who might interfere with the free use of the alien of its premises and its facilities. Or, simply by forbidding an alien to sell his property, a government could effectively

> deprive that property of its value (Explanatory Note to the 1961 Harvard Draft Convention, 1991: 532).

Compensation

The payment of compensation for expropriated property is one of the major elements of a lawful act of expropriation. In some countries, the law stipulates that adequate compensation, corresponding to the prevailing market value and in convertible currency shall be paid without delay.[24] In others, the law may stipulate that "just" compensation shall be paid in convertible currency and without delay.[25] In some instance, the law specifies the period within which compensation should be paid.[26]

The term "adequate" has quite often been used in practice interchangeably with "full", "just", or "fair" compensation. Schwarzenberger, for instance, states that:

> The difference between the terms "full" and "adequate" compensation is merely one between synonyms. A claimant is likely to consider full compensation in accordance with his own petition alone to be adequate. Conversely, compensation considered adequate by an impartial third party, but falling short of a claimant's exaggerated expectations is not necessarily less that full compensation (Schwarzenberger, 1969: 10).[27]

On the other hand, developing countries have long been arguing that the traditional formula of "adequate compensation" should be modified in light of their financial situation and difficulties, which they consider were not of their own making. They say that insistence on strict compliance with "orthodox standards of compensation" would thwart their efforts to carry out badly needed social and economic reforms (Jain, 1983: 124). Thus it is quite often argued that in deciding the amount of compensation to be paid, the ability of the expropriating state to pay should be taken into consideration. Moreover, a large number of lump sum compensation agreements arrived at on the basis of partial compensation[28] indicate that in many of them the expropriating State's ability to pay was taken into account.

The Transfer of Funds The transfer of funds is one of the core elements of investment protection. The ability to transfer capital and earnings is critical for any foreign investor. Most countries provide in their laws guarantees of one form or another with regard to the right to transfer funds.

The scope of funds the transfer right covers, however, varies from country to country. In the developed countries, the scope is usually broader and it includes the principal investment and additional amounts to maintain or increase an investment, the returns, the repayment of loans, the proceeds from liquidation or the sale of the whole or any part of the investment, and the compensation in case of expropriation, war, civil disturbance, and similar events (OECD, 1995: 142-43). In many developing countries, on the other hand, the scope is narrower. In Zimbabwe, for example, foreign investors were allowed to remit 25-50% of their after-tax profits, and in the case of disinvestments, an amount equal to the amount of the original investment less the amount of income from the investment remitted before the disinvestments. In addition, foreign investors would be provided with the necessary foreign exchange for their transactions abroad (Government of Zimbabwe, 1991: 18).

The IMF Agreement distinguishes between restrictions affecting capital transfers and those concerning "current transactions".[29] While a member state may impose restrictions on capital transfers, it cannot do so with regard to current transactions without the approval of the Fund.

It may be argued that the best protection for the foreign investor would be an unconditional transfer guarantee. However, very few countries, mainly industrial countries, provide such an unconditional guarantee. The majority of countries guarantee the transfer of capital, profits, debt service payments and portions of employees' salaries and wages but expressly make this guarantee subject to foreign exchange or other regulations.[30] In some countries, there are additional restrictions, such as that capital may not be transferred prior to liquidation.

To sum up, every country has laws controlling FDI in one form or another. The laws of host countries sometimes specify the legal vehicle through which FDI can be made, the nature of capital resources that can be brought from abroad, the performance and other requirements the FDI is subject to, the incentives provided to the investor, the legal protection accorded to FDI, the circumstances of the termination of the FDI, and other similar matters.

Most restrictions on FDI are explained by considerations that appear at face value to be justifiable. They may be intended to improve the balance-of-payments or benefit local industry; to train or increase the employment of nationals, to develop specific sectors or geographical areas, to develop local technology or, more generally, to limit the role of foreign factors in the economy. Excessive restrictions, however, underestimate the benefits of open competition and a liberal environment. They can also discourage investors and lead them either to turn to other countries where their investments will not be subject to similar limitations or to overcome such obstacles in other costly or objectionable ways, such as corrupting government officials.

The general economic health and degree of political stability in the host country, along with the presence of resources and market, are probably the essential requirements for attracting FDI. Given the satisfaction of these basic conditions, investors may still have a wide choice of locations to choose from. In order to influence this choice, governments provide a wide variety of incentives aimed at promoting both investment in general and investment in select economic sectors of locations or with certain characteristics. However, competition among host countries in offering investment incentives is quite intense and may create a loss of important revenue for the government because the role some of the incentives play in influencing investor decision is at least doubtful. Incentives may be justified in limited circumstances, such as in the case of infant industries.

The laws of most countries contain provisions on investment protection. The provisions usually contain guarantees against the expropriation of FDI without payment of compensation. The value of these unilateral guarantees has, however, been differently assessed in the literature.[31] Some say that a guarantee given by one government cannot be binding on a succeeding government, particularly if there has been a revolutionary change of government (Delupis, 1987: 27-32). Others argue that guarantees that are held out to foreign investors do have legal implications, despite a regime change.[32]

There is a principle of traditional international law that there must be no discrimination in the treatment of nationals and foreigners. This principle has been supported by a number of writers, judicial decisions and State practices. Gillian White, for example, writes as follows:

> It is an established rule of international law that persons residing within the territory of a foreign State are entitled at least to the same protection of their persons and property as is afforded by the local law to nationals of that State... If the property of aliens is nationalised and the property of nationals remains unaffected by the nationalisation decree, the measure is discriminatory and involves the responsibility of the legislating State towards the State whose nationals have been affected (White, 1961: 119).

A number of writers insist that the non-discrimination principle applies when there is a discrimination between foreigners, and not when the discrimination is between nationals and foreigners. Thus, responsibility is incurred if the nationalisation measure affects the property rights of foreigners of nationality "A" and not those of nationalities "B" and "C" who also own property rights of the kind specified in the nationalisation measures (White, 1961: 119; Friedman, 1953: 189).

The non-discrimination principle appears to have found some support in judicial decisions as well. In its advisory opinion regarding the settlers of German origin in the territory ceded by Germany to Poland, the Permanent Court of International Justice found that:

> The facts that no racial discrimination appears in the text of the law of July 14, 1920, and that in a few instances the law applies to non-German Polish nationals who took as purchasers from original holders of German race, makes no substantial difference... There must be equality in fact as well as ostensible legal equality in the sense of the absence of discrimination in the words of the law.[33]

However, the extent of the application of this principle has always been controversial. Some writers say that "what really matters is not whether the treatment of foreigners is better or worse than that accorded to a State's own nationals or is equal to their treatment, but whether it measures up to the minimum standard of international law" (Schwarzenberger, 1969: 159; see also Amerasinghe, 1967: 141). According to De Lupis, a discriminatory nationalisation measure would not be contrary to international law if it is for the public purpose. "It is the public purpose of nationalisation which is of paramount importance and such valid purpose appears to outweigh the necessity of non-discrimination" (Detter Delupis, 1987: 70).

When most of the developing countries were decolonised, the first thing the newly independent States did was to take measures which, in their view, would end their economic dependence on the former colonial powers. As the economies of these countries were largely dominated by MNCs from the former colonial powers, they directed their nationalisation measures against these corporations, hence discrimination becoming inevitable. It is said, therefore, that the non-discrimination principle should not be allowed to operate in these circumstances (Sornarajah, 1986: 184). This view has also been shared by the German Court which considered the Indonesian nationalisation measures:

> The equality concept means only that equals must be treated equally and that the different treatment of unequals is admissible. For the statement to be objective, it is sufficient that the attitude of the former colonial people to its former colonial master is of course different from that toward other foreigners.[34]

It has long been the practice of States to intervene diplomatically to protect property situated abroad which belongs to their nationals. On the other hand, many developing countries regarded diplomatic protection in connection with foreign investments as an instrument of interference in their internal affairs, according private interests primacy over national development plans (UNCTC, 1988: 93). For example, it has been the practice of many Latin American countries that in making concession contracts with foreign investors, they insert a "Calvo Clause".

The Calvo Clause originated from a doctrine advanced in 1868 by an Argentinian jurist, Carlos Calvo.[35] The Calvo doctrine thus set forth the principle that no State may intervene, diplomatically or otherwise, against another sovereign to enforce its citizens' private pecuniary claims. The doctrine exercised a profound influence in the sphere of contracts concluded between States and foreigners. The Calvo Clause has appeared in contracts in various forms; however, there have been basically four variations of the stipulation in the Constitutions of many Latin American countries. They are:

- A Calvo Clause excluding diplomatic protection under any circumstances;
- A Calvo Clause granting the right of diplomatic protection only in case of denial of justice;
- A Calvo Clause similar to (2) but requiring a denial of justice to be more than merely a verdict unfavourable to the claimant; and
- Those constitutional provisions which do not contain a Calvo Clause but which incorporate the Calvo Doctrine providing that, for all purposes, foreign investors are subject to treatment and obligations on an equal basis with nationals.

The validity of a Calvo Clause under international law has always been debatable. Latin American countries advanced two basic arguments in support of the validity of the Calvo Clause. The first is that if foreigner were accorded treatment on basis equal to that accorded to nationals of the State, they would have no right to legally demand more. Hence, "by waiving the right of the special privilege of diplomatic protection, the Clause merely formalises this rule of equality into a contractual commitment". The second argument is that "there is no sound logical or judicial reason under international law for not holding an alien to their contractual waiver of diplomatic protection" (Graham, 1970: 290).

On the other side of the debate, it is said that equal treatment is all that foreigners may demand only if the international minimum standard is maintained. If it is not maintained, there exists a valid justification for diplomatic interposition" (Graham, 1970: 294). In rejecting the argument that the individual's voluntary waiver of diplomatic remedy must be respected, it is said that "an injury to a national is, in actuality, an injury to the State of that national... Thus, a private citizen who is not an accredited agent of the State is unable to sign away the right of his country to intervene" (Graham, 1970: 294).

International Agreements

National laws can be changed with a change of government or an alteration of political ideology. This could have impacts on the effectiveness, continuity and enforceability of these laws. International rules, on the other hand, contribute to the alleviation of such problems, and give security for foreign investors. In fact, as early as 1954, the UN General Assembly passed a resolution urging both capital-exporting and capital-importing countries to "take such other steps as may be feasible and mutually acceptable to stimulate the flow of capital...and more especially to negotiate appropriate treaties, agreements or other arrangements..." (General Assembly Resolution 824(IX), 1954).

International agreements may be categorised as bilateral and multilateral. The multilateral agreements, in turn, may be classified as regional/sectoral and global. The next section briefly discusses the different types of treaties or agreements concluded by governments for the purpose of facilitating the flow of and protecting FDI.

Bilateral Investment Treaties (BITs)

Since Germany and Pakistan signed the first bilateral investment treaty in 1959, over seven hundred BITs have been concluded by over 140 countries (UNCTAD, 1999: 8). Their signatories include all of the world's principal capital-exporting countries and many developing countries. Thus in just over four decades, the bilateral investment treaty has become one of the most important legal instruments affecting private foreign investment.

BITs set out the rules according to which the investments made by the nationals of the two contracting states would be treated and protected in each other's state. Writers are however divided as to the effect of these treaties. One view is that they give "important support for those standards of customary international law which had seemed to be slipping away" (Denza and Brooks, 1987: 912). Others cast doubt as to the existence of a customary international law in the field covered by BITs.

> The existence of such customary international law is difficult to establish as a large part of the world objected to the creation of such customary law...It is possible that an accumulation of bilateral investment treaties which subscribe to the same standard of conduct could make that standard of conduct a principle of customary international law (Sornarajah, 1994: 226).

The view that BITs can lead to the creation of customary international law is however opposed by those who say that this is not possible because the states making such treaties create *lex specialis* as between themselves in view of the uncertain state of the existing international law on foreign investment.[36] Moreover, there is so much divergence in the standards in BITs that it may be premature to conclude that they give rise to any significant rule of international law (Sornarajah, 1986: 79).

There has been a flurry of treaty-making activity over the last forty years. The reason appears to be the strong drive by MNCs to undertake FDI in other countries and the consequent need to create a stable international legal framework to facilitate and protect those investments. The desire of host developing countries to encourage investment and increase the amount of foreign capital flowing to their territory by reducing some of the investor's fears through BITs could be the other reason.

The structure of all BITs are very similar. Virtually every BIT addresses the following issues:

- Statement of purpose;
- Scope of application of the BIT;
- Conditions of entry;
- Standards of treatment;
- Monetary transfer;
- Protection against dispossession;
- Compensation; and
- Settlement of disputes.

Most treaties contain definitions of investments that are broad. They include both tangible and intangible property (see, for example, Article 1 of the United Kingdom treaty with Singapore). The BIT's definition of investment has a time dimension. While most BITs cover both existing and future investments, a few limit the coverage to investments at the time the treaty was made. A compromise position, found particularly in some of Germany's treaties, provides that the BIT will cover existing investments on the condition that the capital-exporting country makes a special request, and the host government approves such request.[37]

Once the investment is made, a basic question is the standard of treatment it is to receive from the host government thereafter. The general standards of treatment found in BITs are "fair and equitable treatment", "national treatment", and "most-favoured-nation treatment" (MFN). In some of the bilateral investment treaties the national treatment clause is combined with the MFN clause so that the foreign investor may take advantage of whichever standard of treatment is more favourable to it. Some BITs also refer to the possibility of derogation from national treatment and/or MFN. For instance, the treaty concluded between the Federal Republic of Germany and Uganda contains the following clause:

> In the interest of national economy either contracting party may, in approving an investment by nationals or companies of the other contracting party, make specific stipulations deviating from the treatment provided for in Article 2. If specific stipulations of that nature have been made, the provisions of Article 2 shall, to that extent, not be applicable (Article 2(d)).

Most BITs apply only post-entry and reserve the right of the host country to regulate entry. But this changed with the adoption by the US of its Model BIT in 1992, so that the US BITs apply a pre-entry national treatment standard. Some Canadian BITs too adopt the US Model.

Provisions on monetary transfer are among the most important in BITs for both the foreign investor and the host country. Naturally, home countries of foreign investors press for unrestricted guarantees to make monetary transfers. On the other hand, balance-of-payments problems and other difficulties reduce the host country's ability and willingness to grant investors unrestricted rights to make monetary transfers. As a result, host developing countries usually press for limited guarantees. Many of the British treaties provide that the right of repatriation of profits may be restricted "in exceptional economic or financial circumstances". In some of the British treaties, there is a requirement that the repatriation of a percentage of the profits should be permitted every year in circumstances of foreign exchange difficulties. The Treaties concluded with the Netherlands[38] provide a non-exhaustive list of the types of transfer which are guaranteed. Stabilisation clauses are included in some treaties to ensure that the transfer of currency will be governed by the laws existing when the agreement entered into force. The United Kingdom - Lesotho Agreement, for instance, guarantees the transfer of capital and returns subject to the host country's "powers conferred by its laws existing when this Agreement entered into force".

The security of private investment in a host country is one of the vital considerations which influence foreign investors in deciding whether or not to invest their capital in that State. Bilateral investment treaties are regarded as useful instruments for providing effective protection of foreign investment. Article 3 of the German-Tanzania Treaty, for example, provides that investments by nationals or companies of either contracting party must be protected to the fullest extent and be secured in the territory of the other contracting party.

On the issue of compensation for expropriated property, many BITs adopt the "Hull Formula", that is, compensation must be "prompt, adequate, and effective".[39] The treaties then proceed to define the meaning of these words. For example, the United Kingdom - Costa Rica Treaty states: "Such compensation shall amount to the market value of the investment expropriated immediately before the expropriation or impending expropriation became public knowledge, shall include interest at a normal commercial rate until the date of payment, shall be made without delay, and be effectively realisable and be freely transferable." On the other hand, the Japan - China treaty adopts a slightly different formulation. It states:

> Compensation...shall be such as to place the nationals and companies in the same financial position as that in which the nationals and companies would have been if expropriation, nationalisation, or other measures...had not been taken. Such compensation shall be paid without delay. It shall be effectively realisable and freely transferable at the exchange rate in effect on the date used for the determination of amount of compensation (Article 5).

On its face, this provision does not provide for the payment of interest and might allow less than market value. To clarify its meaning, China and Japan agreed to an explanatory minute annexed to the Treaty that states:

> It is confirmed that with reference to the provisions of Article 5 of the Agreement, the compensation...shall represent the equivalent of the value of the investment and returns affected at the time when expropriation, nationalisation, or any other measures...are publicly announced or when such measures are taken, whichever is the earlier, and shall carry an appropriate interest taking into account the length of time until the time of payment (Agreed Minute, Paragraph 3).

Most of the bilateral investment treaties contain clauses for the settlement of investment disputes arising between the foreign investor and the host State. The existence of such clauses in the treaties forms an essential part of the protection which a foreign investor requires (see for example Japan - China Treaty). Most BITs specify arbitration in a neutral forum as the method of resolution of the dispute. There are different types of clauses creating different obligations as to such arbitration. Some merely direct the parties to arbitration as a way of solving disputes from foreign investment transactions. Others entitle the foreign investor to initiate a claim before an ICSID tribunal.

But, despite references to ICSID, all provisions containing such references do not create jurisdiction automatically in the ICSID (Broche, 1982: 63). Whether such jurisdiction is created depends on the precise words used in the treaty. Broche makes a distinction between four types of arbitration provisions in BITs. The first type merely states that the dispute "shall, upon agreement by both parties, be submitted for arbitration by the Centre" (see also Wegen, 1985: 67). Such a clause does not constitute consent to arbitration in the absence of an agreement after the dispute has arisen. The second type that requires "sympathetic consideration to a request for conciliation or arbitration by the Centre" does not amount to consent but according to Broches, it may imply an "obligation not to withhold consent unreasonably". The third type of clause requires the host state "to assent to any demand on the part of the national to submit for conciliation or arbitration any dispute arising from the investment". Refusal to assent may amount to an international wrong but the clause itself does not create jurisdiction in ICSID. The fourth type of clause creates jurisdiction in the Centre by giving consent in anticipation of the dispute (see for example the Agreement between the United Kingdom and Lesotho).

To conclude, there has been intense activity in the past four decades in the area of bilateral investment treaties. In the absence of clear rules on investment protection, capital-exporting countries have found it desirable that they should give as much protection as possible to their investors by negotiating BITs with clear rules. Despite their limitation in scope, BITs have more or less served this purpose. However, even though BITs have so far played an important role in the expansion of the acceptance and application of certain standards, it is doubtful if they are suitable for the increasingly globalised economy. In addition to their limitations in scope, there is a risk that continued reliance on BITs would produce a wide range of non-uniform and inconsistent arrangements that could become increasingly inefficient, complex and non-transparent.

Regional/Sectoral Agreements

There are several regional or sectoral agreements that address the regulation of FDI dealing with several issues.[40] Among them are the OECD Codes of Liberalisation of Current Invisible Transaction and of Capital Movements, the OECD Declaration on International Investment and Multinational Enterprises, the North American Free Trade Agreement (NAFTA), and the APEC Non-Binding Investment Principles. Decision 291 of the Andean Pact is another useful illustration, not only in terms of its contents but also because of its history. The Lome Conventions, between the European Economic Community and the ACP countries, also include provisions on FDI, on the basis of which the Community adopted a statement on investment protection principles. Since the list is a long one, only a few of those treaties will be discussed here briefly.

OECD documents The OECD Codes on Liberalisation of Current Invisible Transactions and of Capital Movements are legally binding Decisions of the OECD. From the start, they were bottom-up procedures, committing members to progressive relaxation of controls based on standstill and rollback, within a framework of peer review and reciprocal concessions (OECD, 1987). The specific provisions cover the creation of new enterprises, expansion of existing enterprises, mergers, take-overs and participation in domestic enterprises by non-residents. However, it was only since the mid-1980s was there in practice a significant relaxation of capital controls. In April 1984, agreement was reached to make these provisions fully effective by requiring that Member Countries apply the National Treatment principle when considering applications for licenses, or other authorisations needed for conducting business in the country concerned. Taken together, the Codes on Liberalisation of Capital Movements and of Current Invisible Transactions, and the National Treatment instrument provide:

- National Treatment, both before and after establishment,
- Repatriation of profits, dividends, rents, and the proceeds of liquidated investments,
- Transparency of regulations,
- A mechanism of consultation to deal with complaints, and
- Peer review to promote rollback of remaining restrictions.

The objective of the Codes is the progressive liberalisation of all the operations falling within their purview. They provide a framework of notification, examination and consultation through which their prescriptions can be monitored and liberalisation achieved.

The areas of operation the Members are required to liberalise are specified under List A and List B of the Code. Additional reservations are not permitted on any of the items in the Current Invisibles Code or in List A of the Capital Movements Code (Article 2 of the Code). This implies a standstill which, under normal circumstances, allows no reduction in the degree of liberalisation of the operations concerned. In respect of the items in List B of the Capital Movements Code restrictions may be imposed or reimposed and reservations may be lodged at any time (Article 2 of the Code). When a reservation is lodged, the reasons for this action must be notified forthwith to the Organisation, and the Member must submit a periodic examination of the reservations it maintains.

Remaining restrictions must be applied in a non-discriminatory manner as between OECD Member countries (Article 9 of the Code). Members that have not liberalised must not be discriminated against and must continue to receive the benefits of liberalisation (Article 8 of the Code). Members of a "special customs or monetary system" are permitted to apply to one another additional measures of liberalisation without extending them to other Members (Article 10 of the Code).

The APEC investment principles The APEC Principles on foreign investment are a set of non-binding guidelines for the treatment of foreign investment in the Asia-Pacific region. They were adopted at the APEC Conference held in Bogor, Indonesia, in November 1994, following a recommendation made by a group of Eminent Persons (APEC, 1993). The principles cover the treatment of foreign investments/investors, investment incentives, performance requirements, expropriation and compensation and dispute settlement.[41]

The North American Free Trade Agreement (NAFTA) NAFTA is an Agreement signed between the United States, Canada and Mexico on trade and investment liberalisation. It contains a Chapter on investment which consists of a number of principles (national treatment, MFN, minimum standard of treatment) and obligations (e.g. expropriation and compensation; the free transfer of profits; performance requirements; nationality requirements for senior management and directors) governing a Party's regulation of investment.

The Agreement requires each Party (and its states and provinces) to accord to investors of another Party and their investments national treatment and MFN (or the better of the two) with respect to the establishment, acquisition, expansion, management, conduct, operation, and sale or other disposition of investments (Articles 1102 and 1103). It prohibits the imposition of a number of performance requirements (Article 1106).

NAFTA also contains provision on monetary transfer covering five categories of transfers, and provides that all the transfers be made "freely and without delay", in "freely useable currency at the market rate of exchange" (Article 1109).[42] Article 1110 of the Agreement provides for the protection of foreign investments against nationalisation, expropriation, and other forms of interference that are "tantamount to nationalisation or expropriation". It also stipulates that payment of compensation must be made in accordance with the following principles (Article 1110):

- compensation shall be equivalent to the fair market value of the expropriated investment immediately before the expropriation took place (the date of expropriation);
- the fair market value cannot reflect any change in value occurring because the intended expropriation had become known earlier;
- valuation criteria shall include going concern value, asset value, including declared tax value of tangible property, and other criteria, as appropriate, to determine fair market value;
- compensation must be paid without delay and be fully realisable;
- if payment is made in a G7 currency, compensation shall include interest at a commercially reasonable rate for that currency from the date of expropriation until the date of actual payment; and
- on payment, compensation shall be freely transferable.

Sub-Chapter B of the Investment Chapter establishes an arbitration mechanism for the settlement of investor-state and state-state disputes (Article 1115). A disputing investor may submit a claim to arbitration under one of the following three sets of arbitration rules (Article 1120):

- the ICSID Convention, provided that both the disputing Party and the Party and the Party of the investor are parties to the ICSID Convention;
- the Additional Facility Rules of ICSID, provided that either the disputing Party or the Party of the investor, but not both, is a Party to the ICSID Convention; or

- the UNCITRAL Arbitration Rules.

Global Rules

Although there are numerous bilateral and regional/sectoral agreements around the world, there isn't a single global investment agreement to date that would cover all aspects of investment. All attempts made so far to come up with such an agreement have failed (see Chapters Five and Eight).

Some existing WTO agreements contain provisions relating to investment, notably the Agreement on Trade-Related Investment Measures (TRIMs) and the General Agreement on Trade in Services (GATS). TRIMs protect investment from certain types of performance requirements such as local content and trade-balancing requirements.[43] The GATS explicitly recognises FDI as one of the four "modes of supply" of services. The Agreement includes provisions concerning notification, transparency, MFN, national treatment, market access, subsidies, and foreign exchange restriction on capital account and current account transactions These rules attempt to regulate foreign investment within the framework of reducing trade distortions. However, the WTO plans (if its members agree) to include investment regulation in its domain (see Chapter Eight).

Conclusion

The high growth in FDI flows over the past decade has been supported by widespread liberalisation policies and increasing competition for foreign investment. As governments increasingly realised that FDI could contribute positively to the economic growth of a country, they have progressively liberalised their foreign investment regimes to facilitate FDI flows. In 1998, 94% of FDI regulatory changes around the world improved the environment for FDI (UNCTAD, 1999: 8). Table 3:1 shows that national regulatory changes favourable to FDI outnumbered the less favourable ones by large margins. In part, this represents the route of dependency theory policy thinking (which had been prominent beyond the 1970s) by neo-classical liberalism (see Chapter Two).

Bilateral investment agreements were also increasing progressively in the past several years, reaching a total of 1,726 by the end of 1998 (UNCTAD, 1999: 8). By the end of 1998, the number of treaties for the avoidance of double taxation had reached a total of 1,871 (UNCTAD, 1999: 8). Even though BITs have so far played an important role in the expansion of the acceptance and application of certain standards, it is however doubtful if they are suitable for the increasingly globalised economy. In addition to their limitations in scope, there is a risk that continued reliance on BITs would produce a wide range of non-uniform and inconsistent arrangements that could become increasingly inefficient, complex and non-transparent. At the multilateral level, there have been intensive rule making activities, mainly in connection with the creation or expansion of regional integration schemes, and involving rules for the liberalisation and protection of FDI (UNCTAD, 1999: 8).

Despite all these rule making activities, however, the international system still lacks a broad set of global investment rules. Whatever international agreements we have, their scope is limited either geographically (as in the case of BITs and regional agreements) or in scope (as in the case of TRIMs and BITs). National laws, too, although broader in scope, have geographical limits in their applicability.

By its nature, foreign investment falls within the jurisdiction of more than one country. More importantly, modern communication and financial integration have encouraged firms to operate on a regional or even global basis. Cross-border mergers and acquisitions (M&A) and other forms of strategic alliances have become the norm, rather than the exception. In 1998, the absolute value of all cross-border M&A (sales and purchases) amounted to $544 billion, representing an increase of about 60% over that of 1997 (UNCTAD, 1999: 18). This has enormous implications on national regulatory regimes.

Table 3:1 Changes to National Regulatory Regimes on FDI, 1991-98

Item	**1991**	**1992**	**1993**	**1994**	**1995**	**1996**	**1997**	**1998**
Countries that introduced change	35	43	57	49	64	65	76	60
No. of regulatory changes, of which:	82	79	102	110	112	114	151	145
More favourable to FDI♣	80	79	101	108	106	98	135	136
Less favourable to FDI♦	2	-	1	2	6	16	16	9

♣ Including liberalisation changes or changes aimed at strengthening market functioning, as well as increased incentives.

♦ Including changes aimed at increasing control as well as reducing incentives.

Source UNCTAD, World Investment Report 1999: Foreign Direct Investment and the Challenges of Development, Table IV.1, p.115.

The global expansion of FDI inevitably necessitates the transfer of tangible and intangible assets between parent companies and their foreign affiliates. How to establish prices for such cross-border transfers is a thorny issue for policy-makers makers and regulators. The issue is even more pressing for developing countries, given the more limited resources and expertise of such countries in the field of transfer pricing. The problem is also aggravated by the absence of an international agreement on transfer pricing.

Globalisation of the world economy is said to have brought economic activities closer, such as trade and investment which, in the past, were treated as discrete (Fatouros, 1996: 59). Trade and investment increasingly intertwine to use inputs efficiently and sell outputs across borders. The successful conclusion of successive trade negotiations within the GATT/WTO framework also reduced trade barriers and stimulated global FDI flows. Such frameworks, however, do not address FDI in a satisfactory manner.

The current regulatory framework for FDI is, therefore, unsatisfactory on a number of grounds. Moreover, the diversity of national and international legal regimes governing FDI introduces excessive distortions as between countries and sectors (Fatouros, 1996: 59). The emergence of global investment rules would, among other things, give coherence to the regulatory environment facing foreign investment.

There appears to exist an opportunity for the emergence of global investment rules. The increasing realisation by host countries that FDI can contribute positively to their development endeavours has created an unprecedented positive environment for the negotiation of such rules. Moreover, the ever-diminishing appeal for dependency theory, the rapidly expanding bilateral investment treaties, and the flurry of regional/sectoral agreements that have impacts on FDI would make a global investment agreement possible.

Notes

1 The International Centre for the Settlement of Investment Disputes (ICSID) has compiled the investment legislation of countries in loose-leaf volumes under the title "Investment Laws of the World".

2 These industries include domestic air transport, production and utilisation of nuclear energy, most domestic maritime transport, broadcasting and telecommunication, etc.

3 The Exon-Florio Amendment is formally known as Section VII of Title VII of the Defence Production Act of 1950, 50 U.S.C. app. 2071, and it regulates acquisition of US firms by foreign firms.

4 See, for example, Tanzania, The National Investment (Promotion and Protection) Act 1990; The Investment Code 1991 (of Uganda); Government of Zimbabwe, The Promotion of Investment: Policy and Regulation, 1991. Some of the activities of these Centres include:
- receiving all applications for investment licenses from potential investors;
- determining the terms and conditions which may be imposed in relation to the operation of a business enterprise;
- issuing licenses, approvals, authorisations, permits, and certificates of incentives; and assisting potential investors in identifying and establishing investment projects in the country.

5 See, for example, Investment Proclamation No. 37/1996 (of Ethiopia).

6 In Australia, for example, foreign investors are not allowed to buy developed residential real estate. In Ethiopia, foreign investors are not allowed in the banking and insurance sectors.

7 See, for instance, Australia's Foreign Investment Policy, on the Department of the Treasury web page at *www.treasury.gov.au*, accessed on 30 April 2000.

8 For a comprehensive discussion on this issue, see Turcon (1993); Graham & Krugman (1991).

9 For a further discussion on joint ventures, see Herzfeld & Wilson (1996).

10 The International Convention on the Elimination of All Forms of Racial Discrimination permits discrimination between nationals and foreigners; Article 1(2) reads "This Convention shall not apply to distinctions, exclusions, restrictions or preferences made by a State Party to this Convention between citizens and non-citizens." It also reads: "The Convention does not interfere in the internal legislation of any State as far as rights of citizens and not-citizens are concerned..." See Lerner, (1980: 30). However, there is also disquiet about the wisdom of entry requirements. Many say that they are serious obstacles to the establishment of FDI and are far more significant barriers to FDI than are TRIMS. See Bale (Jr), (1990: 62).
11 See, for example, Afro-Asian Legal Consultative Committee (1974).
12 The 1995 WTO General Agreement on Trade-Related Investment Measures (TRIMS) prohibits certain types of performance requirements (see Chapter Eight for details).
13 Several studies have analysed host countries' incentive laws and policies. See, for example, Yelpaala (1985: 208); Kofele-Kale (1990: 369); Boadway & Shah (1992).
14 See, for example, Investment Incentives Council of Ministers Regulation No. 7/1996 (of Ethiopia), Article 11.
15 See, for example, Investment Incentives Council of Ministers Regulation No. 7/1996 (of Ethiopia), Articles 3,4 and 5.
16 For a comprehensive reading on EPZs, see Basile & Germidis (1984); UNCTAD/ILO (1988); Roberts (1992).
17 One of the distinctive features of foreign investment is that almost all modern foreign investments are undertaken by corporations and not by individuals.
18 For a general survey of the tax rules pertaining to foreign sourced income in many capital-exporting countries, see OECD (1989).
19 The term "taking" is used here to denote the exercise by the state of its power to interfere with private property rights, such as expropriation, nationalisation, confiscation, etc, irrespective of whether the interference is "direct" or "indirect". Also, throughout the discussion, "expropriation" and "nationalisation" are used interchangeably.
20 For a comprehensive reading on non-discrimination, see also White (1961); Foighel (1957); Sornarajah, (1986); Amerasinghe (1967).
21 The Oscar Chin Case, PCIJ Series A/B, 63 at 87, cited in Garcia-Amador (1984).
22 See ICSID, AMCO Asia Corporation et al and Indonesia (Award on Merits), November 21, 1984, reproduced in 24 ILM 102 (1985).
23 See, for example, Iran - United States Claims Tribunal, Case Concerning Starrette Housing Corporation et al and the Government of the Islamic Republic of Iran et al (Interlocutory Award), reproduced in 20 ILM 231, (1981). See also Jain, (1983: 34).
24 See, for example, Investment Proclamation No. 37/1996 (of Ethiopia), Article 21.
25 See, for example, Foreign Investment Act 1990 (of Namibia).
26 See, for example, Investment Code, 1991 (of Uganda).
27 See also Iran - United States Claims Tribunal, SEDCO v National Iranian Oil Company and Iran, (Interlocutory Award), March 1986, p.8, reproduced in 25 ILM 629m (1986).
28 For instance, under the United States-Mexico Settlement of 1942, Mexico agreed to pay a sum of about $US24 million for nationalised oil property, although America's claims totalled 260 million dollars. Similarly, an interest free amount of 28.3 million Egyptian pounds was agreed upon as compensation for the nationalisation of the Suez Canal Company in 1958 as against the Company's claim of 204 million pounds; cited in Jain (1983:156).

29 Article XXXd of the IMF Agreement defines "current transactions" as payments related to international commercial contracts, interest and net returns from investments, and payments of moderate amounts for amortisation of loans or for depreciation of direct investment.

30 See for example Investment Law No. 230 for 1989 (of Egypt); Law on Foreign Investment, 1987, of Vietnam.

31 Vagts observed that these guarantees "seldom have significant legal effect although it is conceivable that they could later disable the country from making various arguments to international tribunal in defence of measures taken against foreign investment" (Vagts, 1990: 104).

32 See for example SPP v Egypt, in 22 ILM 752, (1983).

33 Certain Questions Relating to Settlers of German Origin in the Territory Ceded by Germany to Poland (1923), in PCIJ Series B 6, at 24, as cited in F. Garcia-Amador, 1984: 287).

34 N.V. Verenidge Deli-Maatschapijen and N.V. Senembaj-Maatschapij v Deutsche Indonesische Tabak-Handelsgesellschaft, quoted in Sornarajah, 1986: 184. On the other hand, one should be careful that such measures do not amount to racial discrimination. In the 1970s the Ugandan Government nationalised Asian-owned businesses in Uganda. That measure was criticised as discriminatory based on ethnicity. It is said that since the principle against racial discriminating is a part of "ius cogens", a nationalisation measure the purpose of which is racial persecution of a particular ethnic or alien group is illegal even if there is also an economic purpose behind the nationalisation. Therefore, as nationalisation motivated by economic nationalism could easily bring about racial animosities, the task of balancing the economic and racial reasons of the nationalisation would not be easy.

35 For a comprehensive disucussion of the Calvo Doctrine, see Brownlie, (1990); United Nations International Law Commission (1958; Graham, (1970); Lipstein, (1945); Summers, (1932-33).

36 See, for example, Asia Agricultural Products LTD. v. Sri Lanka, reproduced in 17 YCA 106 (1990).

37 See for example, Germany's bilateral investment treaties with Guyana, Paraguay and Kuwait, in ICSID, Bilateral Investment Treaties, Volumes 3, 5 and 6 respectively.

38 See for example Agreement on Economic Cooperation between the Government of the Kingdom of the Netherlands and the Republic of Uganda, Articles VIII and IX(2).

39 In 1938, the United States Secretary of State Hull, in response to Mexican agrarian nationalisation measures, declared in correspondence to the Ambassador of Mexico that "under every rule of law and equity, no government is entitled to expropriate private property, for whatever purpose, without provision for prompt, adequate, and effective payment thereof" (Henkin et al, 1980: 688). Since that time, this phrase (prompt, adequate, and effective) has sometimes been referred to as the "Hull Formula".

40 UNCTAD has compiled in compendium 39 of such agreements (UNCTAD, 1996a).

41 For a detailed discussion of the APEC Investment Principles, see Chapter Eight.

42 The five categories are remittance of profits, dividends, interest, capital gains, different types of fees etc.; proceeds from the sale or liquidation of an investment; payments made under contract; payments made as compensation for expropriated property; and payments arising from settlement of disputes.

43 For a wider discussion of TRIMs, see Chapter Eight.

Chapter 4

Methodology

Multiple methods have been used in the research that will be explained below (Blaxter, et al, 1996: 77). The whole research process could be divided into two: data collection and analysis. The main sources of data in the research were review of literature, interviews with people, observation – largely in cyberspace and legal policy analysis. These were all oriented to securing a balanced, triangulated understanding of the progress of the MAI negotiations and the perspectives of the key players and the lessons this has for a redesign of FDI regulation.

Literature Review

Both primary and secondary materials have been reviewed in this research. Most primary materials were obtained from international organisations either during my visits to those organisations or through the Internet. In addition, a large number of books, newspaper reports, public recordings, policy papers and statistics have been reviewed. Monitoring e-mail networks was a strategy for keeping up with literatures that often appeared in obscure places (see Section III).

Interviews

I conducted 48 partially structured interviews in 1996 and 1997. The main aim of the interviews was to understand what the strategies of each of the key players were for a global investment agreement, the issues they saw as important and their views on other key players' strategies and positions. The interviews were conducted in Canberra (Australia), Paris, Geneva and Brussels. Nineteen of the interviewees were officials of developed and developing countries; sixteen were officials of international organisations; and thirteen were from NGOs (see Table 4:1). Three potential interviewees refused an interview due to unavailability, and one due to an unwillingness to cooperate.

The choice of interviewees was guided by the search for the diversity of opinions and experiences needed to understand the positions and strategies of the key players and clarify the analysis (see generally Burgess, 1982; Glaser & Strauss, 1967; Lofland, 1971). Hence, the different key international players in the debate for global investment rules were selected based on their activities, voices and influence on different international fora. The strategy was not to determine the distribution and frequency of opinions, but to study the range of types of opinions. Following snowballing techniques (Minchiello et al, 1990), a few individuals, who were said to be knowledgeable/prominent in the field, were initially contacted and asked to nominate other potential interviewees who would have a different opinion from them, and so on. Due to the transport and other costs involved in reaching all of these players around the world, three cities (Paris, Geneva and Brussels) were selected because all of these players have representatives in one or more of these places. Then, letters/faxes were sent to diplomatic missions (if it was for governments) and heads of the relevant sections of international organisations requesting meeting arrangements for the interviews. In some cases, particularly for NGOs, the letters/faxes were addressed to specific individuals who had been recommended as more appropriate for the interview.

Table 4:1 Interviews Conducted in 1996 and 1997

Government Officials	Developed Countries	9
	Developing Countries	10
International Organisations	OECD	2
	UNCTAD	8
	UNEP	2
	WTO	2
	EC	2
Non-Governmental Organisations	Consumer	3
	Environment	1
	Labour	3
	Business	4
	Development	2
Total Number of Interviews		**48**

The choice of partially structured interviews, rather than structured or unstructured interviews, was deliberate. Prior to the interview, I knew from the literature most of the contentious issues and I had a definite framework of topics to be covered; hence, the manner and sequence in which the questions would be asked was not important. What was important was to have the freedom to explore reasons and motives, to probe further in directions I thought would afford clues within the framework of the topics. The interviewees were free to express completely their own lines of thought, but the direction of the interview was mainly in my hands.

Jack Douglas' technique of creative interviewing has been used throughout the interview process. Creative interviewing is "the use of many strategies and tactics of interaction, largely based on an understanding of friendly feelings and intimacy, to optimise cooperative, mutual disclosure and a creative search for mutual understanding" (Douglas 1985:25). Depending on the status, taste and feelings of the interviewees, I sometimes shared my own personal feelings on certain issues, sometimes unrelated to the subject of the interview. Such disclosures would occasion the interviewee's reciprocal revelations. Attempts were also made to make the interviews as informal as possible. Hence, one interview was conducted in a shopping mall; two interviews were conducted over lunch; a number of others were conducted in coffee shops. Such informalities were useful in creating the environment of intimacy.

Notes were taken during most of the interviews. Only four interviews were tape-recorded. After the meetings, the notes were re-read and anything which I did not have time to write during the interview was added.

Interviews were made concrete by focusing upon the specific policy debates on FDI that were prominent at the time of the fieldwork. Pre-eminent among these was the negotiating positions players were adopting toward the MAI. Indeed it was these MAI negotiations that made this a strategic research topic at this historical conjuncture.

Observation in Cyberspace

Observation as a research technique covers a variety of situations and approaches. It can be done in a natural setting such as shops or in formal situations such as laboratories. The observer can be a participant (or visibly present), or his/her presence can be concealed (Kane, 1983: 53). Participant observation is usually used when one wishes to learn from people's actions what they do, as opposed to what they say they do or what others say they do (Kane, 1983: 53).

As the discussion in Chapters Five and Seven shows, NGOs around the world coordinate their activities, among other ways, through the Internet and e-mail "discussion forums". This has significantly made their actions effective and swift. Hence, I subscribed to no less than four e-mail "discussion forums" administered by members of NGOs, as a result of which I would receive 70-80 e-mails, on average, every day. This has enabled me to observe who the participants were and how they were related to one another. It helped me understand what they were doing, how, and with whom they did it. Usually, I knew in advance what actions they were planning to take, and what the genesis of it was. This also helped me prepare to closely monitor the reactions of the other side. Sometimes there would be disclosures of what players on the other side were saying as well. In all of these, I had to be very careful not to be biased by what they advocated. Hence, I deliberately refrained from participating in the discussions, even when some of the suggestions were to my liking.

In addition, I was able to observe a conference where the MAI negotiators and NGO representatives participated. Moreover, I was able to observe certain negotiations in my role in the Australian public service as an investment official. Indeed, I chose this position in the Australian public service so that I would have this direct observational opportunity. I was able in this role to observe directly what governments were saying to each other. Typically, at the time there were strict confidentiality constraints on these communications. But in time these positions also found their way into the public arena, and then I have been able to rely on them more explicitly in this research.

Data Analysis

The interview notes, and any other notes taken during literature review and observation were divided according to main topics and analysed. They were then compared and contrasted throughout the research process. The comparisons and contrasts were made with the views of players from different groups, as well as with members of the same group. New pieces of information were also constantly compared with previous information in the same topic. The relationships and differences between the categories of information were again analysed and incorporated in the book. Some of the relatively unique pieces of information were presented as quotations.

The book started with analysing the theories that have had major impact on national and international FDI rules, as well as the shortcomings of these theories. Discussing these theories at the beginning of the book was important in order to adequately understand the theoretical background of the positions and strategies of each key international player. Many of the utterances of the key players are found in this research to be framed in discourse of the theories outlined in Chapter Two.

Institutional and Legal Analysis

Finally, the theories from Part I of the book and the empirical evidence from Part II are brought together and put in context through the normative analysis in Part III. The pros and cons of the opposing positions of the key international players are analysed in light of these theories. But the empirical findings from Part II are not used to settle normative questions so much as to generate an exhaustive list of the normative issues that must be addressed. The weaknesses and strengths of current international and national regulatory arrangements for FDI are analysed. Moreover, the suitability of global organisations such as the WTO, UNCTAD and the World Bank for developing and implementing a future global FDI agreement is examined in light of the opposing positions of the key players. Then the book asks what would be the best kind of FDI agreement from the starting point of the reality of the key players' positions. This has lead to the development of a hybrid position, "regulated openness", grounded on compromise and principled pragmatism.

Part II
Strategies for a Global Investment Agreement: The Key Players

Chapter 5

The OECD Countries and the OECD Agenda

In Part One of the book (particularly Chapter Three), we have discussed the scope of the current regulatory framework on FDI, both nationally and internationally. We have identified the gaps where the current framework does not adequately address issues related to the regulation of FDI. A case has also been made on the need for a global agreement on FDI. Part two of the book, comprising four Chapters, examines the strategies and positions of the key global players on a global investment regime. These key players are OECD countries, developing countries, public interest groups (such as consumer advocates, environmentalists, labour unions and business associations) and inter-governmental organisations.

The strategies of the OECD and its Members for a future global investment regime could best be explained within the context of the OECD Multilateral Agreement on Investment (MAI).[1] Although OECD countries as a group hoped that the MAI would remove barriers to market access and enhance the multilateral trading system, each of the three main players within the group, namely the United States, the European Commission and Japan had their own distinct priorities when they first decided to start negotiating the Agreement. This Chapter first examines the policies and strategies of the three major players within the OECD briefly. Then it discusses the background and content of the MAI, to be followed by a discussion on why the MAI has so far failed to materialise.

The Three Major Players

The United States

The history of US policy on foreign investment shows a mixture of both restriction and openness. From the end of World War II, US policy on foreign investment was that of openness. With the exception of restrictions on investments originating from communist and some "unfriendly" countries, foreign investment was by-and-large welcome in most sectors of the economy (Kang, 1997: 302).

Table 5:1 Flows of Direct Investment out of and into the US, 1970-90 (in billions of US dollars)

Year	Capital Outflows	Capital Inflows	Net Outflows
1970	7.6	1.5	6.1
1971	7.6	0.4	7.3
1972	7.8	1.0	6.8
1973	11.4	2.8	8.6
1974	9.1	4.8	4.3
1975	14.2	2.6	11.6
1976	12.0	4.4	7.6
1977	11.9	3.7	8.2
1978	16.1	7.9	8.2
1979	25.2	11.9	13.3
1980	19.2	16.9	2.3
1981	9.6	25.2	-15.6
1982	1.0	13.8	-12.8
1983	6.7	12.0	-5.3
1984	11.6	25.4	-13.8
1985	13.2	19.0	-5.9
1986	18.7	34.1	-15.4
1987	31.1	46.9	-15.8
1988	16.2	58.4	-42.2
1989	31.7	72.2	-40.5
1990	24.0	46.1	-22.1

Source *US Department of Commerce*, Survey of Current Business, Various Issues. (in Kang, 1997: 316)

This policy of openness began to change around the first half of the 1970s, when European and Japanese firms began to make significant investment in the US (Kang, 1997: 302). For example in 1970, the net outflow of investment from the US was US$6.1 billion; this was reduced to $2.3 billion by 1980, and to a deficit of $22.1 billion in 1990 (Table 5.1). In the meantime, foreign investment that flowed into the country increased from US$1.5 billion dollars in 1970 to $46.1 billion in 1990. As Table 5.1 shows, the amount of foreign investment coming into the US consistently outpaced the amount of US foreign investment throughout the years 1981 to 1990. In fact, this trend has continued in the years following 1990 too (see UNCTAD World Investment Report for every year). This apparently ignited a fear that the economy was being dominated by foreign firms, particularly European and Japanese, thereby encouraging some elected policy-makers to examine the openness policy and reintroduce restrictions on foreign investment firms.

In the meantime, there was a feeling by some US officials that US firms were being discriminated against in Europe and Japan, while the latter's firms were free to invest in the US. An official of the United States Trade Representatives Office (USTR), an OECD Director, and an EC official all told me during my field work that the US felt that their firms had been excluded, particularly from the film, television, aerospace and electronic industries in Europe. An UNCTAD official, whom I interviewed in Geneva in 1996, also believed that penetrating the expanding European market and Japan was a top priority for the US:

> Americans could not easily penetrate the European and Japanese markets. This is not only because of the laws, but also it has a cultural aspect. A European car has a better chance of being sold in Europe than an American car. The Americans want to be physically present in Europe. That is only how their companies sell their products in Europe...The US does not worry about China, India and others coming to the MAI. They can deal with these countries unilaterally. Their interest is Europe and Japan.

Therefore, the United States, as a key player in putting up the agenda of negotiating the MAI, was primarily concerned in doing something about what is saw as the discrimination against its investors in Europe and Japan.

The European Commission

The EC strategy was directed to two fronts: the US and Asia (Interview with an OECD Director). With the US, the EC was keen to dismantle restrictions on European investment in the US which were made on grounds of "national security", abolish conditional national treatment, and restrict the extraterritorial application of US laws. On the Asian front, on the other hand, the Europeans thought that they were left out of investment in Asia, and they wanted to reverse this situation. In the aftermath of the Asian crisis of 1997-98, some of the heat has been lost from this motive, with Asian investment having much less allure.

Restrictions on "National Security" Grounds Section 5021 of the 1988 Omnibus Trade Act (most commonly known as the Exon-Florio Amendment) authorises the President to investigate the effects on US "national security" of any merger, acquisition or takeover which could result in foreign control of a US firm. It also gives the President power to take action to suspend or prohibit any such transaction, or even order expropriation, should he/she decide that the investment threatens US "national security".

This law, at the very least, has significantly extended the investment-blocking power of the federal government, for foreign investments could easily be blocked through a broad or creative interpretation of "national security". Furthermore, the law has made it easier to demand changes in the condition of investment before granting acceptance to investment proposals. In effect, the law has created a *de facto* screening mechanism that can bar foreign investment in virtually all sectors of the US economy based on vague "national security" grounds. The Exon-Florio Amendment is also reinforced by the 1993 Defence Authorisation Act that requires the President to report to Congress on the results of each investigation done pursuant to the Exon-Florio Amendment, including the potential effect of the proposal or pending transactions on the US's international technology leadership in areas affecting US "national security". Moreover, the US restricts FDI, again on "national security" grounds, from domestic and coastal shipping and certain other sectors of the economy.[2]

The Europeans, therefore, believe that all these laws blur the line between industrial and national security policy and the scope of application of such rules could easily be carried beyond what is necessary to protect essential national security interests (European Commission, 1996: 13). Hence, the European Commission (EC) sought to limit the application of "national security" considerations by the US through a multilateral agreement.

Conditional National Treatment Conditional National Treatment (CNT) refers to the granting of national treatment to foreign investors subject to certain conditions such as, in the case of the US, reciprocity and performance requirements. As a result of a reciprocity requirement, European investment may be allowed in the US only to the extent that "comparable" or "equivalent" opportunities are available to US firms in the home country of the investment (European Commission, 1996: 29). It also refers to "cross-sectoral reciprocity", that is, the requirement may not even be related to the sector in which the foreign company wants to be economically active in the US (European Commission, 1996: 29). Performance requirements, on the other hand, refer to either the potential contribution the foreign company could make to the US economy and employment or to the realisation of specific parameters of production (European Commission, 1996: 21).[3]

Extra-Territoriality The immediate concerns for the EC in this regard were the Cuban Liberty and Democratic Solidarity Act of 1996 (LIBERTAD), commonly known as the Helms-Burton Law, and the law which would punish foreign firms investing $40 million or more a year in oil and gas projects in Iran and Libya. The Helms-Burton Law permits US citizens with claims to property expropriated by Cuba to bring suit in US courts against persons who "traffic" in such property (LIBERTAD, Title III, Sec. 302). Furthermore, persons who "traffic" in such property and their families may be denied entry to the US (LIBERTAD, Title IV, Sec. 401). "Trafficking" is defined to include transferring, distributing, dispensing, brokering or otherwise disposing of confiscated property; purchasing, receiving, obtaining control of, or otherwise acquiring confiscated property; or improving or investing in (other than for routine maintenance) or beginning to manage, lease, possess, use or hold an interest in confiscated property. It also covers entry into a commercial arrangement using or otherwise benefiting from confiscated property (LIBERTAD, Title IV, Sec. 4(13)).

Following the signing of these two bills by the President, many countries expressed their opposition to them. The Canadian Government, for example, introduced legislation to counter the Helms-Burton Law. It also lodged a formal protest under NAFTA. The EC too expressed its objection by taking the matter to the WTO. The EC also believes that the extraterritoriality of US laws is a growing feature of the US legal system and, with a multilateral rule such as the MAI, the US would become less and less able to enforce its own laws onto others.

Asia and Beyond Regarding EC strategy towards Asia, the EC has in fact designed a number of support programs for European firms wishing to invest in Asia, as part of an overall strategy to strengthen European standing in Asia. These include (UNCTAD, 1996: 17):

- The Asia-Invest program, a program which consists of a wide range of instruments designed to promote business contacts between Asian and European investors, such as assistance to market research and monitoring activities, part-financing for business meetings between potential European and Asian investors, and identifying, evaluating and promoting specific investment activities in Asia;
- The European Community Investment Partners, a scheme consisting of facilities that assist in the formation of joint ventures between European and Asian partners;
- Financing Facilities of the European Investment Bank. The Bank has so far approved ECU340 million for joint ventures between Asian and European firms for various types of projects.

In addition to the above measures, the EC wanted to get greater access for its investors in Asia either by bringing Asian States into the MAI or by taking the MAI to the WTO.

> The European countries have agreements among themselves that are not less important than the MAI. The MAI will be insignificant if it remains within the OECD. The idea from the beginning was to attract Asian and Latin American countries. Without them, it will not have any significance. But there is nothing we can do if they refuse to join (Interview with an official of the European Commission).

On the other hand, if bringing these countries to the MAI were not possible, the European Commission's second strategy was to negotiate a similar agreement at the WTO and get those countries on board. According to the EC official quoted above, "the EC always favoured the WTO process. Even after the MAI is concluded, [the European Commission] wants negotiations to start at the WTO". In fact, from the outset the EC was more interested in a multilateral agreement with the broadest participation, and that was one of the reasons why the European Commission was skeptical about the OECD process in the beginning. A white paper released by the Commission in 1995, stated:

> A considerable number of OECD members have shown inclination for negotiations on a Multilateral Investment Agreement open for accession by third countries in the OECD framework. However, one can question whether the OECD is ultimately the best forum for the negotiations on future rules governing world-wide FDI...Limiting a negotiation on multilateral investment rules to OECD members would exclude important actors, such as China, Korea, Brazil and South Africa, and also the countries of ASEAN and Central and Eastern Europe...To present these countries with the result of an exclusive OECD negotiation contains certain risks. Not only would it be politically difficult for many countries to accept such a procedure, they might well have sound economic grounds for not doing so if the OECD agreement, negotiated without their participation, did not adequately reflect their concerns. Consequently, an initiative for the elaboration of foreign investment rules should involve the countries of Central and Eastern Europe and the CIS Republics, the New Industrialised Countries and developing countries from the start. A worldwide phenomenon such as FDI should be discussed with broad multilateral participation, if broad acceptance is to be achieved (EC, 1995).

The EC believed that there was a better than ever chance of successfully negotiating multilateral investment rules within the WTO framework. It also believed that the TRIMs agreement review due in the year 2000 would be a good opportunity to start negotiations on broader investment rules (EC, 1995: 9). However, an official of the EC told me that the US did not seem to be keen on the WTO process:

> The Americans think that the influence the developing countries have at the WTO is so big and, as a result, it will be difficult to come to an agreement at the WTO. They also believe that they have more influence at the OECD.

A similar view was echoed by the South Centre, a think-tank for developing countries:

> Americans do not want the WTO process because any negotiations at the WTO will be attended by developing countries too, and there will be give-and-take. Any proposal they make at the WTO will have to be watered down. They would rather like to see the WTO ultimately incorporate the MAI without any further negotiations on it (Interview with a consultant of the South Centre).

Japan

The Japanese strategy was to get more market access for their investors in the US and Europe. Like the Europeans, they believed that there had been a growing tendency in the US of closing its doors, while the rest of the world had been opening up.

Although the US was generally experiencing a relatively high level of incoming foreign direct investment in the 1980's (Table 5:1), the rapid increase in the magnitude of Japanese investment in the US was most notable (Table 5:2). With the economic power of Japan revealing itself in the US-Japan bilateral trade imbalance, this phenomenon apparently made many in the US concerned about Japanese "takeover" (Glickman & Woodward, 1989: 32).[4] With the ever-increasing trade deficit, Japanese trading practices were seen by many Americans as unfair and actually harmful to the United States. Interview informants told me this situation apparently fuelled a new kind of politics in Washington that combined protectionism with concerns about economic security. And it was in the midst of this atmosphere that Fujitsu Limited attempted to purchase the US computer and semiconductor firm, Fairchild Semiconductor Corporation.

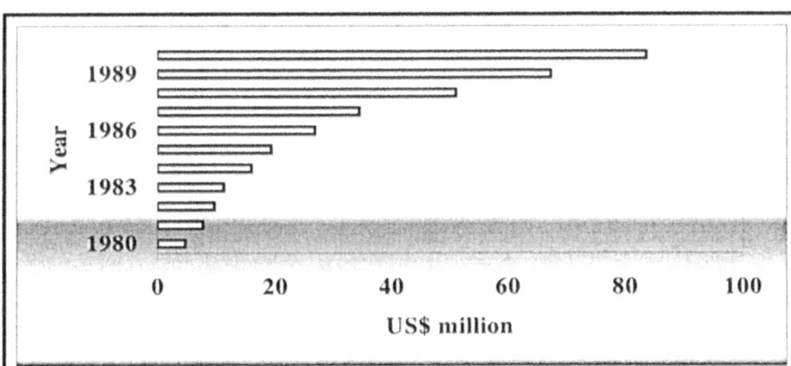

Figure 5:1 Japanese Investment in the US, 1980-90 (in billions of US dollars)

Source US Department of Commerce, *Survey of Current Business, Various Issues* (in Kang, 1997: 320).

Table 5:2 High Technology Acquisitions in the US by country (October 1988-April 1992)

Country	Number of Acquisitions
Japan	399
United Kingdom	65
France	41
Germany	17
Canada	14
Switzerland	14
Taiwan	11
Australia	4
South Korea	4
Netherlands	3
Other	33

Source Economic Strategy Institute Database, May 1992 (cited in Kang, 1997: 320).

Table 5:3 Japan's High Technology Acquisition in the US (October 1988-April 1992, by industry)

Industry	Japanese Acquisition	Total Foreign Acquisition	Japanese Acquisition as a Percentage of all Foreign Acquisition %
Advanced Materials	40	63	63
Aerospace	19	32	59
Biotechnology	17	27	63
Chemicals	25	54	46
Computers	93	142	65
Electronics	33	56	59
Semiconductor Equipment	30	39	77
Semiconductor	51	60	85
Telecommunication	31	64	48
Other	60	71	85

Source Economic Strategy Institute Database, May 1992 (cited in Kang, 1997: 320).

In October 1986, Fairchild announced that the firm was to be sold to Fujitsu Limited. At the time, Fairchild provided over a hundred million dollars of high-speed circuitry annually to the US defence and intelligence community.[5]

When the deal became known to the public and the reaction was negative, many members of Congress became eager to block the transaction (Malone, 1987). The proposed transaction also sparked adverse media reaction in leading US newspapers against the Japanese. For example, the *New York Times* reminded its readers, on 26 January 1987, that "Japanese businessmen were accused of stealing secrets from IBM and are suspected of technology diversions through Hong Kong". Such hostile reaction from many corners of American society apparently made an impression on the Japanese, and Fujitsu backed out of the deal to buy Fairchild. The irony about this controversy was, however, Fujitsu was not even an US-owned company when it received Fujitsu's bid. The firm was purchased several years ago by a French firm, Schlumberger Ltd., which ran it as a wholly owned subsidiary (Kang, 1997: 321). The real force behind the controversy was, perhaps, the desire to overhaul the rules on foreign investment in the US.

Against this background, therefore, the Japanese saw an urgent need to prevent backsliding by the US, and stop the rest of the world from being dragged by it. They were also keen to abolish similar discriminatory practices against their companies in Europe.

Other Developed Countries

Although I only interviewed Australian officials about their roles in the rule making process, it was evident for me from my other interviews, observations and from the documentary record that the rest of the OECD members play very little leadership role in shaping the global agenda. For instance, when the US first proposed the MAI negotiations, the only resistance it met was from Europe, not from Australia, Canada, or Mexico. Non-European OECD members tend to follow the US in any such activities.

Summary of the Positions of Key Players

Each of these main players wanted to open up the markets of the others while at the same time trying to maintain the *status quo* in their domestic investment policy to the extent it was possible. The US sought to achieve this by trying to make national treatment the central principle of the MAI, and discrimination on the ground of "national security" legal. "National Security" has always been the pretext for commercial protectionism in the US. The Europeans, for their part, attempted to make Regional Economic Agreements immune from the MAI, so that they would continue giving favourable treatment to European companies, and at the same time narrow the definition of "national security" as much as possible. The Japanese did not come up with such a sophisticated approach, but generally supported the liberalisation agenda. As the discussion later on in the Chapter reveals, this approach has to some extent contributed to the failure of the MAI negotiations.

In sum, it becomes clear that most of the developed countries' aspirations were incorporated into the MAI. It therefore becomes necessary for us to have a more detailed understanding of these aspirations as drafted in the MAI. The rest of this Chapter is devoted to that detailed understanding.

The Multilateral Agreement on Investment (MAI)

Background to the Negotiations

Proposals to include investment rules as part of the WTO were made during the Uruguay Round, band after their rejection by developing countries the issue was taken up in the OECD. The idea of negotiating the MAI in the OECD was first initiated by the US (Interviews with a Netherlands negotiator, an OECD Director, and a US diplomat/negotiator). A US negotiator at the OECD told me that "Assistant Secretary of State for Economic and Business Affairs, Mr. Alan Larson, has always been one of the few people who were the ardent promoters of the idea".[6] It is also believed that US business and industry, through the powerful US Council for International Business, had been lobbying hard for a binding investment agreement that would abolish restrictions on FDI, guarantee investment protection, and allow investors to bring their disputes against a host country to international tribunal.[7] An EC official, who was also a member of the MAI Negotiating Group told me during my interview:

> The MAI is a brainchild of American business. Which corporations in the US are pushing hard for it? I am not sure.

A similar view was suggested by a top official of the Union of Industrial and Employers' Confederations of Europe (UNICE):

> I do not know exactly which US companies are behind the MAI. I am however sure that US business and the US Administration are behind it.

Others saw it as a purely OECD Secretariat initiative:

> There is a feeling within the OECD that the Secretariat may no more be relevant as most of its work is being taken up by the WTO. It is possible that the people at the Secretariat have felt that they should do something serious to portray the importance of the Secretariat. The MAI could be the result of that feeling (UNCTAD official).

According to the Officials at the OECD Secretariat, on the other hand, "the MAI is a natural outgrowth of the OECD work on investment for the past thirty years" (Interview with a Director of the OECD). The OECD already has fragmented instruments that attempt to regulate FDI. One such instrument is the Capital Movements Code, which calls for a legal standstill in investment restrictions and requires members to notify certain policies to the relevant OECD Committees as well as undergo periodic reviews of policy. In 1986, Member Countries agreed on binding National Treatment on establishment and on a political commitment to progressively apply the principle post-establishment, subject to their needs to maintain public order, protect their essential security interests and fulfil commitments relating to international peace and security.[8] There was an attempt by the US to upgrade the National Treatment instrument later on. That attempt failed because of US insistence on the abolition of cultural exceptions, which Canada and France opposed, and Canada's and France's insistence on the extension of the application of National Treatment to sub-nationals (states), which the US opposed (Interviews with an OECD Director and a Netherlands negotiator). According to Mr. Alan Larson:

> It was the failure of this effort that led OECD countries to decide that they should be more ambitious, not more cautious. It was this determination to develop a state-of-the-art agreement with binding dispute settlement rules that led to the launching of negotiations on the MAI.[9]

Another relevant OECD document is the Decision on Investment Incentives and Disincentives. This document was later revised in 1984 to cover "measures which provide significant incentives and disincentives" rather than only those "specifically designed" for those purposes, as in the earlier formulation. Other OECD documents relevant to investment include the non-binding OECD Guidelines for Multinational Enterprises, and the binding Codes of Liberalisation. Indeed, these and other instruments, and the consultations and reviews under them resulting in "clarifications" or revisions, have produced a considerable body of OECD practice and policy. Therefore, the MAI could well also be seen as an agreement consolidating the various OECD instruments, in addition to being an international instrument open for accession by non-member countries.

Although the OECD countries had divergent strategies when they decided to start negotiations, they all had a common view that trade and investment are so interrelated that facilitating the free flow of investment would make a significant contribution to the enhancement of trade. They argue that FDI and FDI policies greatly influence the size, direction and composition of world trade. FDI increases the exports of the home country through inter-firm and cross-firm sales. They also say that, especially since the mid-1980s, technological developments and the liberalisation of rules have greatly enhanced the movement of goods, services, capital and intangible assets. This new environment, coupled with competition, has forced firms to combine their ownership advantage with the location advantages of host countries and establish an integrated production system. As a result, any part of the production chain can be located wherever it contributes most to the firm's overall performance. This means that FDI and trade flows are determined simultaneously, both becoming consequences of the same location decision. Hence, they say, the decision to trade has become the decision to invest, and it becomes an FDI decision if a foreign location is chosen (UNCTAD, 1996).[10] More trade eventually leads to more investment.

This common position on the relationship between investment and trade may have helped rival members of the OECD reconcile their differences, at least temporarily, and adopt a common strategy to negotiate an Agreement with "high standard" rules for the liberalisation of investment, investment protection and "effective" dispute settlement. Whatever the motive behind the decision to negotiate the MAI the US proposal to start a feasibility study, to be followed by a negotiation, on a "comprehensive" investment instrument was neither strongly opposed nor fully welcomed by the other member countries in the beginning. An OECD Director told me that most members "thought that they were not ready for such an ambitious treaty. Through time, however, they digested it and convinced themselves that it [was] also in their interest to have such an agreement". Working groups were established, and the feasibility study started in 1991. This activity culminated in the mandate issued by the Ministerial Council to start negotiation on the MAI in 1995. Although the preparatory studies were done in the Committee for International Investment and Multinational Enterprises (CIIME), the actual negotiations took place outside the main OECD committee structure, entrusted to a "high-level negotiating group".

Content of the Draft MAI[11]

The draft Agreement is divided into twelve Sections, consisting of several Articles and paragraphs, under the headings General Provisions, Scope of Application, Treatment of Investors and Investments, Investment protection, Dispute Settlement, Exceptions and Safeguards, Financial Services, Taxation, Country Specific Exceptions, Relationship to Other International Agreements, Implementation and Operation, and Final Provision. It was also supposed to have several annexes that were to be considered as integral parts of the Agreement. Each of these Sections of the draft Agreement will now be discussed briefly.

General Provisions Under General Provisions came the Preamble of the Agreement. The Preamble described liberalisation of investment regimes, investment protection and effective dispute settlement as the overriding aims of the Agreement. It also recognised the contribution foreign investment would make to economic development. Furthermore, it made references to sustainable development, environmental protection, and core labour standards. Such references were, however, late additions that were opposed by some delegations and the paragraphs that refer to these issues remained in brackets to indicate that no agreement had been reached upon them. The non-binding and voluntary nature of the OECD Guidelines for Multilateral Enterprises was also stressed in the Preamble.

Scope of Application The scope of application of the MAI was very broad in that it covered all economic sectors, all forms of investment, all stages of investment and all types of measures. The MAI adopted a "top down" approach, as opposed to the WTO's "bottom up" approach, and all sectors were included in the scope of the Agreement, except those against which specific reservations have been made by a Contracting Party.

"Investor" was defined as any natural or legal person, and it included all entities with the capacity to invest (Section II, Art.1). The draft Agreement defined investment in terms of assets and it covered "every kind of asset owned or controlled, directly or indirectly by an investor" (Section II, Art.2). This included not only the traditional forms of foreign direct investment (e.g. establishment of branches and subsidiaries, acquisition of permanent holdings in local companies, purchase of tangible assets), but also portfolio investment (e.g. equity participation for investment purposes), financial investment (e.g. bonds, debentures, loans), intangible property (e.g. intellectual property rights) and new forms of investment that were likely emerge in the future. It also included state-owned enterprises where the State is an economic actor. In principle, at least, the definition extended to contractual rights, including concessions, and rights to receive payments, for example under financial contracts such as derivatives, although possible limitations were under discussion.

The negotiators had divergent views on whether or not the definition of investment should cover investments indirectly owned or controlled by investors of a party. Four possible scenarios were considered (MAI Commentary, 24 April 1998: 6):

a) investment by an investor established in another MAI Party, but owned or controlled by an investor from a non-MAI Party (e.g. an investment in Austria by Belgian subsidiary of a non-MAI parent company);
b) investment by an investor established in a non-MAI Party, but owned or controlled by an investor from a MAI Party (e.g. an investment in Canada by a non-MAI subsidiary of a Danish parent company);
c) investment by an investor established in another MAI Party, but owned or controlled by an investor of a third MAI Party (an investment in France by a German subsidiary of a Hungarian Parent); and
d) investment in a MAI Party by an investor there covered by the MAI (e.g. an investment in Italy by an Italian subsidiary of a Japanese parent company).

There was a consensus that (c) and (d) investment would be covered by the MAI. There was also a wide support for covering case (b) investment, although a final decision was to be made at a later stage. The view on case (a) investments was divided, with most delegations favouring providing for certain exclusions in a denial of benefits clause which would permit, but not require, exclusions in circumstances where, for example, the investor was constituted "for no other reason than obtaining MAI benefits"(MAI Commentary, 1998: 6).

The Agreement also covered all stages of investment, including the establishment, acquisition, expansion, operation, management, maintenance, use, enjoyment and sale or other disposition of investment (Section III, Art.1). All types of normative measures, such as laws, regulations, judicial decisions, and international treaties, taken by all levels of government, including those agencies to which government authorities have delegated their prerogatives, fell within the coverage of the Agreement.

Attempts had been made to set some limitations on the scope of application of the Agreement. Not meeting the transparency obligation would be permitted in certain situations (Section VII). The Agreement also allowed governments to take any measures necessary to protect their vital national security interests or to maintain public order or in performance of their obligations under the United Nations Charter for purposes of maintaining international peace and security. Such measures could even be permanent. Furthermore, the Agreement allowed governments to temporarily suspend the application of certain provisions of the Agreement in times of serious balance-of-payments and external financial difficulties (Section VI). Such measures, however, would be subject to review by the Parties Group and the IMF. Overall, save the few limitations listed above, the scope of application of the MAI was broader than any other previous agreement.

Treatment of Investors and Investments The MAI sought to liberalise investment rules through, among other things, non-discrimination and the abolition of performance requirements. Non-discrimination was said to be achieved by way of National Treatment and MFN. The MAI required member countries to accord foreign investors treatment no less favourable than the treatment they accord to their own investors, at both pre- and post-establishment phases of the investment (Section III, Art.1). During the negotiations, some delegates had proposed the "same" or "comparable" treatment as the appropriate standard rather than "no less favourable treatment". This proposal was rejected by most delegates on the ground that it "would unacceptably weaken the standard of treatment" to be accorded to the foreign investor (MAI Commentary, 1998: 10). Therefore, theoretically a country could have laws that discriminate between foreign and domestic investors, but not one that puts the foreign investor in a less advantageous position than domestic investors. MFN on the other hand refers to the automatic extension, to the foreign investors of a country, of any more favourable treatment accorded to the foreign investors of another country (Section II, Art.2). It was anticipated that some departures from NT and MFN could be allowed in very limited circumstances, such as the protection of national security interests. However, departures would not be allowed for considerations such as development objectives, economic needs or culture (Interview with an official of the USTR).

On the other hand, the fact that the MAI did not prohibit discrimination between foreign and national investors as long as it was in favour of the foreign investor, makes it discriminatory. Indeed, there is a real possibility, particularly in countries that are not favourably placed to attract sufficient foreign investment, that such discrimination could happen. Indeed it happens already as a result of competition for investment and competition for bribes. Moreover, the draft Agreement did not specify if treatment accorded to foreign investors by a province or a sub-national state should be compared with the treatment accorded to domestic investors in that particular province or sub-national state, or with those of another state or province, for the purpose deciding whether or nor there was national treatment.

The MAI prohibited the imposing performance requirements on foreign investors. The Article on Performance Requirements was divided into five paragraphs (Section III). The first paragraph set forth what would be totally prohibited. The other four paragraphs were exceptions or clarifications to the first paragraph. Paragraph one listed twelve categories of requirements covered by the prohibition (Section 3, Art.1 (a-l)). Such prohibited requirements included export quotas; domestic content; to purchase, use or accord preferences to domestic goods and services or suppliers; to relate imports to exports or to the inflow of foreign exchange; transfer of technology; employment quotas; research and development; joint ventures; etc. Some of these requirements have already been prohibited by the WTO TRIMS Agreement or by other Agreements such as the Energy Charter Treaty of the OECD. The categories of requirements listed under Article 1(a) through 1(e) would be prohibited in all circumstances, whether when they would be imposed as a condition for allowing various phases of an investment (such as establishment or operation) to proceed, or when the host country would offer an incentive in connection with the requirement. The remainder of the list would be prohibited only when they are imposed as a condition for allowing an investment to proceed. This means a country would not be prohibited from offering an advantage to an investor in connection with the categories of requirements listed under Article 1(f) through 1(l).

Section III of the draft Agreement also covered a vast number of other issues, including movement of key personnel, employment requirements, privatisation, monopolies, investment incentives, not lowering of standards, and so on. The Article on the movement of key personnel would ensure that individual investors, managers, and business executives would not face restrictions in relation to their temporary entry, stay and work beyond what follows from the normal application of immigration laws in the host country, that is, the host country would not be allowed restrict the entry of such people by numeric quotas and/or economic need tests. The investor would also be free to employ any person of his choice regardless of nationality or citizenship. Moreover, National Treatment and MFN would apply to all phases and kinds of privatisation. Countries would also be required to publish or make publicly available the essential features and procedures for participating in prospective privatisations.

The draft Agreement allowed countries to designate, maintain or eliminate monopolies as they wish, provided that they would apply the principles of National Treatment and MFN (Section III). Some delegates had the view that demonopolisation operations would generally be favourable to liberalisation because they would open up new investment activities. Others, however, had the view that this would extend the obligations of the MAI into a new area. It was finally agreed that the MAI should allow Contracting Parties to lodge country specific exceptions at the time of demonopolisation, even if the instance arises after the coming into effect of the Agreement (MAI Commentary, 1998: 17).

Investment Incentives remained to be one of the stickiest issues in the MAI negotiation. The negotiators were divided on whether or not it would be advisable to have an article on Investment Incentives in the first place, and secondly what the scope of such an article would be if it were decided to have one. Many delegates were of the view that "disciplines on investment incentives would be important for the overall credibility of the MAI" (MAI Commentary, 1998: 18). One delegate had in fact proposed a definition of investment incentives along the lines of the definitions of subsidies found in the WTO Agreement on Subsidies and Countervailing Measures (MAI Commentary, 1998: 18). The proposal was, however, rejected by other delegates on the ground that "since WTO members were still grappling with related issues, it would be premature to include disciplines in the MAI that could duplicate or detract from WTO obligations", and that "there has been insufficient analysis of the nature and impact of incentives" (MAI Commentary, 1998: 18). Some delegates were even concerned that regulating investment incentives through the MAI could divert foreign investment to non-member countries, thereby putting members of the MAI at a disadvantage in their ability to attract or retain foreign investment. They also argued that it could discourage non-member countries from acceding to the MAI (MAI Commentary, 1998: 18).

Investment Protection The Section on investment protection dealt with the general treatment of foreign investors and their investments, expropriation, protection from strife, transfer of funds, subrogation, and protection of investor rights arising from investment agreements between the investor and the host country (Section IV). The host country would be obliged to give foreign investors/investments "fair and equitable" treatment as well as "full and constant protection and security". Such treatment would have to be no less favourable than that required by international law (Section IV, Art.1). Some delegates had suggested that it would be essential to form a link between "General Treatment" and NT/MFN. But it was finally agreed that it was justified to separate the two because while "General Treatment" is an "absolute" principle, NT/MFN are "relative" principles (MAI Commentary, 1998: 29).

Expropriation or any other "measure having similar effects" would be permitted only if it is in the public interest, on non-discriminatory basis, and against the payment of prompt, adequate and effective compensation, and in accordance with due process of law (Section IV, Art.2). The loss of an investment as a result of the violation of criminal laws would not be considered expropriation (MAI Commentary, 1998: 30). "Indirect expropriation" was covered by the term "measures having equivalent effect" under Article 2. The negotiators had identified four options for calculating compensation. The first option was that the compensation to be paid should be calculated by summing the fair market value of the expropriated property on the date of expropriation and interest at a commercial rate from the date of expropriation until the date of actual payment. The sum should be expressed, at the option of the investor, on the date of expropriation, in either the currency of the host state, the currency of the investor's home state, another freely useable currency, or any other currency acceptable to the host government. The second option was similar to the first except that the sum would be expressed, at the option of the host government, in either a freely useable currency, the ECU, or any other currency acceptable to the investor. The third option stipulated that the sum total of the fair market value of the expropriated property on the date of expropriation and interest until the date of payment would be expressed in any freely convertible currency chosen by the host government. The fourth option did not specify the currency of payment, but stipulated that compensation should include interest until the date of actual payment, at a commercially reasonable rate established on a market basis (MAI Commentary, 1998: 31-32). The negotiators remained divided on which option to adopt, and the draft paragraph on the payment of compensation was left with brackets to indicate that no agreement had been reached on it.

Section IV of the draft Agreement also consisted of an Article that would protect the investor from strife. It dealt with the situation where an investor would suffer losses in the host country due to war, any other armed conflict, state of emergency or similar events. The Article stipulated that the host country would be obliged to pay compensation in two situations: firstly, in instances where the armed forces of the host country requisitioned the property of the investor and, secondly, in instances where the property destroyed by the armed forces of the host country and the demolition was not necessitated by the situations (Section IV, Art.3).

Finally, the subrogation provision attempted to address instances where the home government of the investor or its designated agency would enter into all the rights and claims the investor had vis-à-vis the host country following payment of compensation to the investor by the home country with regard to the loss the investor had suffered in the host country (Section IV, Art.6). However, it was not clear whether this provision should deal with both "commercial" and "non-commercial" risks, or with just one of them.

Dispute Settlement The dispute settlement provision was the other core element of the MAI. The negotiators believed that the establishment of a binding, effective dispute settlement mechanism was necessary for the implementation of high standards of treatment and protection of foreign investors (Interview with a US negotiator). The provision would apply to both state-state and investor-state disputes.

The MAI adopted the usual procedure in State-State dispute settlement, that is, consultation conciliation and arbitration. The disputes would be arbitrated by ad hoc MAI panels. The actual Panellists would be selected from the MAI roster on the recommendation of the Secretary – General of the International Centre for the Settlement of Investment Disputes (ICSID), or failing an agreement by the parties to the dispute, by the "appointing authority" (Section V, Art.C (2)). The tribunal would decide on disputes in accordance with the provisions of the MAI, interpreted and applied in accordance with the applicable rules of international law. If gaps in the MAI rule appeared during a dispute and the parties were not able to agree on supplementary rules, UNCITRAL rules would serve as default rules. Domestic law would be taken into account but the MAI would override any domestic law. Awards issued by a Panel would be final and binding save in some exceptional circumstances (Section V, Art.C (6)).

In the case of investor-state disputes, the choice of what procedure to follow and where to submit the dispute would be left entirely to the foreign investor. The foreign investor could choose to submit the dispute to courts or administrative tribunals of the host country, to arbitration under ICSID (if the host country is a party to ICSID), the rules of the ICSID Additional Facility, the UNCITRAL Rules, or the ICC Court of Arbitration. The Panel of Arbitrators would be selected from the MAI roster of potential panelists. The decision of the panel would be binding on all parties (Section V, Art.D).

The dispute settlement provision would give wider rights to the foreign investor while at the same time it undermined the sovereignty of the host country. It would also put the foreign investor in a more privileged position than the national investor because the choices the foreign investor had were not also at the disposal of the national investor.

Exceptions and Safeguards This Section of the Agreement dealt with general exceptions, actions taken in relation to monetary and exchange rate policy, and temporary safeguards. The Article on General Exceptions allowed states to take measures, in certain limited circumstances, contravening any of the provisions of the MAI except those of investment protection provisions (Section VI). The limited circumstances under which the general exceptions were to be allowed included:

a) the protection of essential security interests:
   - in times of war, armed conflict or other emergency;
   - relating to the non-proliferation of weapons of mass destruction;
   - relating to the production of arms and ammunition;
b) the pursuance of one's obligations under the United Nations Charter for the maintenance of peace and security; and
c) taking any measures necessary for the maintenance of public order, provided that such measures do not constitute a means of arbitrary or unjustifiable discrimination, or disguised investment restriction.

Monetary authorities of member countries would also be allowed to take discriminatory measures in pursuit of monetary or exchange rate policies. Moreover, member countries would be allowed to ignore the Articles on free transfer of funds and National Treatment if they would be in, or face a threat of, serious balance-of-payments and external financial difficulties, or where the free movement of capital could cause or threaten to cause serious difficulties for macroeconomic management. However, such measures would have to be temporary and consistent with the Articles of Agreement of the International Monetary Fund. They should not also exceed what would be necessary to deal with the particular situation (Section VI).

Financial Services The section on financial services dealt with matters such as the definition of financial services, prudential measures that may be taken by host countries, investment approval procedures of host countries, transparency, information transfer, and payment and clearing systems (Section VII). Two categories of financial activities were listed under the definition: (a) all insurance and insurance related services, such as direct insurance (including co-insurance), reinsurance and retrocession, insurance intermediation, and all services auxiliary to insurance, and (b) banking and other financial services, including public deposits and repayment of funds, lending of all types, financial leasing, all payment and money transmission services, money market instruments, foreign exchange, exchange rate and interest rate instruments, securities, money brokering, asset management, clearing services for financial assets, etc.

The draft Agreement allowed countries to take "prudential measures with respect to financial services, including measures for the protection of investors, depositors, policy holders…or to ensure the integrity and stability of its financial system" (Section VII). These measures could be taken in contravention of National Treatment, MFN or any other provision of the Agreement, provided that they would not be used as a means of avoiding one's commitments and obligations under the MAI.

Taxation The Section on taxation was aimed at preventing two types of measures by host countries: discriminatory taxation and expropriatory taxation (Section VIII). It prohibited host countries from discriminating against foreign investors using tax laws. It also outlawed taxation measures that would have the equivalent effect of expropriation. It did not however prohibit laws that would give more tax advantages for foreign investors, such as tax incentives to attract foreign investment.

It was generally felt during the negotiations that "tax havens", which are usually characterised by low (or zero) tax rates and/or extremely narrow tax bases as well as bank secrecy laws restricting exchange of tax information, provide opportunities for tax evasion and, therefore, pose a serious threat to countries' tax revenues. Hence, it was generally agreed that a) taxation measures aimed at preventing the avoidance or evasion of taxes would not be considered to be expropriatory (Section VIII, Footnote 3), b) tax policy considerations should be taken into account during accession to the MAI, and c) tax authorities should be involved in the process by which accession of candidates are judged (MAI Commentary, 1998: 58).

Country Specific Exceptions Once the Agreement was signed, or acceded to, countries would generally be prohibited from introducing new more restrictive measures to the minimum standard of treatment. Section IX of the draft Agreement set out the principles by which countries may be allowed to maintain some of their restrictive laws ("non-conforming measures"), as opposed to the liberalisation principles of the MAI.

Countries would be asked to annex to the Agreement a list of their laws that do not conform with the liberalisation requirements of the Agreement, but would not be permitted to introduce new restrictive measures after the coming into force of the Agreement. This mechanism was designed to ensure that investment restrictions are put to a "standstill", and any future laws would be more liberal than the current ones. Standstill would not apply, however, to any general exceptions (e.g. national security) or to any temporary derogations (e.g. balance-of-payments) (MAI Commentary, 1998: 59). Although agreement had been reached on a draft Article, the negotiators had also explored ways of achieving more liberalisation through a "rollback" provision, which would require member states to eliminate in the future all restrictive measures that were grandfathered by the "standstill" provision (MAI Commentary, 1998: 60).

As the MAI was primarily about liberalisation, countries were expected to submit fewer exceptions. Instead, each country tried to preserve the *status quo*. The

US alone submitted over 54 pages of exceptions. Australia submitted a list of 29 "non-conforming" measures, which apparently covered almost every restrictive measure it had at the time. The list of such exceptions finally filled over 600 pages, much bigger than anticipated in the beginning. This practically rendered the liberalisation objective of the Agreement impossible to achieve.

Relationship to other International Agreements This Article attempted to make sure that the MAI would not contradict two international agreements, namely the Articles of Agreement of the International Monetary Fund, and the OECD Guidelines for Multinational Enterprises. It stated that the provisions of the IMF Agreement take precedence over those of the MAI. The coverage of the IMF Agreement includes, for example, cases where the Fund would request the imposition of capital controls in accordance with the Fund's Articles of Agreement. With regard to the OECD Guidelines, it was stated that the Guidelines would remain as non-binding recommendations.

Implementation and Operation This Article laid down the rules for the establishment of the Preparatory Group and the Parties Group. The Preparatory Group would be an *ad hoc* assembly of signatories to the Final Act and the Agreement. Its main function would be to prepare the conditions for the coming into force of the Agreement and the establishment of the Parties Group. It would also conduct negotiations with non-OECD countries with a view to their becoming signatories to the Agreement. The Parties Group would be an assembly of members signatory to the Agreement. Some of its functions would include clarifying the interpretation or application of the Agreement and considering "any matter that may affect the operation of the Agreement". It would also establish its rules and procedures. Decisions of the Parties Group would be by consensus.

Final Provisions This Article laid down the rules of becoming a signatory to the Agreement, entry into force of the Agreement, accession, amendment, withdrawal, etc. The Agreement was intended to be open for accession by all those who were not members of the Negotiating Group. Once a member, a country would withdraw from the Agreement only after five years of membership and by giving six-month advance written notice. Moreover, for investments existing in the country at the date of withdrawal, the Agreement would continue to apply for 15 years following withdrawal.

Why did the MAI Collapse?

By the end of 1996, ten negotiating sessions had been held by the MAI Negotiating Group (OECD/DAFFE/INV/IME(96)44: 2). The Progress Report submitted by the Negotiating Group to the Ministerial Meeting of May 1996 indicated that the negotiations were in full swing, and that everyone in the group was confident of accomplishing the task by the set deadline (OECD/GD(96)78: 3).

The negotiations were more or less progressing smoothly until around mid-1996, mainly because they were kept largely secret and most of the stickiest issues were not yet dealt with. However, the secrecy did not last for long. A seminar was organised jointly by Consumers International and CUTS (an Indian consumer advocacy group) in Geneva in October 1996, where OECD officials and various NGO representatives were present. I was able to attend as part of the data-gathering process for this book. It was evident in Geneva that there was a clear communication breakdown and mistrust between the MAI negotiators and the NGO representatives. The NGOs' main demand, made to the OECD officials at the seminar, was to be involved in the negotiation process, either through formal and regular consultations or by nominating their representatives to sit at the negotiation table. They also demanded to be provided with whatever draft text of the Agreement existed at the time. The OECD officials, on the other hand, made it clear that they were only prepared to organise information workshops from time to time, and that any NGOs wishing to attend those workshops would be invited. Shortly after the Seminar, in December 1996, the OECD Secretariat arranged a public briefing about the MAI in Paris and a few NGOs were invited to attend and express their views. The meeting ended without a positive outcome.

In the meantime, a Canadian NGO posted the draft text of the MAI on the Internet in early 1997. Activists around the world immediately started to analyse the effects of the Agreement on their respective communities. Internet sites distributing information against the MAI flourished almost overnight.[12] A formidable virtual coalition coalesced. In addition to the already existing anti-MAI NGOs such as the Council of Canadians, Friends of the Earth, Public Citizen, WWF, the Third World Network, new ones such as the MAI-not (in Canada), MAI *niet gezien* (in the Netherlands), and later Stop-MAI (in Australia) were formed. As the campaigns against the MAI intensified in every OECD country, the negotiators found it increasingly difficult to make concessions in order to conclude the negotiations by the set deadline, that is, April/May 1997. As a result, very little progress was made from the previous year when Ministers met in May 1997. The negotiators were therefore given one more year and were urged to conclude the negotiations in time for the 1998 Ministerial Meeting (OECD News Release, 27 May 1997).

The OECD Secretariat had released very little information on the MAI until the text of the draft Agreement was posted on the Internet by the NGOs. Once this happened, however, the Secretariat started releasing more information on the OECD Internet site and organising meetings with NGOs and developing countries more frequently. Among such meetings, the one called by the OECD in October 1997 to consult NGOs was spectacular. The NGOs came to Paris for the meeting from different parts of the world and held a meeting of their own beforehand to take a common stand. They prepared a joint statement and presented it to the OECD with a warning that unless their demands were met in full, they would each return to their home countries and "launch massive campaigns to kill the MAI". They also called on the OECD Secretarial and member countries to:

- Undertake an independent assessment of the social, environmental and development impact of the MAI with full public participation;

- Require multinational investors to observe binding agreements incorporating environment, labour, health, safety and human rights standards;
- Eliminate the investor-state dispute resolution mechanism;
- Eliminate the MAI's expropriation provision;
- Suspend the MAI negotiation and extend the 1998 deadline;
- Increase transparency in the negotiations;
- Broaden the active participation of government departments in the official negotiations;
- Renegotiate the terms of withdrawal.

The OECD representatives rejected most of the demands listed. The NGOs then immediately began strategising for the grassroots campaigns to defeat the treaty.[13]

By the end of 1997, public campaigns against the MAI had significant results in some countries. In Canada, for example, three provincial governments had declared that they would not recognise the MAI even if signed by the Federal Government. In the US, a lobby campaign spearheaded by Public Citizen (led by consumer advocate Ralph Nader) and environmental groups like Friends of the Earth-US had won support from many members of the Congress (Third World Resurgence, Feb-March 1998). As delegates from OECD countries met in February 1998 in Paris to continue the negotiations on the MAI, the coalition of NGOs intensified their campaign by launching an "International Week of Action" against the MAI in many of these countries. Anti-MAI demonstrations were staged and phone calls were made to parliamentarians throughout the OECD countries. In the Netherlands, activists occupied the entrance of the office of the Chairman of the MAI Negotiating Group, Mr. Engering, on 12 February 1998 and left only after he came out and spoke to them. The voice of protest included even church leaders. The General Secretary of the World Council of Churches wrote to the member churches in the 29 OECD countries:

> The MAI, which is expected to become the international framework for foreign direct investment, is being negotiated by representatives of the OECD economies without the participation of representatives of the majority of the countries of the world. Moreover the Agreement, as it stands, could threaten efforts to create sustainable communities. There are reasons to be concerned about the implications for the environment, working conditions and human rights.[14]

The cumulative effect of such a spontaneously organised and intense campaign obviously created enormous pressure on the negotiators. Although negotiating countries were expected to make fewer country specific reservations, this proved to be practically impossible in the face of such hostile public perception against the Agreement. As a result, each country attempted to maintain the *status quo* by making as many reservations as possible, shattering state by state the dream of achieving high standard liberal rules. Negotiators were also stuck on a number of other disagreements among governments. These included the extraterritorial application of laws such as the Helms-Burton Law, and the inclusion in the MAI of provisions on Labour, the environment and culture.

When the Ministers met at the end of April, the negotiations had already lost much of their momentum, and there was no draft Agreement ready for signature. They therefore suspended the negotiations for six months and decided "on a period of assessment and consultations between the negotiating parties and with interested parts of their societies". They also stated their commitment "to a transparent negotiating process and to active public discussions on the issues at stake in the negotiations" (OECD News Release, Paris, 28 April 1998).

A survey done by Corporate Europe Observatory (CEO) towards the end of the six-month period indicates that no serious consultation and assessment has actually been made by most OECD countries during that period. According to the Report summarising the findings of the survey, countries like the Czech Republic, Luxembourg and Spain had not taken steps at all to consult with civil society in the six-month period. In countries where formal consultations had taken place, such as Belgium, Canada, Ireland, the Netherlands, Japan, UK and US, the negotiators seemed to have been occupied with defending "the government's negotiating position rather than to have an open dialogue about the impacts of the MAI and its overall desirability" (CEO Report, October 1998: 1). The EC and the EU Council of Ministers jointly organised a "dialogue meeting" in September, with around 25 NGOs represented. The EC had itself set the agenda and decided the list of representatives of civil society to be invited. This generated even greater controversy and "the NGOs were very close to calling off the meeting", had the EC not opened the meeting up for more NGO representatives at the very last moment. As was the case with most of the other countries, the Commission's position on the MAI was not revised afterwards (CEO Report, October 1998: 2).

Very few countries conducted and made public an assessment of the impact of the MAI. The list of such countries includes Finland and UK, which had conducted an assessment of the impact of the MAI on the environment before the six-month consultation period, and Norway and Sweden which undertook a similar assessment during the consultation period. The UK government also published the development implications of the MAI, which were heavily criticised by various NGOs (CEO Report, October 1998: 3).

According to the CEO Report, the Norwegian Government study had been criticised both by the NGOs and the Norwegian Justice Department "for its far too limited scope" (CEO Report, October 1998: 3). The Swedish study revealed a large number of potential conflicts between Swedish environmental legislation and Multilateral Environmental Agreements to which Sweden is a signatory, on the one hand, and the MAI on the other (CEO Report, October 1998: 3).

The most extensive consultations and assessments were conducted by the French Government and the Australian Parliament. Although the method used by the two were different, the end results were very similar. The Government of France commissioned Catherine Lalumiere, a member of the European Parliament, and Jean-Pierre Landau, the Inspector General of Finance, to prepare a report on the MAI for submission to Parliament. They conducted interviews with government officials from France and other countries, businesses, NGOs, cultural organisations and unions.[15] The report was critical of the way the negotiations were conducted as well as the contents of the draft Agreement. It also expressed its doubts whether the OECD was the appropriate forum for negotiating this kind of international agreements. While the report concluded that international investment agreements were important, it recommended two options regarding the MAI: either a radical modification of the text or a complete cancellation of the negotiations. It also made seven recommendations for any future international investment agreement:

- exclude portfolio investment and financial flows from the definition of investment;
- limit the dispute settlement mechanism only to states;
- avoid phrases such as "measures having the equivalent effect of expropriation";
- avoid the "general treatment" article of the MAI;
- limit the ban performance requirement to those already controlled by WTO;
- replace "standstill" rules with a right to derogate from the agreement if willing to pay compensation as under WTO rules; and
- ensure the effective participation of developing countries.

Following the submission of the report, France announced that it would not participate in the MAI negotiations scheduled for October 20-21, and the Prime Minister told Parliament that France would rather support investment negotiations at the WTO. Soon after, Germany withdrew its negotiator Mr. Schumeros from his candidacy for Chairperson replacing Mr. Engering of the Netherlands.

The Australian inquiry and assessment of the MAI was conducted by the Senate Joint Standing Committee on Treaties, pursuant to a request made by the Foreign Minister Alexander Downer in March 1998. It was by far the most extensive open inquiry made on the MAI at the time. The Committee received more than 900 submissions (Report 18, 1999: 177). Eighty-six per cent of respondents rejected the MAI, while 7% indicated qualified support for the draft Agreement. Six per cent of respondents said that ratification of the draft Agreement should only be considered after a referendum was held, "while 2% of respondents considered that a government signing the draft MAI would perpetrate an act of treason" (Report 18, 1999: 177).

The Committee expressed its alarm on the "secrecy" surrounding the negotiations and the lack of adequate consultation by Department of the Treasury.[16] It stated that the first source of information for many Australians regarding the MAI was the Internet, personal contacts, and groups formed to oppose the draft Agreement, rather than the Treasury. The Committee took the view that too little information was made publicly available until too late in the negotiation process (Report 18, 1999: 139). Twenty-three per cent of the submissions received raised the issue of perceived secrecy surrounding the negotiations, or the difficulty in obtaining up to date and accurate information on the draft Agreement (Report 18, 1999: 177). The Committee also found that the Treasury was selective in whatever consultations it had made to the point where even local government representatives, the Australian Industry Group, and the Australian Stock Exchange were all excluded from the consultation process (Report 18, 1999: 140). In its strongest criticism of Treasury, the Committee stated:

> Treasury seemed to believe that it owned this document [the MAI] to the point where it did not accept the validity of the concerns of those who opposed it. These people were simply seen as 'misinformed' and largely ignored. In turn, they felt that they were being treated with contempt. Hostility and suspicion was generated against the draft Agreement, and also towards the process of government in the minds of many citizens (Report 18, 1999: 143).

The Committee had also stated in its Report that "if Australia had acceded to this Agreement, there would have been substantial changes to the operation of the Commonwealth Government" (Report 18, 1999: 141). This was consistent with the view taken by 36% of respondents who believed that the MAI would infringe Australia's sovereignty (Report 18, 1999: 177), and inconsistent with what Treasury had all along been saying, that is, Australia's current arrangements would not be affected by the MAI in any way. Furthermore, the Committee took the position that "the OECD was not the most appropriate body to have negotiated an agreement to regulate international investment", and that the WTO would have been the most appropriate forum (Report 18, 1999: 137,144). It also stated that any future international investment agreement should "include clear statements of such matters as the rights and obligations of both host countries and international investors and protection of existing rights, together with an equitable dispute settlement process. These areas were among the greatest deficiencies of the draft MAI. Without such a framework, any successor document would almost certainly fail to gain acceptance in Australia" (Report 18, 1999: 144). Finally, the Committee recommended that:

- Australia continue to be involved in any future agreement for the regulation of international capital;
- the Department of the Prime Minister and Cabinet represent Australia in the negotiations (displacing Treasury);
- all relevant Commonwealth agencies be actively and effectively involved from the beginning of any negotiations;
- all Australians be given the opportunity to put their views on all aspects of any negotiating text as part of an open and public process; and
- written reports be given to the Joint Standing Committee on Treaties on a six-monthly basis about the content and progress of any such negotiations (Report 18, 1999: xv).

At the end of the six-month consultation period, negotiators met in Paris on October 20, 1998 and held a press conference the next day to announce that they would meet again in December after further consultations. In December they announced that the negotiations have been suspended indefinitely (OECD Press Release, 3 December 1998).

Conclusion

The overall strategy of the OECD and its members has been greater liberalisation of investment rules and higher security for foreign investment around the world. The "long dead economists" in whose thrall the OECD member negotiators did their work were decidedly neo-classical. The MAI was aimed at establishing "high standard", comprehensive rules for the liberalisation and protection of foreign investment. Within the OECD grouping, however, each of the big players (the US, EU and Japan) had their own priorities. The US was intent in opening up the European market for its investors, particularly in the film, television, aerospace and electronic industries, while keeping its market as close as possible to the *status quo* under the guise of "national security" and conditional national treatment. Similarly, the EU (particularly France) was keen to open up the US market for its investors and to restrict the extra-territorial application of US laws, while keeping its own market as closed as possible under the guise of cultural sensitivity. The EU was also keen to open up the Asian market for its investors either by drawing Asian countries into the MAI or by initiating a similar agreement within the WTO framework. The Japanese strategy was focused on getting more access to the US and European markets. The other OECD countries were simply followers, as the negotiation was mainly between the US, the EU and Japan (Picciotto, 1998: 741).

The MAI was negotiated exclusively by OECD countries, and largely in secrecy. The intention was to invite other countries to sign once an Agreement had been reached among OECD countries. This strategy was designed to reduce the chances of failure. But it was a strategy built on two mistaken ideas or beliefs: (1) as long as a few developing countries in Asia and Latin America were informed of the ongoing negotiations, there would not be serious opposition arising from other developing countries; and (2) public interest groups (NGOs) were not stakeholders in the process, or their opposition to it would not hinder the process, hence should not be consulted. As it turned out later, this was a fatal mistake. The longer the majority of developing countries were barred from participating in the negotiation process in any meaningful way, the higher their anxiety grew and the stronger their opposition. Even some of those countries that were part of the "outreach" program (such as India and Malaysia) turned out to be extremely vocal in their opposition. Moreover, the exclusiveness of the process made them even more suspicious about the OECD agenda and the benefits of global investment rules. As it was later demonstrated during the WTO Conference in Seattle, more developing countries began to be conscious of their roles in international rulemaking and assert their rights. Although this was a positive development, certainly it was one of the unintended effects of the MAI.

The exclusive nature of the negotiations meant that, as the Joint Standing Committee on Treaties (1999: 137) put it, the Agreement was simply "being negotiated by the wrong group of nations". A global investment agreement such as the MAI needs to address the interests of all major players, and the process of formulating it needs to be an inclusive one (see Chapter Ten for such an alternative model).

The OECD negotiators also miscalculated the level of interest the MAI would generate within the NGO community. Even after realising it, they underestimated the level of opposition the NGOs could galvanise around the world. By the time the negotiators gave in and agreed to make concessions, the NGOs wanted nothing short of the total abandonment of the negotiations. In OECD states as different as the US, France and Australia, NGOs mobilised a political pincer expanding from both the extreme left and the extreme right (Perot, Le Pen, Pauline Hanson), expanding inwards to create a shrinking neo-liberal centre of support for MAI. All this would definitely have enormous implications on how multilateral agreements should be negotiated in the future. The fact that the WTO was willing (albeit half-heartedly) to allow some NGOs to participate in the Seattle Conference was a lesson learnt from the failures of the MAI. In every respect that matters, it was the MAI that sowed the seeds of Seattle.

The MAI's preoccupation with liberalisation and the protection of investor rights meant that all other issues of importance in FDI regulation would be ignored. This preoccupation also made it unbalanced and discriminatory, although the negotiators professed that it would abolish discrimination. How was it unbalanced and discriminatory?

a) The non-discrimination clauses (national treatment and MFN) prohibited host countries from treating foreign investors less favourably than domestic investors, but did not prohibit host countries from according more favourable treatment to foreign investors. In other words, the MAI established a minimum of "no less favourable" treatment of foreign investors only, not a uniform standard for all investors.
b) The dispute settlement clauses put the foreign investor in a more privileged position than the domestic investor because the choices foreign investors were given were not also at the disposal of the national investor.
c) The MAI did not regulate incentives. As more and more countries continue offering incentives to attract scarce FDI, and combined with the effects of the non-discrimination clauses, foreign investors would be offered special privileges, which domestic investors would not be entitled to.
d) The MAI encroached too much on the sovereign rights of host countries:

   - It prohibited host countries from selecting the type of FDI they would like to allow in their territories.
   - The prohibition of performance requirements would mean that host countries would not be able to maximise the benefits they get from FDI through, for example, technology transfer requirements, employment or skill development requirements, and so on.
   - The broad definition of "expropriation" would scare host country governments from taking certain measures, even when the measures would be essential on grounds of protecting the environment, public

health, consumer safety, etc. (the dispute between Ethyn Corporation and Canada is a good example).

- The dispute settlement provision would give a wider right to the foreign investor while at the same time it undermines the sovereignty of the host country.

To sum up, the strategy of the OECD countries and the Organisation's agenda has been liberalisation, higher standard of treatment for foreign investors and investor protection. The liberalisation agenda was mainly directed at members of the Organisation (US against EU and vice versa, Japan against US, etc). But the other two items of the agenda were directed mainly against non-OECD countries, as OECD countries generally have higher standards of investor treatment and protection. Hence, the choice of the OECD as a forum and the exclusion of non-OECD countries from the negotiation process were ultimately fatal decisions, for they defeated one of the very purposes of the Agreement itself. The draft Agreement did not reflect the concerns of these non-OECD countries and the process barely made an attempt to do so. The next Chapter discusses the concerns and strategies of developing countries.

Notes

1 The MAI is a draft investment agreement that had been negotiated by the OECD countries from April 1995 to May 1998 under the sponsorship of the OECD Secretariat. The negotiations were planned to be completed in April 1997 initially, but later the deadline was extended to April 1998. Because of the enormous controversy it generated both within the OECD grouping and around the world, the negotiation was suspended indefinitely in May 1998 and the Agreement has not been signed as of this date.

2 See, for example, Maritime Act and the US Outer Continental Shelf Act, the Commercial Fishing Industry Vessel Anti-reflagging Act of 1987, the Federal Power Act, the Geothermal Steam Act, and the Nuclear Energy Act.

3 Examples of CNT can be found in the American Pre-eminence Act of 1991, the Energy Policy Act of 1992, the National Cooperative Production Act of 1993, and the Defence Application Act of 1993.

4 For examples of views critical of Japanese direct investment in the US, see Burstein (1988); Franz & Collins (1989).

5 For an account of the Fairchild affair, see Warshofsky (1989: 301-33).

6 Mr. Larson was also one of the two Vice Chairmen of the Negotiating Group, the other being Mr. Akitaki Saikai of Japan.

7 A radio documentary entitled "The Quiet Debate", broadcast by Background Briefing (ABC Australia) on November 30, 1997.

8 The principle of post-establishment national treatment is that host countries would treat foreign investors/investments no less favourably that domestic investors/investments in their day-to-day regulation of business activities.

9 Speech made by Mr. Larson on the Conference held in Rio de Janero, Brazil, 16-18 July 1996, on the theme "Investment Policies in Latin America and Multinational Rules on Investment".

10 See also speech by Mr. Larson, Vice Chairman of the MAI Negotiating Group, at the Conference organised by the OECD Secretariat and held in Rio de Janero, Brazil, 16-18 July 1996, on the theme "Investment Policies in Latin America and Multilateral Rules on Investment".

11 The draft MAI used for discussion throughout the book is the 24 April 1998 version. For more discussion of the MAI, see also Henderson (1999); Kelsy (1999); Picciotto and Mayne (1999).

12 For a list of MAI-related Internet sites, see *http://mai.flora.org/*, accessed on 25 December 1999.

13 The NGO campaigns and strategies were extensively posted and discussed at the time at *http://www/flora.org/mai-not/*, accessed on 1 April 1999.

14 The letter was posted at *http://wcc-coe.org/wcc.english.html*, accessed on 10 April 1999.

15 The report is posted on the web page of Ministère de l'Économie, des Finances et de l'Industrie, at *http://www.finances.gouv.fr/pole_ecofin/international/ami0998/*, accessed on 25 April 1999.

16 Treasury represented Australia on the MAI negotiations. Before joining the Australian Public Service, I had some opportunity from the NGO side (as a technical consultant) to observe some of these consultations with Treasury.

Chapter 6

Developing Countries

In recent decades, the marketplaces of the developing countries have been emerging as important destinations of FDI flows.[1] MNCs and the governments of major capital exporting countries seem to be acting together to get the hurdles in FDI flows removed and to facilitate the smooth functioning of foreign investment (Chapter Five). Developing countries, on the other hand, while keen to supplement their meagre resources of development with FDI, seem to be unsure about giving unrestricted market access to foreign investors. There are many areas where the interests of these two groups are at variance, and there are other areas where they coincide.

In the previous Chapter, the strategies of the OECD and its members for a future global investment regime have been discussed. The discussion revealed the common agenda of the OECD countries as well as the particular priorities of the key members. The main features of the MAI and the anticipated next step after its downfall have also been discussed. This Chapter, on the other hand, discusses the strategies of other stakeholders, developing countries, for a global investment regime.

Key Players

The key players in developing countries do not have a common strategy for a global investment regime at this point in time. Their views are divided on whether to have such a regime in the first place, secondly on the appropriate forum for the negotiation and implementation of such a regime, and thirdly on the nature and emphasis of the regime, if at the end of the day a decision would be made to have one.

Latin American countries such as Argentina, Brazil and Chile have been supportive of a global framework of investment rules. Chilean and Argentine diplomats at the WTO told me during interviews:

> We support a multilateral rule on investment. We have a more liberal regime than India, China or Malaysia. We support an initiative that goes in the direction of upgrading the multilateral trading system. We will, however, have concern if the investment rules contradict the trading system.

Over the past decade, the countries of Latin America have made a significant shift in the way they treat FDI. Their policies seem to have departed from the influences of dependency theory and embraced neo-classical economic theory. For example, they have introduced very liberal investment regimes, signed a large number of Bilateral Investment Treaties with several developed countries as well as among themselves, created new regional and sub-regional arrangements to deal with FDI, and started a process of negotiating a hemispheric-wide investment agreement involving the entire Western hemisphere (UNCTAD, 1997: 75). The countries of this region have progressively opened up their economies since the late 1980s and early 1990s, replacing their traditional, inward-oriented policies with a strategy meant to enhance their participation in the world economy. As a result, their national investment regimes have exhibited significant changes, such as:

- the granting of national treatment to foreign investors;
- the elimination or significant reduction of controls on the transfer of funds;
- the opening of economic sectors that were previously closed to foreign investors; and
- the establishment of investment promotion agencies.

In the intellectual heartland of dependency theory, the policy shift away from its prescriptions has been most decisive. According to a senior Argentine diplomat, for Latin Americans, a global investment regime would be a complement to the process they have already started through regional agreements. These countries also believe that, being among those with the most liberal investment regimes, they may not have to do any more adjustment to their investment policies and rules by joining a liberal, global investment framework.[2] This of course is based on the assumption that any global investment framework would have liberalisation as its main objective. They therefore see the MAI or any WTO agreement on investment as complementary (Interview with Chilean and Argentine diplomats).

The second group of countries, led by India, China, Malaysia and Indonesia does not see the need for a multilateral framework for FDI. They were also opposed to the extension of the MAI to non-OECD countries. India's Commerce Secretary, Mr. Tejendra Khanna, in a speech at the World Trade Congress, held in Singapore in April 1996, noted:

> Just as boxing matches are organised in different weight categories and a light weight and heavy weight boxer are not put into the same ring, investment rules which may be equitable and practicable for OECD countries would clearly be out of place and illogical if extended across the board for all WTO members.

Some of these countries (such as Malaysia and India) also doubt if a global investment framework would have any positive effect on the volume of FDI flowing to developing countries. A consultant of the South Centre[3], who is also a Professor of economics in the University of Cambridge, told me:

> FDI is growing any way without a global regime. Many countries have liberal regimes, but they do not get FDI. Moreover, a risk on FDI arises not from lack of a legal regime protecting FDI, but from the basic economic conditions in the host countries. So there is no need for a global investment regime.

The main strategy of this group of countries is to block or delay any attempt to negotiate a global investment regime (Interviews with Malaysian, Egyptian, Chinese and Ethiopian diplomats). Hence, when Japan, Canada and others proposed, at the WTO Ministerial Conference in Singapore in December 1996, to mandate the WTO to host investment negotiations, Malaysia, India, Indonesia, Philippines and others strongly opposed the proposal.

According to the officials of this group of countries who were interviewed during the course of this research, these countries would not support a global investment framework mainly for two reasons. The first is that such a framework could significantly erode their sovereignty by giving "excessive" powers to foreign investors (for example through the international adjudication of investment disputes) and limiting the regulatory power of States. The second is that standardised investment rules would leave very little room to countries to manoeuvre their investment policies according to their development and social objectives and priorities, thereby interfering with their "right to development" (Interviews with diplomats of Malaysia, Egypt, China and India stationed in Geneva).

These divergent positions of developing countries are more or less the culmination of their changing attitudes towards FDI over several decades (see Chapter Two).

From 1980 onwards, the number of nationalisation acts dropped dramatically (see Table 2:1). Countries have become increasingly appreciative of the benefits that can be gained from FDI. In most cases, the countries that have grown the fastest in the past few decades are those which were the most favourably disposed towards FDI (Dunning, 1993: 558). In fact, it now appears that there is an emerging broad consensus among both developing and developed countries that FDI can quicken economic growth and that any adverse effects can be controlled (Shihata, 1991: 488). A United Nations report (quoted in Sornarajah, 1994) described the trend relating to FDI in host countries as follows:

> In the early 1970s, fortified by their strengthened bargaining position as the centres of economic growth and as recipients of investments by transnational corporations in the developing world, most of these countries introduced rigorous regulatory regimes for foreign investment and

> technology...However, since the mid-1970s, many of these countries have initiated policies and strategies that depart in certain respects from these early regimes. These new policies on the whole portray a more flexible and pragmatic approach aimed at facilitating and speeding up foreign investment flows.

In this period of compromise, host countries designed their policies and laws simultaneously along two tracks: inducing FDI, and then harnessing it to their goals. These goals fall generally into four categories: domestic economic objectives, such as reducing poverty; external economic objectives, such as improving balance of payments or breaking into new markets; national ownership or control of certain economic activities; and transfer of technology and knowhow (see Chapter Three).

It has been said above that those countries that oppose a global investment regime do so mainly for two reasons: protecting sovereignty and their desire to preserve their power to channel foreign investment in sectors where they want it to contribute to their development. These two grounds will be discussed in the following part of the Chapter.

FDI and Sovereignty

The protection of sovereignty is presented by some developing countries as one of the grounds for opposing the negotiation of global investment rules (Interview with Malaysian, Egyptian, Chinese and Ethiopian diplomats). It is argued that the unrestricted entry of FDI to developing countries could be a threat to the sovereignty of those countries and the independent development of their social and cultural life. There is also a fear that home countries could use foreign investors to impose "their values and work ethics on the host developing countries, which are different from those of the latter, as well as to lecture developing countries what is good or bad for them" (Interview with a Malaysian diplomat).

Many developing countries see their economic difficulties as both a legacy of colonial policies and a product of current global economic injustices. Hence, they embrace sovereignty not only as an aspiration, but also as a demarcation of property rights within international society. The proposals for a New International Economic Order in the 1970s, the demand for a right to development, and the UN General Assembly Resolution on Permanent Sovereignty over Natural Resources were all supported by developing countries as efforts to bolster their sovereignty (Schachter, 1983: 525-46 and 1986: 29-59; Jackson, 1990; Blaney, 1992).

The United Nations, at its sixth ordinary session in 1952, recognised within the context of Resolution 523/VI referring to "Integrated Economic Development" that developing countries have the "right to determine freely the use of their natural resources" and the need for them to "utilise such resources in order to be in a better position to further the realisation of their plans of economic development, in accordance with their national interests". Shortly after that resolution, at the seventh ordinary session, the General Assembly directly examined the right which developing countries must have to exploit their natural wealth and resources (Resolution 626/VII). Later, on December 12, 1958, the General Assembly passed another resolution affirming "the right of peoples and nations to self-determination...includes permanent sovereignty over their natural wealth and resources" (Resolution 1314/XIII). In order to clarify the extent and effective nature of this sovereignty, the General Assembly further decided to set up a commission which would formulate recommendations (Elian, 1979: 86).

In the years that followed, the UN General Assembly continued to pass other resolutions recognising the sovereign right of states to use their natural wealth for the advancement of their economic development (Resolutions 1803/XVIII, 2158/XXI, 2386/XXIII, etc). The debate over the essence and the extent of application of the doctrine of permanent sovereignty over natural resources also continued. By 1973, many members felt that it was necessary to move on beyond recognition and establish some concrete ways and means for utilising this right (Elian, 1979: 98). Hence, on December 12, 1974, the General Assembly adopted the Charter of Economic Rights and Duties of States (Resolution A/3281) – a document which many developing countries still accord the highest political and economic significance. The adoption of the Charter occasioned a great confrontation of opinions along the North-South divide, both in the negotiations of the working group and in the General Assembly (Elian, 1979: 118). The Charter was adopted through nominal roll call, with 120 members voting for it, 6 against and 10 abstentions (Elian, 1979: 137). The most contentious issues were permanent sovereignty over natural resources, nationalisation and the application of domestic laws on foreign investments, and the status of multinational corporations (Elian, 1979: 118).

Article 2, paragraph 1 of the Charter states that sovereignty is full, including possession, utilisation and disposal of all assets, natural resources and economic activities, and that States hold and exert this right freely (Resolution A/ 3281). The Charter also states that nationalisation or expropriation is a right of the State adopting such measures, in exchange for adequate compensation and taking into account all circumstances considered relevant by the respective State (Resolution A/ 3281).

Given the circumstances of its adoption, it is debatable whether or not the Charter has the full force of international law. Many developing countries, however, argue that it is an international law and, as a result, they are opposed to any agreement that has the effect of diluting its strength (Sornarajah, 1994; also interviews officials of Malaysia, Egypt and Ethiopia). The MAI encountered stiff resistance from some core developing countries partly because it essentially attempted to undo what these countries achieved through the Charter. The National Treatment clause of the MAI required host countries to give unrestricted market access to foreign investors in sectors where their domestic investors are active. The Standstill clause required them not to introduce any restrictive laws and policies in the future. The MAI also gave foreign investors the right to take their dispute with the host country to an international tribunal without the host country's consent. Combined, all of these clauses restrict severely States' ability to exercise complete sovereignty over their natural resources and wealth, contrary in important respects to what is stipulated in the Charter.

When the major interests of MNCs and States are in conflict, there have been various forms of direct, sometimes brutal interference by MNCs in the domestic affairs of States. Alan Sabatier (1975), in a Chapter of his book specifically dedicated to examples of cases in which the sovereignty of States has been damaged through manoeuvres of multinational corporations, cites numerous such pressures and acts of political-military interference by corporations where they have subsidiaries. As the earlier discussion showed, it is only in the past decade and a half that the relationship between many developing countries and multinational corporations has become smoother. However, there is still genuine concern that some multinational corporations are much more powerful, both politically and economically, than many developing countries to the point of endangering the latters' sovereignty. It is unthinkable for many developing country governments to appear before an international tribunal in their dispute with such companies. Hence, several governments from the developing world would like to retain their power to reject any investment proposals by foreign investors they are not comfortable with. Although almost all of them have a generally positive attitude towards FDI, the level of trust they have towards foreign investors has not reached that stage where they would open their doors completely without any fear of adverse consequences.

FDI and Development

Most developing countries generally accept that FDI could make a big contribution to their development efforts. Their concern is however that all types of FDI, flowing in all sectors of an economy, may not necessarily constitute a necessary condition for achieving rapid growth and sustainable development. The countries that oppose a global investment regime argue that FDI could only be beneficial to their economies if they can control, regulate and direct it according to their development objectives. A consultant of the South Centre said during my discussion with him:

> The cost of FDI could be very high. The foreign investor expects a very high return, and the money or profit has to be repatriated. That is why it is essential for a country to have the power to choose the kind of project it needs. FDI is productive if it contributes and links to the country's development. A hamburger shop or a supermarket may not be a productive foreign investment from the point of view of developing countries.

These countries want FDI to complement their domestic capability, not to replace it. They therefore want to foster and protect their local companies with a view to making them competitive both locally and internationally. A Chinese diplomat told me during my fieldwork in Geneva:

> The present system of regulating FDI works very well. It should be up to national governments to decide how much FDI they need and how to regulate it. Developing countries want FDI, but not at the expense of domestic investment.

It is also argued that a rapid increase in FDI stock could exacerbate the balance-of-payment problems of the host country. One of the mechanisms of avoiding this problem would be to constrain the rate of FDI to not exceed the growth rate of local investment (Khor, 1996). Moreover, the pace and nature of investment liberalisation might be determined by considerations such as the capacity of the local sector to withstand greater competition from foreign firms producing locally, the effects such liberalisation would have on the trade balance and balance-of-payments, and the like (Khor, 1996).

There is a large volume of literature on the impact of FDI on development. Some of it shows that FDI has both negative and positive results. Kumar (1996) summarises the literature as follows:

a) FDI (expressed as a ratio of net FDI inflow to GNP) neither increases domestic investment nor does it provide additional balance-of-payments financing, suggesting that FDI appears to have been used in large part as a substitute for other types of foreign investment flows;
b) an increase in FDI reduces national savings;
c) FDI does not exert a significantly different effect from domestically financed investment on the rate of economic growth; and
d) FDI exerts both direct and indirect effects on the current account, the latter appears to be a substantial negative effect.

Some experts have also expressed doubts about the causal relationship between FDI flows and growth. Singh for example suggests that growth stimulates the flow of FDI rather than the other way around (Singh, 1988: 35-82). Another study by Chung et *al* finds that the relationship between FDI and growth is much weaker than that between domestic savings and growth (Chung et al, 1995: 691-703).

Some studies show that FDI has a spillover effect on local enterprises, such as the transfer of technology and know-how (Dunning, 1993: 288). However, MNCs historically tend to concentrate their research and development activities in their home countries (Dunning, 1993). Thus, if the entry of foreign investors into the host country is not accompanied with research and development, the benefit in the transfer of technology and know-how may not be that significant. Very tight control over intellectual property by foreign investors might mean that the technology transfer benefits are not achieved.

The other concern is the effects FDI might have on the balance-of-payments of the host country. FDI makes significant additions to the foreign exchange supply of the host country in the initial phase of its entry. What happens after that largely depends on the type of investment products (Graham and Krugman, 1989). If the investment is export-oriented, its effect on the balance-of-payments would be positive. If the investment is not export-oriented, its effect on the balance-of-payments in the medium and longer term could be negative, particularly if it is a mere acquisition of a non-export oriented domestic company. Moreover, some studies demonstrate that subsidiaries of foreign companies have a larger propensity to import than domestic competitors producing similar products (Graham and Krugman, 1989). Although they were caused mainly by short-term capital flows, the financial crisis in Asia and Mexico have demonstrated indiscriminate inflow of foreign investment may not necessarily make a positive contribution to the balance-of-payments of the host country. Hence, Chile and Malaysia introduced capital control measures, which seem to have produced positive results.[4]

The Asian economic "miracle" is often cited as an example of how well directed and controlled FDI could contribute to the development of a country. In fact, almost all of the major countries that oppose an initiative for a global investment regime come from this part of the world. Hence, it may be useful here to briefly examine the Asian economic "miracle", and its subsequent meltdown, to see the role played by the State in the whole process.

The Asian Economic Miracle/Meltdown

For the decade and a half to 1997, the world was hearing stories of the miraculous success of the Asian economies. Singapore, Hong Kong, Taiwan, South Korea, Malaysia, Thailand and Indonesia had been making impressive economic development for decades. Some of the achievements of these countries included:

- a dramatic reduction in poverty. Income in South Korea, for example, quadrupled from the mid-1970s to the mid-1990s;
- a new Asian middle class arose to become an important market in global terms;
- tertiary education mushroomed. In Hong Kong, for example, the number of undergraduates increased by more than 400% since 1975;
- health standards dramatically improved;
- there was massive infrastructural development; and
- life expectancy increased (Gough, 1998: 101-2).

How did these countries achieve this rapid and sustained development? There is no single answer, and they did not follow a single development model. Perkins suggests that they have followed at least three distinct development models, even though all three have some common features. According to him, there were the manufacturing, export-led state interventionist models of Korea and Taiwan; the free port service, commerce dominated model of Singapore and Hong Kong; and models followed by those economies relatively richer in natural resources (at least in the beginning) but not in human resources, such as Indonesia, Malaysia and Thailand (Perkins, 1994: 655-56).

One thing that seems common in all of these countries, except Hong Kong, is the interventionist role played by the State. Hong Kong has frequently been depicted as a laissez-faire economy (see for example, Friedman and

Friedman, 1980; Balassa, 1988 and 1991; Chen, 1979). These writers argue that it has been the maintenance of a free trade regime that has made Hong Kong's economy a success story. Others, however, argue that the state played a significant role even in Hong Kong (see for example, Lui and Chiu, 1996).

There is now widespread acknowledgment of the role played by the State in East and South East Asian industrialisation. It is also acknowledged that the role, nature and extent of State intervention had considerable variations, and that this has changed over time (Deyo, 1987; White, 1988; Amsden, 1989; Wade, 1990). Malaysia and South Korea are presented below as examples of the variations in the emphasis given by the respective States in their development policy.

Malaysia Malaysia is a multi-ethnic country in which the population is divided between three main ethnic groups: Malays (making up about 57% of the population), Chinese (about 33%) and Indians (about 8%) (Eyre, 1997: 126). During the colonial era, Malays were largely associated with subsistence agriculture, while the Chinese and Indians were (still are) involved largely in the cash economy. As a result, upon independence from British colonial rule, the Chinese and Indians were in a far better position to seize new initiatives in trading, commerce and manufacturing, and to expand their position in the growing economy (Eyre, 1997: 126). In 1970, average income per month for Malays was US$55.8, for Chinese US$127.9 and for Indians US$98.7 (Faaland et al, 1990). Malays were over-represented in those people living below the poverty line, comprising 73.8% poor households (Government of Malaysia, 1976). Moreover, Malays accounted for only 2.4 % of corporate ownership, while 63.3 % was foreign owned, and the remainder was owned by "other Malaysians", mainly Chinese and Indians (Government of Malaysia, 1991).

Upon gaining independence, political control was transferred from the British to a small Malay aristocracy. For the majority of the Malays who were concentrated in the traditional agricultural sector, however, things were not really improving much (Mehmet, 1978). Following the 1969 election, tensions between the major ethnic groups boiled over into a major outbreak of rioting. This resulted in the government undertaking a fundamental reappraisal of its national development policy. A New Economic Policy (NEP), which would run for twenty years, was introduced with the central objective of "eradicating poverty irrespective of race and restructuring Malaysian society to reduce and eventually eliminate the identification of race with economic function" (Government of Malaysia, 1971: v).

The NEP was viewed as "a direct response by the Malaysian government to correct uneven development between different ethnic groups, so ensuring that the racial riots of 1969 would not be repeated" (Eyre, 1997: 130). Creating an atmosphere of political and social stability through affirmative action was the central objective of the NEP. It was decided that employment as well as the management and ownership of commercial and industrial property should reflect the ethnic composition of the population. By the end of the NEP in 1990, Malaysia was a stable and prosperous country. Many attribute this achievement to the unique development policy adopted by the government (Eyre, 1997).

South Korea South Korea's industrialisation started during the early 1960s, with the government making economic development the top priority. At the centre of the government's policy was the creation of large private conglomerate businesses (chaebols), to serve as the main vehicles for economic development. Hence, the government actively helped create large conglomerates, promoting mergers and directing entry and exit of firms, according to the requirements of technological-scale economies and world demand conditions (Singh, 1996: 16). In this, there was much in common with Japanese development through zaibatsus. As a result, Korea's manufacturing industry displayed one of the highest market concentrations anywhere in the world, with the top 50 chaebols accounting for 15% of GDP in 1990. In the same year, 11 of the world largest 500 industrial companies were from Korea (Singh, 1996: 17). A United Nations study observed:

> Such a structure is the deliberate creation of the government, which utilised a highly interventionist strategy to push industry into large-scale, complex technology demanding activities while simultaneously restricting FDI inflows tightly to promote national ownership. It was deemed necessary to create enterprises of large size and diversity, to undertake the risk inherent in launching high technology, high-skill activities that would remain competitive in world markets. The chaebols acted as the representative and spearheads of the government strategy: they were supported by protection against imports and TNC entry, subsidised credit, procurement preference and massive investments in education, infrastructure and science-technology network (United Nations, 1993: 35).

Towards the end of the 1960s, the government embarked in a strategy of export promotion, while maintaining protection of its market. Strong government involvement and building up of the capabilities of domestic private corporations was again at the centre of the strategy. A policy of investment incentives and socialisation of risks was adopted. In economic sectors where domestic private investors were reluctant to invest due to the large amount of capital required as well as technological and market risks, the government provided companies with finance at subsidised rates and other forms of incentives. The story about the success of Samsung Industries perhaps illustrates the policy of the government at the time and how Korean companies benefited from that policy.

Samsung Industries began making microwave ovens in the early 1970s in a cramped old laboratory, turning out a few hundred overpriced ovens annually for the heavily protected domestic market. The government's Economic Development Board was a key player in making Samsung one of the world's biggest producers of microwaves within a relatively short period of time. Government officials were keenly aware that the Republic of Korea could not rely on low wage manufacturing for long and, sooner or later, would not be in a position to compete for labour-intensive manufacturing jobs with other low-wage neighbours such as China and Indonesia. To prepare for that day, government officials, working in consultation with the private sector, developed incentives for new knowledge- and capital-intensive industries. Incentives varied widely and included the government's building industrial parks, subsidising utilities, giving tax rebates for exports, and making cheap loans for investment in new products. By 1980, urged forward by subsidies and incentives, Korean industry had moved into steel, ships, and even cars and was about to leap into world class electronics (World Bank, 1993: 130).

Samsung made good use of these measures, and the company's first break came in 1980, when a US department store, looking for cheaper substitutes, ordered several thousand ovens. Soon production had risen to 100,000. When General Electronics, unable to keep pace with the Japanese competition, decided to stop manufacturing microwaves itself and import the ovens under its own label instead, Samsung was a logical choice (World Bank, 1993: 130).

Another example of heavy State intervention in Korea is the support given by the government to heavy and chemical industries during the recession of the early 1970s. When it was realised that the recession had threatened the financial viability of many of these strategic corporations, the government introduced the Presidential Emergency Decree of August 1972, which declared a moratorium on corporate debt. (Singh, 1996: 20). Corporate loans were converted into long-term loans to be paid on an instalment basis over a five-year period with a grace period of three years. A maximum interest rate of 16.2% was fixed on these loans while the prevailing market rate was over 40% per annum (Kim, et al, 1995). This intervention by the Korean government has been criticised by some economists as an example of inefficiency, waste and general government failure (World Bank, 1993; Kruger, 1995). Others however see it as exceptionally valuable source of Korea's export success in the world market since the mid-1980 (Amsden, 1989; Kim et al, 1995).

Table 6:1 Percentage Share of FDI in Gross Fixed Capital Formation (1971-93)

	1971-75	1976-80	1981-85	1986-90	1991	1992	1993
Korea	1.9	0.4	0.5	1.3	1.0	0.5	0.4
Malaysia	15.2	11.9	10.8	10.5	24.0	26.0	23.7

Source UNCTAD, World Investment Report, 1993, 1994 and 1995.

Role of FDI in East and South-East Asian Development

As the development policies adopted by each of the East and South-East Asian countries vary, so does the role played by FDI in those countries. For example, while South Korea has attracted little foreign investment during the period 1971-93, by contrast, the role of FDI in the growth and exports of Malaysia has been considerably greater during the same period (Table 6:1).

Korea relied on foreign capital mainly as a way to complement domestic investment. According to Rasiah (1996:186), the authorities in Korea utilised foreign capital to enhance the productive capacity of their domestic enterprises. Technological knowledge acquired through licensing arrangements, with limited direct participation of MNCs in the domestic economy confined largely in labour-intensive assembly operations. In Malaysia, however, FDI-controlled enterprises accounted for 40% of fixed assets, 62% of overall manufactured exports, 47% of total manufacturing output and 44% of employment in 1991 (Rasiah, 1995: 81).

Despite the difference in approach, one of the hallmarks of economic policy-making in all of the countries of East and South-East Asia was the pragmatic flexibility of their governments in pursuit of economic objectives. Policies that worked were retained, while policies that failed or impeded other policy objectives were abandoned. Thus, the Korean and Malaysian governments reduced intensive promotion of heavy and chemical industries when the fiscal costs and strains on the financial system threatened macroeconomic stability (World Bank, 1993: 86). Similarly, Indonesia abandoned capital market controls and attempts to control interest rates when they were found to be ineffective, while Japan shifted from highly selective interventions to promote exports in the 1950s and 1960s to industrial policies designed to reduce trade friction in the 1980s (World Bank, 1993: 86). The story is similar in Taiwan, China and Singapore (World Bank, 1993). In essence, what the World Bank concluded in its "Asian Miracle" report was that however authoritarian these societies may have been in other respects, on economic matters there was robust policy contestation, for example between different sections of the bureaucracy. The contest was less one of neo-classical liberal markets versus dependency; it was less about ideology than about selective state intervention based on openness to evidence.

Regulating FDI

Most of the countries that had opposition to a global investment regime are from South and South-East Asia. And one of the main reasons for their opposition emanates from their own experience that there is no single model of development that could apply to all countries, at all times. They believe that a global investment regime would deprive them of the flexibility and pragmatism they need to design, implement and change their investment laws, depending on their particular circumstances. The National Treatment clause of the MAI, for example, obliges host countries not to discriminate against foreign investors. This means that economic sectors that are open for domestic investors should also be open for foreign investors, or any incentives given to domestic investors should also be given to foreign investors. The MAI also requires host countries to stop introducing any more restrictive policies and laws in the future. Such requirements severely limit the governments' ability to manoeuvre their policies and laws to fulfil their current needs. This is essentially one of the main reasons why they were opposed to the MAI.[5] A Chinese diplomat told me in Geneva in July 1997:

> The OECD countries are at a similar stage of development and it is OK for them to have the MAI. But it does not work for countries of different developmental stages. Moreover, the MAI is focused on commitments by governments, not on commitments by business. It is an unbalanced document. Investors should also be committed to certain obligations.[6]

Some do not see any merit in the MAI even for developed countries themselves. An economics Professor at Cambridge University, who is also a consultant of the South Centre, told me:

> The MAI is bad for developing as well as developed countries. It increases the power of capital and reduces the power of Labor. Capital will flow to big developing countries. Unemployment will rise in the developed countries. The MAI is good only for the multinational companies. I think the multinationals have a disproportionate influence on the MAI negotiators and the Office of the United States Trade Representative (USTR).

He further said that if we were ever have to have a global investment regime, it should be one that would enshrine the:

- developing country's right for development;
- right to select development projects;
- discretion of countries to stop the repatriation of profit for a while; and
- protection of the rights of investors.

It is argued by the opponents of a global investment regime that the main purpose of such a regime should not be to give market access for multinational corporations but the creation of an opportunity where FDI contributes to the economic development of the host countries. A Chinese diplomat told me:

> Any FDI agreement must be one that would take into account the developmental dimension. It should be one that would make contributions to the development of developing countries. It should also be one that would put obligations on multinational companies, not only on host countries.

These countries also believe that investment frameworks such as the MAI do not consider issues that are more important to them, as they are mainly about securing a high standard of treatment for multinational companies (Interview with Malaysian and Egyptian diplomats). Moreover, they fear that multinational corporations would be able to cross borders without barriers and set up projects or buy up local companies whilst facing minimal or no regulation in the host countries as to entry, conditions of establishment, ownership, operation, and repatriation of profits and capital. Correspondingly, the rights and authority to regulate foreign investors and the degree of freedom and policy options of host countries would be reduced or constrained significantly (Khor, 1996).

During the period 1997-99, the dynamic economies of Asia have been rocked by economic and financial crisis. A number of, at times conflicting, hypotheses have been suggested as to what caused this crisis. Most people agree that lack of proper financial regulatory frameworks is one of the main reasons (McLeod and Garnaut, 1998; Chang and Singh, 1999). In the past decade or so, developments in the capital market have substantially eroded government regulatory power in financial transactions. Neo-liberal economists say this is a positive development because the markets themselves are capable of correcting any adverse consequences.

It needs to be recognised that external shocks today create greater macroeconomic disturbances than shocks in the past that were caused by changes in the terms of trade. Global capital can react more abruptly and indiscriminately, leading to a crisis and regional instability. What does this mean for developing countries? From a political perspective, this development may represent a power shift from elected governments to speculators, bond traders and fund managers, and that Malaysian Prime Minister Mahathir's visceral reaction to financier George Soros epitomises this painful shift.

During the economic boom since the late 1980s, the Bank of Thailand (BOT) removed almost all of its earlier restrictions on the movement of financial capital into and out of Thailand. To attract foreign investment into the country, the Thai authorities thought it was not enough to show to investors that the entry of foreign investment was open, but exit was unrestricted as well. So the government had removed most of the capital controls that had made maintenance of its fixed exchange rate policy consistent with a degree of monetary independence. "This meant that speculative attacks on the Baht became much easier. When the market began to expect a devaluation, the rate of financial outflow became so great that depreciation became inevitable" (Warr, 1998: 60).

According to some observers, sound capital control regulations could have saved the Asian countries from the crisis. The Economist (1998) writes:

> Chile has been relatively unaffected by the "tequila effect" of the Mexican crisis. Chile instituted three types of controls. First, 30% of all non-equity capital flowing into the country must be deposited interest-free at the central bank for one year. Second, only if rated as high as Chile's government bonds by two bond-rating agencies can Chilean firms and banks borrow from the international capital markets. Third, any foreign money coming into Chile must stay in the country for at least one year.

Similarly, Chang and Singh (1999) argue that India, with fewer reserves and less strong fundamentals than China, has been able to avoid the strong regional contagion by implementing only a strictly limited opening of its traditional comprehensive capital control regime.

Some now argue that probably the overflow of capital in these crisis-affected Asian countries may also have been one of the causes of the problem. According to Chang and Singh (1999), this "excess" capital flowed mostly into financing real estate (especially in Thailand and Malaysia) or excess production capacity in manufacturing (especially in Korea), consequently creating asset bubbles and/or excess capacities. If this is true, it adds weight to the long-standing argument of some developing countries on the need to retain their power to channel foreign investment into sectors that are most important for the long-term economic development of the host country.

At a more micro-level, there clearly was a problem of crony capitalism and corruption, the debilitating effects of which were not so visible during the long boom. The cronies who ran banks often did not put adequate risk management systems in place that could come to terms with the volatility of contemporary money markets. So, there was a failure of macro risk management at the level of aggregate capital flows and a failure of micro risk management at the level of individual banks.

Venue

The ultimate strategy of the countries that oppose a global investment regime is to preserve as much as possible the power of national governments to screen investment proposals, as well as control, direct and regulate the operations of foreign investors. They believe that the global investment framework proposed by the developed countries (such as the MAI) would deprive them of this power, and therefore they oppose such a proposal outright. At the same time, they know that in the longer term the pressure by the developed countries to negotiate such an agreement would be very hard to resist. During my interview with an official of the South Centre, I was told that:

> Developing countries will be under great pressure to accept the MAI. They will be subjected to unofficial sanctions and blackmail. They are being told by the IMF and World Bank that the MAI is good. At the end of the day, the MAI will become a global agreement.

Of course, the MAI has now become history. But the push by the developed countries for a similar agreement has not. Therefore, the other strategy of the opponents is to delay the starting of negotiations as long as possible and, when the time to negotiate comes, negotiate an agreement that lacks teeth. Hence they oppose any investment negotiations within the framework of the WTO, as the WTO is a body capable of making binding rules.

In November 1996, at a meeting of the heads of delegation at the WTO, Indonesia presented a joint statement of eight developing countries (Malaysia, India, Egypt, Tanzania, Ghana, Uganda and Haiti) opposing the starting of any discussion of investment issues within the WTO. These countries, which were later joined by many others, "pointed out that the WTO already has rules to deal with aspects of investment that have a direct and distorting effect on trade and cause material injury to trading partners, and that is sufficient for now." (Khor, 1996a)

At the same time, another group of countries also presented a joint statement arguing that it would be useful if the WTO takes up investment issues.

In the December 1996 Ministerial Conference in Singapore, a group of developed and developing countries led by Japan and Canada made a proposal for the WTO to set up a working party on trade and investment. They proposed that the working party would look into the links between trade and investment, the barriers to investment, existing international investment agreements, and issues on rights and obligations in the area of investment (Ibid). This proposal was quickly supported by all developed countries and a number of developing countries, including Argentina, Brazil and Honduras (Speeches made by their delegations). Brazil, in fact, requested the start of investment negotiations within the WTO as soon as possible (speech of the Minister for External Relations, Mr. L.F. Lamreia).

Other countries, including Indonesia, Philippines, India, and Malaysia opposed the move (Speeches by the delegates of the countries). Indonesia insisted that this task should be left for UNCTAD (Speech by the Indonesian Minister of Industry and Trade, Mr. Tungky Ariwibowo). After intense, behind-the-scenes discussion between the various parties, however, agreement was reached to start only exploratory and educative work on the relationship between trade and investment. The Malaysian Minister of International Trade and Industry, Ms. Rafidah Aziz, said in her speech to the Conference:

> On the issue of the relationship of investment to trade, Malaysia cannot accept or subscribe to any move towards the formulation of multilateral investment rules in the WTO, although work on an educative process can be supported, provided it does not lead to negotiations within the WTO.

Finally, the Conference adopted a resolution to "establish a working group to examine the relationship between trade and investment" (WTO Press Release).[7]

The countries that oppose the WTO as a venue also have a number of other reasons for doing so. Firstly, they argue that the areas of competence of the WTO are not wide enough to cover the many facets of investment issues. For example, development issues as well as issues of investment linked with social and financial equity among different communities, political and sectoral policies could not be discussed within the framework of the WTO (Interview with a Malaysian diplomat in Geneva). A Chinese diplomat in Geneva told me:

> WTO is basically a trade organisation. But investment is one of the factors of economic development; it is not basically a trade issue. So, WTO is not well suited to handle negotiations on investment rules.

Those aspects of investment with more direct relation to the WTO trade rules have already been covered in TRIMS. It is therefore argued that pushing the discussion on investment policy through the narrow framework of the WTO would distort the issues (Khor, 1996: 13).

Secondly, these countries feel that, lacking the necessary human resources and negotiating capacity, developing countries would be in a disadvantageous position if negotiations took place within the framework of the WTO (Khor, 1996: 14). Thirdly, a WTO investment agreement would be subject to the WTO dispute settlement mechanism, which has provisions on cross-retaliation. Developing countries would not want this (Interview with an official of the South Centre).

These countries, therefore, believe that it would be much better for them if UNCTAD assumes the responsibility of overseeing any such negotiations. They think that UNCTAD has a number of comparative advantages over the OECD or WTO for the following reasons (Khor, 1996: 14):

a) as UNCTAD is not a rule making body, the discussions and the seeking of consensus could be conducted in an atmosphere that does not carry the implication of rule making;
b) UNCTAD has a broader paradigm of trade and development. It also has expertise in dealing with international frameworks in other areas such as technology transfer, restrictive trade practices and competition, which are relevant to the investment issue;
c) UNCTAD's framework is less likely to place developing countries in a less disadvantageous position in the discussions on multilateral rules;
d) UNCTAD has a more diverse membership and is a more open forum (Interview with a Chinese diplomat); and
e) UNCTAD already has a mandate and work program for handling the issue of a multilateral investment framework and years of research experience on the subject. At its ninth conference in 1996 in Midrand, South Africa, UNCTAD has been given the mandate, among other things, to focus on:

> ...identifying and analysing implications for development of issues relevant to a possible multilateral framework on investment, beginning with an examination and review of existing agreements, taking into account the interests of developing countries and bearing in mind the work undertaken by other organisations. In this regard, the role of the OECD and the activities of its outreach program in explaining recent developments in that organisation should be noted (UNCTAD, 1996).

The Midrand resolution was supported by all member countries, both developed and developing. However, some countries are not keen to support the idea of upgrading the mandate given to UNCTAD in the Midrand conference to that of hosting negotiations. A Chilean diplomat told me:

> The WTO is the appropriate forum for negotiating investment rules. UNCTAD is not a rule-making body, and one cannot negotiate rules at UNCTAD. Although at the WTO trade is the main focus, this is basically done in the interest of development, not by ignoring it.

A somewhat similar opinion was echoed by an Argentine diplomat:

> UNCTAD has a format of an expert workshop. It helps the learning process, but there can't be negotiations there. I am very much sceptical about the UNCTAD process. On the other hand, though we are not opposed to it, the WTO process at the moment is similar to the UNCTAD process. Our view is that one should not waste time discussing issues that have already been dealt with by UNCTAD, but to go forward and discuss new issues.

Conclusion

Developing countries do not have a common strategy on how to tackle the issue of global investment rules. Their views are divided on:

- whether to have such a regime in the first place;
- where to negotiate and which institution to entrust with the implementation of it; and
- the nature and emphasis of the regime, if at the end of the day a regime is constructed.

While Latin American countries such as Argentina, Brazil and Chile support a global framework of investment rules, other countries such as Indonesia, India, China, Malaysia, Egypt do not see the need for such rules. They are also opposed to the extension of the MAI to non-OECD countries. Their main grounds of opposition for such a framework are twofold. The first is that such a framework could significantly erode the sovereignty of host countries by giving "excessive" powers to foreign investors and limiting the regulatory power of States. The second is that standardised investment rules would leave very little room for countries to manoeuvre their investment policies according to their development and social objectives and priorities, thereby interfering with their "right to development".

Most developing countries generally accept that FDI could make big contributions to their development efforts. There is however concern that, when the major interests of MNCs and host States are in conflict, MNCs may use their muscle as well as the influence of their home countries to interfere in the domestic affairs of weaker host countries. Moreover, a global framework that would allow foreign investors to take the host country to international tribunals without the latter's consent is seen as a measure that would severely erode the sovereignty of host nations. There is also a genuine fear that, given the enormous economic and political power of multinational corporations, many developing countries would not be in a position to defend their case in international adjudications successfully and pay the required legal and other bills.

The other main concern is that all types of FDI, flowing in all sectors of an economy, may not necessarily constitute a necessary condition for achieving rapid growth and sustainable development. FDI that replaces domestic capabilities, rather than complementing them, is not necessarily a good thing. It is therefore argued that FDI could only be beneficial to the host economies if host countries can regulate it according to their development objectives.

There is also concern that a rapid increase in FDI stock could exacerbate the balance-of-payments problems of the host country. FDI makes significant additions to the foreign exchange supply of the host country in the initial phase of its entry. What happens after that largely depends on the type of the investment. Moreover, the inability to regulate the entry of FDI in the host country would increase the foreign share of equity and profits in the economy. This could create a strain on the balance-of-payments of the country, particularly if repatriation of profits is too high. It is therefore argued that the pace and nature of investment liberalisation should be determined by considerations such as the capacity of the local sector to withstand greater competition from foreign firms producing locally, the effects such liberalisation would have on the trade balance and balance-of-payments, etc. All this can be done if the host country retains the power to regulate the entry and operation of FDI into its economy.

The model of agreement proposed by the proponents of the MAI was opposed by many developing countries partly because it required host countries to give up their right to adopt a selective approach to foreign investment to promote their chosen development strategy. This right is seen as very important by many of these countries. Moreover, any proposal that gives rights and protection to foreign investors, but not corresponding obligations is not acceptable to these countries. Hence, they argue that any future global agreement on investment needs to address the following issues:

- developing countries' right for development;
- the right to select development projects;
- discretion of host countries to temporarily stop the repatriation of funds in a crisis situation;
- protection of the rights of investors;
- obligations and duties of foreign investors;
- rules regarding business conduct and restrictive practices; and
- technology transfer.

The question of venue has been as controversial as the substantive content of the future agreement itself. While there are some developing countries that want to negotiate the global agreement within the framework of the WTO, others reject this and propose that UNCTAD would be the appropriate forum. At this stage, both UNCTAD and the WTO have been given the mandate to do exploratory works on FDI and its effects on Trade and Development.

Notes

1 For the trend in the flow of FDI to developing countries, see UNCTAD, World Investment Report, 1993, 1994, 1995, 1996, 1997, 1998, 1999.

2 Speech made by Mr. J. Riaboi, Minister at the Argentine Mission to the UN in Geneva, at the Seminar organised jointly by Consumer International (CI) and Consumer and Unity Trust Organisation (CUTS), in Geneva from 18-19 October 1996.

3 The South Centre is an organisation established and financed by developing countries to serve them as a think-tank. Its headquarters is in Geneva.

4 For discussions on capital control measures taken by Malaysia and Chile, see Buckley (2000); Edwards (1999).

5 See, for example, the comment by India's Commerce Secretary Tejendra Khanna at the World Trade Conference held in Singapore in April 1996, quoted on page 100 above.

6 We will see in Chapter Ten that this Chinese line of an imbalance that lacks "commitment by business" was even more fundamental to the NGO critique of the MAI.

7 See Chapter Eight for more discussion on the role played by the WTO in investment matters.

Chapter 7

Consumer, Labour, Environmental and Business Groups

International non-governmental organisations (NGOs) play key roles in shaping international rules and institutions (Braithwaite & Drahos, 2000). Although most of the prominent NGOs tend to be from Europe and the US (Braithwaite & Drahos, 2000: 36), some NGOs from the developing world, such us Third World Network, CUTS and the South Centre have been playing crucial roles during the GATT negotiations and the MAI debate. NGO growth has actually been more rapid in the South than in the North in the past decades (Braithwaite & Drahos, 2000).

If the strategies followed and positions taken during the MAI debate are of any indication, consumer advocates, environmentalists and labour unions have commonality on most of the issues regarding FDI regulation, while business representatives stand on the opposite side. The first three groups formed a broad coalition in their stand against the MAI and made a rigorous campaign to kill it, in which they finally succeeded[1] (Chapter Five). Business representatives, particularly the Business and Industry Advisory Council (BIAC) and the United States Council for International Business gave strong backing to the MAI, to the extent of being singled out as the initiator and driving force behind the negotiation process (Chapter Five).

The NGO alliance against the MAI was built and information shared primarily through the Internet. Without the Internet, the alliance could not have been created so spontaneously. The Internet enabled the campaigners to disseminate information to a global audience quickly and help NGOs with fewer resources, especially in developing countries, to engage in a highly technical international negotiation. The Internet was also very cost effective. In most instances, the campaigns were coordinated from either already existing NGO offices or home-based computers (Goodman, 1999).

The campaign against the MAI was very broad based, bringing together anyone that had something to oppose from the draft Agreement. The social movements organised and sought support from the centre-left and much of the centre. In Australia, for example, the Stop-MAI group actively sought support from the Democrats, Greens[2] and the Labour Party, but deliberately avoided association with One Nation Party (led by Pauline Hanson) and other right-wing organisations. However, the far right, such as One Nation Party, saw a populist opportunity and joined the campaign. As a result the OECD and some member Governments initially branded the NGO alliance as xenophobes or nationalists (Chosky, 1998; Goodman, 1999). Australia's Foreign Minister Alexander Downer said that "allegations made against the MAI are driven by closed-border nationalism which is afraid of globalisation and the opportunities which it offers for job creation, investment and a better standard of living for all Australians" (Downer, 1998a). He then attacked Labour, Democrat and Green critics of the MAI in parliament for befriending "... the League of Rights,[3] the Member for Oxley[4] and their kind – the kind of far left and far right [who] are running around saying that the MAI is some sort of deathly secret" (Downer, 1998b).

In the previous two Chapters of Part II, an attempt has been made to present the strategies and positions of developed countries and developing countries. This Chapter discusses the strategies and positions of social movements and key international business associations for global investment rules. The key international social movements that played significant roles in shaping global investment rules are the consumer, environmental and labour movements.

The Consumer Movement

Consumer movements around the world have been expressing their concerns on the regulation of FDI for some time. Consumers International (formerly IOCU), which is a global federation of over 210 consumer organisations in about 84 countries, has particularly been at the forefront of pursuing the matter. From a perspective of more uncompromising opposition of any global investment agreement, consumer groups loosely associated with Ralph Nader that are not members of Consumers International, often in coalition with Northern trade unions, have also been important players, particularly in North America.

Although consumer advocates generally recognise the benefits foreign investment brings to host economies, at the same time there is a fear that the great economic power wielded by MNCs could be open to abuse (Chapter Six). Through their sheer size and, in some instances lack of accountability to host countries, MNCs have the potential to limit competition. As MNCs dominate national economies, consumers could face less choice and higher prices (CI, 1996: 1). MNCs may damage local competitors and consumers by engaging in anti-competitive practices. They may trigger the lowering of environmental, labour and other standards as host countries compete to attract investors to their territory. They may also behave unethically by, for example, artificially avoiding taxes or using bribes. As investment becomes transnational, it would be practically impossible for individual national governments to regulate alone all the activities of foreign investors (CI, 1997: 3).

Therefore, consumer advocates believe that there is a need for an international agreement on FDI to ensure healthy competition between the many players and benefits for consumers and domestic economies (Interview with officials of ACCC[5] and ACA[6]). A submission made by Consumers International to the OECD with regard to the MAI states:

> ...foreign companies may damage local producers and consumers by engaging in anti-competitive practices; they may lower consumer, environmental, labour and other standards as countries compete to attract investors to their territory; or they may behave unethically by, for example, artificially avoiding taxes or using bribes. There is an urgent need to create balancing mechanisms for overseeing and regulating investment to ensure that the gains of liberalisation are dispersed to consumers and not monopolised by a few producers (CI, 1997: 3).

Consumer advocates have identified three broad issues any global agreement on FDI needs to address. These are the regulatory power of national authorities, competition policy and consumer protection (CI, 1997: 3)

The Regulatory Power of Governments

The position of consumer advocates on this issue has similarity with that of developing countries discussed in Chapter Six. In its submission to the Australian Treasury with regard to the MAI, the Australian Consumers Association (ACA), for example, stated that:

> The National Treatment clause [of the MAI] requires all member countries not to treat foreign investors less favourably than national investors... This provision greatly diminishes the Government's power to screen FDI applications, if not abolishing it altogether in practical terms. However, in order to protect the Australian economy, Australian culture, the environment or the safety of consumers, there may be a need on occasion to restrict FDI....ACA is of the view that the democratic process should dictate which policy measures to adopt under various circumstances and opposes restricting by international agreement the powers that sovereign governments have in this regard.

FDI can contribute to a cycle of investment, technological progress, innovation, human resource development and improved environmental standards by linking the various elements that determine growth. As a result consumers can benefit from a wider range of products, higher standard goods and competitively-priced services. However, Consumers International does not believe that just any FDI is necessarily good for the host country and its people:

> Any foreign direct investment, however generous, which has the effect of supplanting or undermining local capacity is in

> the end not positive for the development of a country and its people. Oxfam found that in countries such as Chile, Mexico, the Dominican Republic and Bangladesh unregulated foreign direct investment in the context of highly unequal national and international markets brought few benefits to local communities and, in some cases, did substantial harm. To avoid this, the host country government must retain the sovereign right and ability (even if they do not choose to exercise it) to select and direct such investment to priority areas (CI, 1997: 22).

Competition Policy

In markets where companies have to compete to persuade the consumer to buy their products, the consumer movement believes consumers benefit from a choice of products and lower prices. Competition encourages companies to innovate and be cost effective in order to keep ahead of their rivals. Competition also benefits the economy by encouraging the efficient allocation of resources, entrepreneurship and a more flexible economy able to adapt to changing circumstances This in turn could bolster productivity and nourish investment, allowing national income to grow and the country to retain its comparative and competitive advantage in the global economy. In its submission to the MAI negotiating group, Consumers International stated:

> In a competitive market, firms are obliged to perform the best they can to satisfy consumer needs and demands. They will try to satisfy future demands through R&D and innovation. However, the preferred situation for any supplier in any market is to achieve monopoly control. Unless competition laws are in place and properly implemented, firms may be tempted to indulge in their natural instinct to increase their market share and to influence prices from their dominant position (CI, 1997: 18).

In the absence of competition regulation, companies, particularly bigger multinational corporations, could exploit the situation to earn excess profits or to influence government behaviour by:

- using inflated internal transfer prices between parent companies and overseas subsidiaries;
- exploiting monopoly power to set higher prices than would exist in a competitive environment;
- manipulating the final prices for exported goods (especially if such goods compete with the output of a local subsidiary); or
- ignoring, subverting or challenging local regulations which smaller companies are forced to observe (CI, 1995).

In developing countries, foreign multinational companies could be tempted to indulge in restrictive business practices[7] more often than domestic companies because of their greater efficiency, possession of company-specific assets such as technology or brand names, financial strength, size, vertical integration or global orientation (CI, 1997: 18).

To counter the adverse effects of monopolistic business practices, Governments normally introduce rules and regulations to ensure that competition is maintained.[8] The coverage of competition policy includes limiting the market share of dominant firms by regulation, control of mergers and acquisitions, and control of anti-competitive practices such as tied selling and predatory pricing.

Although all of the major developed countries have policies and laws that ensure competition among companies, many developing countries and "transitional" economies do not have such policies and laws. Many of these countries lack the expertise even when they see the need to have such laws and policies. In 1995 alone, 35 developing countries approached UNCTAD for advice on competition issues as they introduced or upgraded their competition laws (CI, 1996: 2). Even in countries that have the expertise and infrastructure, national competition laws and policies may not be totally effective because of the increasing globalisation of trade and economic relations as well as the highly mobile nature of capital.

Consumer advocates believe a global investment agreement that addresses competition issues could help overcome these problems. Moreover, the establishment of international mechanisms to deal with anti-competitive business practices by foreign investors could persuade governments to reject control measures on FDI that pre-empt anti-competitive practices by foreign investors. This might encourage further liberalisation of foreign investment regimes (CI, 1997: 19).

Senior officials of ACA and ACCC told me that there are three major competition-related issues that an international regulatory regime needs to address. These are: cross-border mergers and acquisitions, international cartels, and strategic alliances.

Mergers and Acquisitions Cross-border mergers and acquisitions (M&A) could pose problems of regulation for national agencies as they involve firms operating in more than one country, having an effect on more than one country. The situation could also lead to different national regulatory agencies arriving at different conclusions in evaluating proposed mergers and acquisitions (CI, 1996: 3). The following are some examples of such instances:

a) The Canadian government supported a proposed merger between de Havilland (Canada) and a European firm, ATR, because de Havilland was likely to go out of business unless the merger went ahead, potentially causing loss of jobs and other benefits to the community and the State. Canada was willing to approve the merger because there was not a potential competition problem in Canada. The European Union, however, blocked the merger on the ground that the resulting company would have a dominant position (50%) in the world market for turbo-prop commuter aircraft (CI, 1996: 3).

b) The leading tea suppliers in Pakistan accounted for over half of the market. When the suppliers' parent companies merged, the price of tea rose. Under investigation, it was found that the average price of tea imported from sister companies in Kenya was higher than the prices paid by them to other sellers in the international markets (CI, 1996: 3).

Cooperation and networking between the authorities of the countries concerned may help solve the problem. However, if countries have different priorities or if the merger would have different effects in different markets, cooperation may be difficult to achieve.

International Cartels International cartels are joint actions by corporations from different countries under which they agree to divide markets, set prices or divide up bids for projects. As the agreement is an international one, and since there is no single agency at the moment capable of dealing with the agreement on an international level, it is up to national authorities to cooperate or tackle the cartel alone. The following two instances serve as illustration:

a) A Pakistani enterprise had invited quotations for the purchase of electronic tinplate. It received quotations from six foreign firms and found that the quality of the three lowest bids corresponded exactly to the total of the quality required. The Monopoly Control Authority of Pakistan found that this was unlikely to have occurred other than as a result of collusive tendering. In the end, no action was taken because there was not practical substantive law covering effects of anti-competitive arrangements agreed upon abroad and there was a lack of investigative powers to collect sufficient evidence (CI, 1996: 3).
b) The Organisation of Petroleum Exporting Countries (OPEC) decided in the 1970s to restrict supply and raise prices, triggering a global recession. More than 20 years later, the effect of the increased price of oil can still be felt in many countries around the world (CI, 1996: 3).

Powerful countries such as the US have mechanisms to act against firms outside their territories whose anti-competitive practices affect their economies. However, most countries are not in such position. The development of a global control mechanism could protect particularly those countries that are less powerful than the companies they deal with.

Strategic Business Alliances Another consumer movement concern strategic business alliances; a cooperative arrangement between two or more companies in which:

- a common strategy is developed in unison and a win-win attitude is adopted by all parties;

- the relationship is reciprocal with each partner prepared to share specific strengths with the other, thus lending power to the enterprise; and
- a pooling of resources, investment and risks occurs for mutual gain (Harbison, 1996: 2).

In the past few years, there has been a surge in strategic business alliances between companies. In 1994 and 1995 alone, more than 20,000 alliances have been formed worldwide, and approximately 75% of those have been cross-border (Harbison, 1996: 1). In many industries (including communications, electronics, health care, transportation, energy and services), the global demands on technology and financial resources are forcing companies to ally in order to compete, often at the same time that industry boundaries are blurring and new capabilities have become critical (Harbison, 1996: 2).

Strategic business alliances could pose a threat to domestic competition law because they are designed to foster cooperation between competing firms. Although they could offset costs and spread the costs for the companies involved, they also have the potential to step over the line between cooperation and cartelisation (CI, 1993: 3). Moreover, because they usually involve companies from different countries, they are often difficult to regulate by one particular national regulatory agency (Interviews with officials of ACA and ACCC).

Consumer Protection

The consumer movement has identified eight "consumer rights" that need to be protected through national regulation as well as international agreements. These are the right to basic needs, safety, information, choice, a fair hearing, redress, consumer education and healthy environment (CI, 1997a). The movement alleges that a large number of companies, including MNCs, violate one or more of these rights on a regular basis. Examples of such violations include the following (CI, 1995: 2-3):

- Pressure from oil companies against the introduction of unleaded petrol in Kenya;
- The production of pesticides, herbicides and fungicides by Shell in Nairobi, that are banned in other countries;
- The promotion of tobacco products in developing countries using advertising techniques disallowed in the multinational corporations' home countries;
- Dumping of hazardous waste by Asia Rare Earths – a subsidiary of Mitsubishi – in Malaysia; and
- Promoting powdered milk as a breast milk substitute by giving free samples to hospital maternity wards or gifts to staff and health officials and through other promotional techniques that do not correspond to agreed international guidelines.

Consumers International has adopted three major strategies for controlling the violation of these rights: a (now moribund) voluntary code of conduct for companies (Consumer Charter for Global Business), Model Law for national governments, and actively supporting the development of global competition and consumer protection laws.

There are many multinational companies that have developed their own code of practice or helped to develop codes of practice for their respective industry group. The Consumer Charter for Global Business developed by Consumers International sought to complement these codes by setting out best practice for business across all industries in areas such as ethical standards, competition, marketing practices, product standards, labelling of products, disclosure of information and consumer redress.

The aim of the Charter was to develop company practice in light of these consumer concerns and to be the basis for national regulation of business practices. The Charter also aimed to provide a focus for consumer education campaigns and highlights how different corporate activities can affect consumer rights (CI, 1997). Given the clutter of more specialised codes and the revival of debate on reinvigorating the OECD Guidelines for Multinational Enterprises after the collapse of the MAI, CI has put its Charter on the back burner.

First introduced in the 1980s by Consumers International's Regional Office for Latin America, the *Model Law* strategy aims to respond to particular regional realities in "ways that the broader set of universal guidelines cannot" (CI, 1999: 8). A *Model Law* is a series of legal principles that could serve as guides for national government legislation and consumer activists (CI, 1999: 10). In Europe, the existence of the European Union Single Market has led to the development of regional directives regulating standards and quality of products. Consumer rights are one of the "four freedoms" on which the Single Market is based.[9] These directives could also serve as the *Model Law* for Central and Eastern European countries (CI, 1999: 11).

To summarise, the international consumer movement does not support a liberalisation move that significantly reduces the regulatory power of national governments. It also identifies competition policy and consumer protection as issues of importance for global regulation. This summary is equally true of the Consumers International and Naderite coalitions in the consumer movement. The main difference in their positions is that while the Naderite groups would see any more negotiations toward a TRIMS agreement at the WTO as an unequivocally dangerous threat to national sovereignty, Consumers International is not opposed in principle to liberalising global agreements so long as rights to investment access are balanced by enforceable obligations of investors.

The Labour Movement

The labour movement has concern that globalisation of product and labour markets, coupled with the emphasis on open, deregulated markets could lead to a situation where basic labour standards are ignored, workers' rights to form or join trade unions are suppressed, trade union members are targeted with violent repression and trade union organising becomes a high-risk activity in many countries (ICFTU, 1996: 3).

The United Nations held the 1995 World Summit for Social Development in Copenhagen. This *Social Summit* reached a consensus that there was a clear link between respect for basic workers' rights and development (United Nations, 1995). Similarly, the 1995 World Development Report of the World Bank stated that efficient labour market outcomes depend upon sound industrial relations practices, in which employment conditions are determined through a negotiated labour contract guided by core labour standards (World Bank, 1995). A number of cooperation and trade arrangements such as the Social Charter of the European Union, the Generalised System of Preferences (GSP), trade arrangements between the United States and the European Union, and the NAFTA attempt to address in various degrees the issue of workers' rights (ICFTU, 1996: 3).

The labour movement accepts the fact that FDI could play a significant role in raising working people's economic and social welfare (Interview with an official of ICFTU). However, the pursuit of return on investment could also lead to violations of *core* labour standards. As a response to their inability to match the financial incentives offered to inward investors by richer countries, some poor countries suppress "core" labour standards in order to attract FDI (Interview with officials of TUAC[10] and ICFTU). Some activists call this "a race to the bottom" (ICFTU, 1996: 3).

Many developing and transition economies have promoted certain geographic areas as Export Processing Zones (also known as free zones, industrial free zones, special economic zones, etc.). Investors in such zones would usually be permitted to import machinery and equipment, raw material, and component parts free of duty and without customs control. However, according to the UN:

> It is primarily in the Export Processing Zones that workers' rights to join a national union for collective bargaining and/or to strike largely restricted by Governments, based on the belief that unions will discourage FDI in the country... In some instances these restrictions were introduced in response to conditions laid down by TNCs as a pre-requisite for investment.[11]

Core Labour Standards

The labour movement argues that the incorporation into all multilateral investment and trade agreements of *core* labour standards would prevent the most extreme forms of exploitation and guarantee the basic rights of workers (Interview with officials of TUAC and ICFTU). Following the adoption by the Copenhagen World Summit for Social Development, in 1995, of "basic worker's rights", the subsequent renewal of commitment by States to observe internationally recognised *core* labour standards during the Singapore WTO Ministerial Conference in 1996, the International Labour Organisation (ILO) adopted a Declaration on Fundamental Principles and Rights at Work.[12] The labour standards that have been identified as *core* by the ILO Declaration as well as by the ICFTU and TUAC are those rights covered by seven ILO Conventions, namely:

- ILO Convention 87 (the right to freedom of association);
- ILO Convention 98 (the right to collective bargaining);
- ILO Conventions 29 and 105 (the abolition of forced labour);
- ILO Conventions 100 and 111 (non-discrimination in employment and remuneration); and
- ILO Convention 138 (minimum age for employment – elimination of child labour).

The labour movement believed that the respect for these *core* standards would establish a social minimum at the global level to respond to the realities of globalisation. The ICFTU also argues that these *core* labour standards:

- provide a cornerstone of democratic rights;
- provide the basis for the sustainable operation of labour markets;
- enable labour markets to be organised in a way both efficient and democratic;
- are included in the commitment agreed at the United Nations Social Summit; and
- represent an almost universal consensus about what constitutes a minimum of decent treatment of workers everywhere, regardless of the stage of development of the country (ICFTU, 1996: 4).

The ICFTU states that these *core* labour standards are meant to be for all countries, irrespective of their level of economic development (Interview with an official of the ICFTU). The organisation also argues that:

> Adherence to [them] would prevent the most extreme forms of exploitation and cut-throat competition. It would not end developing countries' comparative advantage, but it would establish a process by which conditions of employment could gradually be improved as trade increases. This would encourage the growth of consumer markets, stimulating both domestic and foreign investment and, most importantly, jobs (ICFTU, 1996a: 3).

However, there are several countries and business representatives that oppose the inclusion of labour standards in a global investment agreement (Chapter Five). One of the grounds for the opposition is that given the cultural diversity of the world's nations, it is not possible to have universal labour standards. It is also said that setting universal labour standards is not a necessarily appropriate method of addressing labour related issues such as child labour (Chapters Five and Six). According to the officials of TUAC and the ICFTU I interviewed, however, the proposed *core* labour standards are principles whose precise translation into law and practice could vary according to the institutions and customs of the country concerned.

Regarding child labour, the labour movement's position is that a three-pronged approach should be taken to eliminate child labour altogether.

> The problem of family poverty which can drive parents to send or even sell their children for work needs to be addressed. The availability of school places needs to be increased. And labour laws need to be adopted and implemented to ensure that children who should in their own, their families' and nation's interest be at school, are not at work. The priority must be to get rid of the most blatant forms of commercial exploitation of children (ICFTU, 1997: 4).

Developing countries express concern that the incorporation of labour standards into an international investment agreement would diminish their comparative advantage in abundant supply of cheaper labour (Chapter Six). But an official of the ICFTU told me that the standards should ensure that competition focus on improving productivity rather than on forcing down wages and working conditions.

The OECD Guidelines for Multinational Enterprises

The OECD Guidelines are one part of the 1976 Declaration of the OECD on International Investment and Multinational Enterprises. They address a wide range of issues related to business activities, such as general policy, information disclosure, competition, taxation, employment and industrial relations, environment and science and technology. They are non-binding, but have considerable moral weight as they express OECD governments' collective expectations concerning the behaviour and activities of multinational companies.

During the MAI negotiations, the labour movement argued that the MAI needed to incorporate the OECD Guidelines in their current status, that is without giving them a binding nature. In its submission to the MAI negotiating group, TUAC stated that:

- there should be an extensive reference to the Guidelines in the preamble of the MAI;
- the full text of the Guidelines should be annexed to the Agreement;
- the text of the Agreement should include the OECD Decision in 1991 to establish National Contact Points in Member Countries to implement and promote the Guidelines (OECD, 1996: 2).

The position taken by the labour movement to demand the incorporation into the MAI of the Guidelines without making them binding stood, at the time, in stark contrast from the position taken by the consumer and environment movements. An official of TUAC told me that this was so because the labour movement believed that "in the current circumstances it would not be realistic to make the Guidelines a binding legal instrument. On the other hand, incorporating them into the MAI in a non-binding way would save them from being forgotten in the OECD machinery".

In the post-MAI environment today, however, there is more flux on this issue. The labour movement is at one with the other social movements in wanting the OECD Guidelines to become more enforceable.

Venue

The labour movement stood at odds with the other social movements (which in most respects were allies) on the question of the venue for a multilateral investment negotiation. While the consumer and environment movements preferred UNCTAD over the OECD or WTO as the venue for such negotiations, the labour movement preferred the OECD or WTO over UNCTAD. In a statement made at UNCTAD IX conference, the ICFTU stated:

> The ICFTU considers that a comprehensive and universal framework for foreign direct investment is needed to promote growth of international investment under the optimal condition for host country and TNC alike. This may well come about as a result of initiatives to negotiate a Multilateral Agreement on Investment through the OECD, which could be extended to the global investment environment through WTO... UNCTAD IX should give a clear mandate to the UNCTAD secretariat:
>
> - to continue to provide information on the extent and role of transnational companies (TNCs) in the world economy;
> - to provide analysis of the main emerging issues on the agenda of the WTO, including labour standards, investment and the environment (ICFTU, 1996: 5,7).

To summarise, the labour movement believes that there is a need for a global framework for foreign direct investment. It also believes that *core* labour standards (seven ILO Conventions) should be part of any international framework on investment, that in particular a "social clause" should be recognised through the WTO. It argues that adherence to these seven Conventions would prevent the most extreme forms of exploitation of workers around the world.

Environmental Groups

A large number of international and national environmental NGOs were at the forefront of the campaign against the MAI (Chapter Five). The most prominent of these were Friends of the Earth-International[13] and the World Wide Fund for Nature (WWF).[14] At the national level, groups such as Friends of the Earth Canada and the Australian Conservation Foundation were also involved. As revealed during the campaign against the MAI, the main concerns of environmentalists with regard to FDI are centred on issues of environmental protection, sustainable development, environmental standards, the regulatory power of national governments and corporate responsibility. The following section of the book discusses these issues separately.

Environmental Protection

Environmental factors are more and more influencing the locational decisions of foreign investors. In 1992, the World Bank and OECD sent questionnaires to the 1001 largest mining, construction and manufacturing companies in North America and Western Europe asking them to rank the importance of environmental issues in their investment decisions in Central and Eastern Europe. Approximately 38% of these companies rated environmental risks at least as important as any other risk, including economic and business risks (Klavens and Zamparutti, 1995: ix). Some companies reported that they had rejected investment opportunities because of environmental problems. Eighty-five per cent of the companies indicated that they conduct significant environmental assessment at potential investment sites. The issue of potential liability arising from past environmental practices was the most important environmental issue for the investors (Klavens and Zamparutti, 1995: ix). The ratings agencies – Standard and Poors and Moody's – and insurance companies also more critically assess investments in terms of environmental risk than used to be (Braithwaite and Drahos, 2000).

The environment movement, however, is concerned that not all investors and Governments give environmental issues serious consideration. The World Wide Fund for Nature (WWF) described the interrelationship between investment and the environment as follows:

> The potential ecological and social impacts of increased investment are profound. Increasing foreign direct investment could fund cleaner technologies and contribute to poverty alleviation or it could speed up short-sighted environmental destruction, over-exploitation of natural resources and further marginalisation of the world's poor. A comprehensive international legal framework is necessary to ensure that investment supports, rather than threatens, sustainable development. Whilst international investment is a necessary condition for sustainable development, it is certainly not a sufficient one. The positive impacts outlined above will only arise if the correct systems of regulatory and economic incentives are in place before markets are liberalised. Otherwise, increasing investment is more likely to exacerbate global income differentials and accelerate the current trend of unsustainable resource use and pollution (WWF, 1996: 3).

Environmentalists cite the serious incident in Bhopal that caused enormous human damage, the Ok Tedi river pollution that caused the displacement of thousands of people from their villages, and the "pollution havens" in some parts of the world as examples justifying their concern (Interview with an official of WWF).

The Bhopal Disaster In December 1984, methyl isocyanate (MIC), a poisonous substance had been accidentally released into the atmosphere from Union Carbide's plant in Bhopal (India). The result was immediate and devastating, killing thousands of people and injuring hundreds of thousands (Cohen, 1996; Kalelkar, 1998). More than ten years after the incident happened, the effects of the incident were still serious. In 1996, the International Medical Commission on Bhopal (IMCB) identified likely neuro-toxicological damage and evident post-traumatic stress syndrome among the inhabitants of Bhopal, in addition to the widely recognised damage the gases did to lungs and eyes. The IMCB also found that as many as 50,000 survivors may be still suffering from partial or total disability as a consequence of the Bhopal disaster (ICMB, 1996). The Commission further stated that:

> The Bhopal disaster resulted in severe social and economic disruption including grieving for deaths of family members and providers, loss of jobs or ability to work, social stigma, especially for girls of marriageable age, relocation to smaller overcrowded living quarters... Survivors have not received adequate compensation for their losses of loved ones, their property and their earning power. Furthermore, the termination of most sheltered work programs has led to additional disruption, inequities and severe hardships for survivors (IMCB, 1996: 2).

In the aftermath of the incident, two separate major technical investigations of the event were authorised. One investigation, sponsored by the Government of India, was conducted by a staff of scientists and engineers from the Indian Council of Scientific and Industrial Research (ICSIR) and other experts (ICSIR, 1985). A second investigation, sponsored by the Union Carbide Corporation (UCC), was conducted by scientists and engineers from UCC, Union Carbide India Ltd., outside experts and attorneys (UCC, 1985). The two separate investigations concluded that the incident was caused by the inadvertent entry of a large quantity of water into one of the MIC tanks. This large quantity of water reacted with the MIC in the tank, causing its temperature to rise rapidly, and ultimately causing the major release (ICSIR, 1985; UCC, 1985).

The Indian Government filed a civil suit against UCC in the United States, asserting that the Government was the sole representative of the Bhopal victims. Later, Union Carbide agreed to pay $470 million for more than 550,000 claimants, to be distributed through compensation courts set up by the Indian Government (Gary Cohen, 1996: 2). However, the International Medical Commission on Bhopal concluded that:

- The compensation courts had little understanding of health problems related to gas exposure. They did not recognise nor compensate the people suffering from any post traumatic stress disorders, any neurological diseases, any reproductive abnormalities, nor any children seeking health-related claims;

- Union Carbide India failed to acknowledge or respond to earlier accidents, warnings from their employees, or even censure from their own corporate headquarters in the USA. They contributed to the lack of a rational medical care strategy by failing to provide any information about the toxicology of the chemicals released and other hazardous products and by-products of their industrial activities to local officials and emergency workers.
- The Indian Government also contributed to the failure of both compensation and medical care by adopting a policy of complete secrecy regarding its own health studies conducted following the disaster. Additionally, the Government misdirected expenditures that were meant to support the victims of the incident (IMCB, 1985).

The Ok-Tedi Disaster The Ok Tedi copper mine, located in the Star Mountains of Western Papua New Guinea (PNG), was one of the largest copper mines in the world. BHP, an Australian multinational corporation, and the Government of PNG were the two major owners of the mine, operated as Ok Tedi Mining Limited (OTML).

When the OTMS started production in 1984, the Ok Tedi River became the outlet of the mine waste, affecting the entire Ok Tedi and Fly River systems. It was estimated that the OTML discharged a total of 66 million tonnes of waste material into the Ok Tedi/Fly River systems each year. Of this total, about 31 million tonnes was assumed to travel 200 kilometres down the length of the Ok Tedi River and enter the Fly River at D'Albertis Junction, while the other 35 million tonnes was stored in the valleys around the mine and the main channel of the Ok Tedi River itself (Eagle and Higgins, 1991: 50). The extent of the environmental damage caused on the ecosystem of the two river systems was expressed by one of the villagers as follows:

> Fish of all species that lived in the [Ok Tedi River] died and floated up to the surface... The river bed has filled up with sediment causing the river level to rise. Sediment has also been deposited along the river banks, leaving a mud effluent of one meter deep. The Ok Tedi River overflows its banks, depositing waste and sediment along what was the most fertile area for gardening... The sediment also contains copper particles, which are deposited on the banks and can cause a serious risk to our lives... Riverbanks and floodplains have disappeared during sudden flooding of the river and the trees are dying out completely. The forest is being inundated. This has forced animals to migrate to other areas. Mining is affecting over 100,000 hectares of fertile agricultural land and almost an equal area of natural forest (Maun, 1997:113-14).[15]

One of the most serious physical impacts of the discharge was the constant degradation of the Ok Tedi river bed and the periodic floods which then deposit waste materials along its banks. By 1995, some 30 square kilometres of land had already been directly affected by this overbank deposition of mine sediments (Post-Courier, 12 September 1995). According to a report prepared for the Australian Conservation Foundation, the sediment load plus a variety of toxic exposure related to the mine waste rendered the first 70 kilometres of the Ok Tedi River almost biologically dead (Rosenbaum and Krockenberger, 1993).

Stuart Kirsch, an American anthropologist, conducted ethnographic field work in the Yonggom-speaking village of Dome from August 1987 to May 1989. He explained that the resulting diminution in the availability of subsistence resources due to the environmental disaster was matched by a less tangible impact on the cosmology of the Yonggom people.

> The damage to their ecosystem ultimately weakens the intimate association between Yonggom myths, religious beliefs, and their environment. For example, an important male cult myth is told about certain fish that used to live in the Ok Tedi River. As the fish have not survived the impact of the mine and do not live in the smaller creeks, the myth no longer has the same significance. As events and actions are seen as mapped onto the physical world, environmental destruction also erases social histories and memories of the deceased (Kirsch, 1989: 57).

At independence, Papua New Guinea made a constitutional commitment to protect the environment through sustainable development. The country also enacted a series of environmental protection laws soon after independence and signed the South Pacific Convention on Environmental Protection (Taylor, 1997: 15, 22). However, the Government did very little to prevent the Ok Tedi environmental disaster.

As the pollution level increased, so did the concerns of environmental groups both within PNG and outside the country. Dissatisfaction with the pollution and opposition to the mine and OTML culminated in 1995 when a group representing villagers along the Ok Tedi and Fly Rivers began legal action in Melbourne (Australia) to sue BHP, as the largest shareholder and manager of the mine, for its negligence in allowing extensive pollution of the river system (King, 1997: 94).

The PNG Government responded by enacting legislation that would establish a national Compensation Tribunal with exclusive powers to deal with all compensation claims and retrospectively rule out both the validity of the lawsuit in Melbourne and the agreement made between the lawyers and the villagers (Compensation Act 1995 (PNG)). The leader of PNG's parliamentary opposition even described the lawsuit in Melbourne as the work of "foreign spivs, crooks and carpetbaggers" (Post-Courier, 5 May 1994). The PNG Government's actions were not surprising given the fact the Government was a joint-owner of OTML and that it had turned a blind eye to the environmental problems for quite a long time. This would make the Government partly responsible for the environmental damage caused in pursuit of profit.

Finally, in June 1996, BHP agreed to spend up to A$150 million to compensate the villagers for the environmental damage caused by the Ok Tedi mine. The company also agreed to build a full tailings retention system within two years and meet the legal costs of the villagers, which amounted to A$7.6 million. The agreement was reached in an out-of-court settlement (The Ok Tedi Settlement and Text of the Agreement).

"Pollution Havens" An official of the WWF in Geneva told me of the fear environmentalists have that the intense competition to attract FDI could force some countries to lower environmental standards. Pollution- and resource-intensive industries (such as chemicals, metals and natural resources) that are susceptible to environmental costs could show a locational preference for areas of low environmental standards (Braithwaite, 1980; Castleman, 1979). The most commonly cited examples of this phenomena include Export Processing Zones (EPZs) in countries such as Mexico, Brazil and India. In the case of Mexico, some argue that the NAFTA agreement has proved to be an incentive for US firms to move to Mexico in order to escape better-enforced US environmental standards.

Sustainable Development

Foreign investment is not incompatible with sustainable development. In fact, the transfer of technology and capital through foreign investment could enhance sustainable development. However, environmentalists argue that growth and sustainable development are not necessarily synonymous. They say that unless the actions of the market are regulated, the environment could become a victim of growth (Interview with an official of WWF).

In 1992, the United Nations Environment Programme (UNEP) took an initiative to form the UNEP Financial Services Initiative to engage a broad range of financial institutions – from banks to venture capitalists to the insurance industry – in a constructive dialogue between economic development, environmental protection, and sustainable development. The main objective of the Initiative was to promote the integration of environmental considerations in all aspects of the financial sector's operations and services. A second objective of the Initiative was to foster private environmental investment (UNEP, 1996: 1). Shortly after the formation of the Initiative, UNEP brokered a statement by the financial institutions on the environment and sustainable development. The statement included:

- A commitment to increase environmental management;
- The adoption of best industry practices in such core areas as credit risk management, energy efficiency, and environmental impact assessment; and
- The implementation of precautionary principles (UNEP, 1996: 1).

In October 1995, UNEP hosted a second round table meeting on banking and environment. The meeting agreed, among other things, to "move beyond liability management that is purely regulation-driven toward a commitment to environmental responsibility" (UNEP, 1996: 2). In May 1997, 350 leading bankers and financial experts from around the world met yet again in New York to consider and try to agree on new strategies for investments and loans for environment initiatives. Part of the statement issued after the meeting read:

> We members of the financial services industry recognise that sustainable development depends upon a positive interaction between economic and social development, and environmental protection, to balance the interests of this and future generations. We further recognise that sustainable development is the collective responsibility of government, business, and individuals. We are committed to working cooperatively with these sectors within the framework of market mechanisms toward common environmental goals (UNEP, 1997: 3).

By June 1997, the Statement on Environment and Sustainable Development was signed by 97 banks and 70 insurance companies from several countries (UNEP, 1997). These commitments were not however binding. They covered only parts of the banking and insurance industry. Environmental groups demand an agreement that commits all businesses to ensuring sustainable development. In its statement about the MAI, the WWF demanded:

> The MAI must signal that its ultimate aim is sustainable development, and not merely economic growth, by including an unambiguously worded preamble which will guide the remaining text. This preambular commitment must then be translated into action by legally binding provisions in the main text body of the MAI text (WWF, 1997: 3).

Environmental Standards

Environmental groups fear that, in their desire to attract FDI and under the pressure of competition, some countries might lower their environmental standards or refrain from enforcing them (Interview with an official of WWF). In Papua New Guinea, for example, several foreign-owned mining companies were exempted from the Contaminants Act and the Water Resources Act (MPI, 1995). Similar exemptions occur in the Export Processing Zones of many countries. Environmentalists argue that a minimum international environmental standard needs to be established to prevent a "race to the bottom".

The ties foreign investors have with the host country, especially in the natural resource sector in general and the mining sector in particular, often ceases as soon as the natural resource is exhausted. This would allow them to dissolve their operations without fulfilling their legal obligations to clean up pollution, restore damage, or compensate for unsustainable practices, even where such actions are required by laws of the host country. Therefore, environmental groups demanded the MAI negotiators to make deliberate lowering of environmental standards a breach of the MAI provisions which may be referred to the dispute settlement mechanism (WWF, 1997: 4). They also demanded that foreign investors comply with the highest standard prevailing in either the investor's home country or the host country (WWF, 1996: 5).

Regulatory Power of Host Countries

Environmentalists argue that the positive impacts of foreign investment "will only arise if the correct systems of regulatory and economic incentives are in place before markets are liberalised. If this is not done, increasing investment is more likely to exacerbate global income differentials, and accelerate the current trend of unsustainable resource use and pollution" (WWF, 1996: 3).

Foreign investment sometimes involves the transfer of sub-standard or dangerous technology, particularly to developing countries (Bruno, 1994). In the absence of a general international agreement on what is an "environmentally sound" technology, each country will have to put in place its national regulatory framework to control the transfer of dangerous or harmful technology. The absence of international measures which systematically identify "dirty" technologies and prevent their transfer makes the regulatory power of national governments even more important (Bruno, 1994). Hence, like consumer rights advocates, environmental NGOs do not want a global investment agreement to deny national governments such regulatory power.

Corporate Responsibility

Multinational corporations sometimes practice irresponsible behaviour in the hope of maximising their profit. BHP acted irresponsibly in its mining activity in Ok Tedi (see discussion above). Similarly, foreign-owned nickel mining and smelting operations in Kanany (New Caledonia) resulted in extensive marine damage and air pollution. Although there were environmental laws in place in both countries, the breaches of these laws did not result in government action (WWF, 1997). Therefore, a global investment agreement could address such problems by placing binding obligations on investors to apply the best of home or host country environmental standards to their operations. Moreover, by virtue of their size and the relative advantage they have in terms of access to finance, expertise and technology, multinational corporations need to take the lead in applying responsible business practices (Interview with an official of WWF).

The MAI and the Environment Debate

Environmental NGOs such as the World Wide Fund for Nature (WWF) and Friends of Earth were among the forefront of the groups opposing the MAI (Chapter Five). They were critical of both the negotiation process as well as the contents of the Agreement. In one of its statements on the MAI, the WWF stated that the MAI ignored the commitments codified in the Rio Declaration and Agenda 21 (WWF, 1996: 1). It also stated that "any global agreement must be negotiated with the full participation of non-OECD countries inside a consultative and transparent UN-Organization" (WWF, 1996:1).

According to my informants in the environment movement, the most important issues a global investment agreement should address are sustainable development, environmental standards, power of national governments and corporate responsibility.

To summarise, environmental factors are increasingly influencing the locational decisions of foreign investors. Environmental groups, however, are concerned that not all investors and Governments give environmental issues serious consideration. While foreign direct investment could fund cleaner technologies and contribute to poverty alleviation, it could also speed up environmental destruction, over-exploitation of natural resources and further marginalisation of the world's poor.

Environmental groups believe that a comprehensive international legal framework is necessary to ensure that investment supports, rather than threatens, sustainable development. They have identified certain principles that a global investment agreement should address. They refer to sustainable development, environmental standards, power of national governments and corporate responsibility.

The Business Community

Key international business representatives such as the International Chamber of Commerce (ICC) and the OECD Business and Industry Advisory Council (BIAC)[16] have made their positions clear in a number of occasions that they support an international investment regime. In its submission to the MAI negotiating group, the ICC, for example, stated:

> Currently, a patchwork of rules governing investment exists in many hundreds of bilateral investment treaties (BITs), freedom of commerce and navigation agreements (FCNs), regional or plurilateral agreements...and in the Uruguay Round agreements on Trade-Related Investment Measures (TRIMS), Trade-Related Aspects of Intellectual Property Rights (TRIPS), and the General Agreement on Trade in Services (GATS). Given the increased volume and growing importance of international investment...the time is ripe for establishing a multilateral set of investment rules which removes current investment impediments and enshrines the principle of national treatment, provides protection for investment, and establishes a mechanism for resolving disputes (ICC, 1996: 14).

Similarly, BIAC stated in its submission to the MAI:

> BIAC's position continues to be that the development of a multilateral framework for rules affecting foreign direct investment, resulting in the removal of direct or indirect obstacles to FDI in national legislation, practices and other

> government measures, will be the OECD's single effective contribution to promoting business confidence and improving global economic performance (BIAC, 1995: 1).

Many outside of the business community in fact believe that the MAI was the creation of "big business", particularly the powerful United States Council for International Business. An official of the European Commission, who was also a member of the MAI negotiating team told me:

> The MAI is a brain-child of American business. Which corporations in the US are pushing hard for it? I am not sure.

A similar view was expressed to me by an official of the Union of Industrial and Employers' Confederation of Europe (UNICE):

> I do not know exactly which US companies are behind the MAI. I am however sure that US business and the US Administration are behind it.

There are groups within the business community that do not support a global investment regime. For example, an official of UNICE told me "right now [1997] there is no need for a multilateral investment regime. The situation is not clear enough as to what business wants". More importantly, UNICE did not support the WTO as the forum for any possible negotiations on FDI.

> One thing worries us most. We are not happy at all with the WTO process. We are afraid of seeing too much being done at the WTO. WTO is a trade Organisation, and it would not have the neutrality of a law-making body. A legislator has to take into account the interests of all its subjects. At the WTO, this does not happen. There is a lot of horse-trading there, and most of the horse-trading is done behind closed doors. The OECD is relatively open in this regard. To us, the OECD is a hopeful avenue (Interview with an official of UNICE).[17]

Greater market access and better predictability of rules are the main reasons behind the business community's support for an international investment regime. Although many countries have already liberalised their investment regimes to a large degree, there are still others that have various types of restrictions against FDI, both at the entry and/or operation phases of the business enterprise (Chapter Three). As a consequence, foreign investors are often forced by circumstances into a decision on an investment location that is less than optimal from an economic point of view. The presence of liberal multilateral rules on investment would mean that investors will have a relatively free choice of locations for their investments. An official of BIAC told me that a global investment regime could help accelerate the trend towards liberalisation of investment policies. According to this official, the presence of different, inconsistent and unpredictable rules and requirements in each country makes it difficult for companies to assess the return on their investment over the long term.

The ICC and BIAC supported the MAI process strongly. It was also BIAC's view that the MAI should finally end up in the WTO (Interview with an official of BIAC). The BIAC official I interviewed also told me that they did not want UNCTAD to host investment negotiations because UNCTAD was "inefficient and hostile to foreign investors".

BIAC and the ICC were the only non-governmental agencies to make submissions to the MAI negotiating group in the beginning, although other NGOs too have made submissions towards the end (collapse) of the negotiations. These two prominent business associations made their submissions at a time when the MAI negotiating group did not even have a preliminary draft agreement on the table. It was interesting to note later that the draft agreement developed by the negotiators was more or less in line with the submissions made by BIAC and the ICC.

In their submissions to the MAI negotiating group, BIAC and the ICC demanded that the MAI address the following issues in the manner proposed by them:

- the definition of investment or investor should be as broad as possible to encompass potential new developments in cross-border investment relations;
- unrestricted right of entry and establishment for foreign investors, except in very few areas reserved for national security reasons;
- national treatment and most-favoured-nation treatment;
- unrestricted right to transfer abroad income from the operation or liquidation of investment. Temporary restrictions of such transfer should be limited to only the most serious balance-of-payments problems;
- no operational requirements such as performance requirements, export requirements, etc;
- unrestricted appointment and movement of key foreign personnel;
- no expropriation except for a public purpose, in a non-discriminatory fashion, and against the payment of "prompt, adequate and effective" compensation;
- investor-to-state and state-to-state dispute resolution. Foreign investors should have the choice between arbitration and litigation. In the case of arbitration, foreign investors should be free to select the arbitration rules or arbitral institution. The scope of investment disputes should also include disputes arising from alleged violation of the MAI as well as disputes arising out of other agreements and treaties. With regard to local courts, the foreign investor should have the option, without forfeiting the option to go to arbitration, to resort to local courts prior to initiation or arbitration and use of local courts for injunctive and declaratory relief even after arbitration has been commenced.
- restrict freedom of host countries to provide incentives.

BIAC and the ICC opposed the introduction into a multilateral framework on investment of international environmental, labour or consumer standards, arguing that these are matters that should be dealt with by domestic laws.

> ...the MAI could include language addressed to governments allowing the adoption of domestic measures, consistent with national treatment obligations, which are deemed necessary by signatories to promote national objectives concerning, for example, environmental protection...This approach...would be acceptable to BIAC. However, any change in that language would not be acceptable (BIAC, 1996b: 2).

BIAC also opposed the reference into the MAI of the OECD Guidelines for Multinational Enterprises in a manner that would change the Guidelines' voluntary nature (Interview with an official of BIAC). It did not, however, oppose a specific mention of the Guidelines provided that it was made explicit that there would not be any formal operating linkage between the Guidelines and the MAI. When a text of the draft MAI was produced later, BIAC expressed its satisfaction in the following words:

> [The submission] was furnished to the OECD at a time when neither the OECD Secretariat nor the committees involved had produced any written text of their own on the structure and content of the potential agreement....Subsequently, when the OECD had released the first of its papers, we were gratified to see the government representatives on the committees were much in line with our BIAC thinking and had indeed taken up most of our suggestions.[18]

To summarise, business representatives think that the time is ripe for establishing a multilateral set of investment rules. Greater market access and achieving the predictability of rules are the main reasons behind their support for an international investment regime. They argue that a global investment regime could help accelerate the trend towards liberalisation of investment policies. Basically, the ICC and BIAC got what they wanted in the first draft of the MAI. This was a pyrrhic victory, however, reflecting the fact that to that point they were the only interest groups shaping the text. In the end, the business groups got worse than nothing as a result of dominating a secret process. It was this very business domination that caused the MAI to collapse as politically unsustainable and that contributed so much to the climate of distrust in Seattle that derailed the launch of a WTO Millennium Round.

Conclusion

Consumer advocates, environmentalists and labour unions have commonality on most of the issues related to FDI regulation, while business representatives stand on the opposite side. The first three groups formed a broad coalition in their stand against the MAI and launched a relentless campaign to kill it. Business representatives largely gave strong backing to the MAI, to the extent of being seen with some truth as initiating and driving the negotiation process. There are two points where the majority coalitions of all four groups agree though: the benefits of FDI for the host country and the need for a global investment regime. There are minority fractions, especially of the social movements, opposed to any kind of investment regime and deeply suspicious of FDI. But for the majority coalitions of all the key players, dependency theory has no contemporary resonance for them.

They agree that FDI can contribute to technological progress, innovation and human resource development by linking the various elements that determine growth. As a result, consumers can benefit from a wider range of products, higher standard goods and competitively priced goods and services. FDI can also raise working people's economic and social welfare, fund cleaner technologies and contribute to poverty alleviation.

Despite the potentially positive contributions of FDI, consumer advocates, environmentalists and labour unions fear that the great economic power wielded by multinational corporations (MNCs) could be open for abuse. Through their sheer size and, in some instances, lack of accountability to host countries, MNCs have the potential to limit competition, forcing consumers to face less choice and higher prices. They can also trigger the lowering of environmental, labour and other standards as host countries compete to attract investors to their territory; or they may behave unethically by, for example, artificially avoiding taxes or indulging in corrupt practices. Hence, these three groups demand an international regime that places greater control on the activities of foreign investors.

Consumer groups have identified three broad issues any global agreement on FDI needs to address. These are the regulatory power of governments, competition policy and consumer protection. They believe that any foreign direct investment that has the effect of supplanting or undermining local capacity is in the end not positive for the development of a country and its people. They therefore demand that the national democratic process should dictate which policy measures to adopt under various circumstances, and oppose restricting by international agreement the powers sovereign governments have in this regard.

There are a number of competition policy related activities, including cross-border restrictive agreements, mergers and strategic alliances, which may be beyond the control of national competition authorities and can lead to procedural problems and possible conflicts between authorities. An international regulatory regime is needed to address such problems. Moreover, consumer groups have identified eight "consumer rights" that need to be protected through national regulation as well as international agreements. These are the right to basic needs, safety, information, choice, a fair hearing, redress, consumer education and healthy environment.

The labour movement has its own list of basic rights, which it calls *core* labour standards. It supports an international investment regime because it is concerned that the globalisation of product and labour markets, coupled with the emphasis on open, deregulated markets could lead to a situation where basic labour standards are ignored, workers' rights to form or join trade unions are suppressed, trade union members are targets of violent repression and trade union organising becomes a high-risk activity. It is also concerned that, as a result of the growing policy competition between governments to attract FDI, *core* labour standards could be suppressed. This is especially so in Export Processing Zones where workers' rights to join a national union for collective bargaining and/or to strike is largely restricted by Governments.

The labour movement wants to avoid this by incorporating into all multilateral investment and trade agreements *core* labour standards. The movement has identified seven ILO Conventions, that is 87, 89, 29, 105, 100, 111 and 138 as constituting *core* labour standards. It also argues that these *core* labour standards:

- provide a cornerstone of democratic rights;
- provide the basis for the sustainable operation of labour markets;
- enable labour markets to be organised in a way that is both efficient and democratic;
- are included in the commitment agreed at the United Nations Social Development Summit; and
- represent an almost universal consensus about what constitutes a minimum of decent treatment of workers everywhere, regardless of the stage of development of the country.

During the MAI negotiations, the labour movement argued that the MAI needed to incorporate the OECD Guidelines in their current status, that is, without giving them a binding nature. This position stood, at the time, in stark contrast with the position taken by the consumer and environment movements, which demanded a binding commitment to regulate corporate behaviour. The movement also differed from its allies on the question of venue. While the consumer and environment movements preferred UNCTAD over the OECD or WTO as the negotiating venue for investment rules, the labour movement preferred the OECD or WTO over UNCTAD.

Environmentalists believe that a comprehensive international investment framework is necessary to ensure that investment supports, rather than threatens, sustainable development. In the absence of such rules, the intense competition to attract FDI could force some countries to lower environmental standards. An international agreement is, therefore, needed to address issues of sustainable development, environmental standards, powers of national governments and corporate responsibility.

Key business representatives support an international investment regime, but for a different reason from that of consumer, labour and environmental groups. Greater market access and better predictability of rules are the main reasons behind their support for an international investment regime. Although many countries have already liberalised their investment regimes to a large degree, there are still others with various types of restrictions. The presence of liberal and predictable global rules on investment would mean that the investors would have a relatively free choice of locations for their investments and greater operational autonomy.

Notes

1 The international labour movement was not totally against the MAI but opposed some aspects of the MAI. Some national labour organisations, such as the ACTU of Australia, totally opposed the draft Agreement.

2 It was Senator Brown (Australian Greens) who first raised the issue of the MAI in the Australian Federal Senate in March 1997 (Kemp, 1997).

3 This is a right-wing organisation in Australia.

4 Pauline Hanson (One Nation Party) represented Oxley in the House of Representatives at the time.

5 The Australian Competition and Consumers Commission (ACCC) is an independent statutory body formed by the Australian Government to deal with competition and consumer protection matters.

6 The Australian Consumers Association (ACA) is a non-profit NGO established to lobby and campaign on behalf of consumers to promote their rights, to influence government policy, and to ensure consumer issues have a high profile in the public arena.

7 Restrictive business practices (RBPs) could be horizontal or vertical. Horizontal RBPs or cartel agreements can result in price fixing through collusive tendering or uniform sales conditions, market allocation – geographical or customer, or elimination of outsiders through predatory pricing. Vertical RBPs arise where a dominant firm uses RBPs to take advantage of its strong market power over its suppliers or distributors. They include retail price maintenance, refusal to deal, exclusive dealing, reciprocal exclusivity, differential pricing, predatory pricing, and transfer pricing.

8 For a wider discussion on competition policy, see Consumers International web page at *http://193.128.6.150/consumers/campaigns/competition/competition2.html*, accessed on January 25, 2000.

9 The others are freedoms of movement for people, merchandise and capital and services.

10 TUAC is a Trade Union Advisory Council of the OECD, composed of trade union representatives from OECD countries.

11 Document prepared by the Secretary General of the UN Sub-Commission on Human Rights in July 1995, cited in TUAC, FDI and Labour Standards, Discussion Paper, p.5.

12 For more discussion on the ILO Declaration, see the ILO Internet site at: *www.ilo.org*, accessed on 11 November 2000.

13 Friend of the Earth-International a federation of 61 national Friends of the Earth organisations. Although each national organisation is unique to its own country and culture, defining its priorities and operating methods, they are deeply involved in the debate for sustainable development. For more information, see *www.foe.org*.

14 WWF is an international conservation NGO, claiming to have 5 million supporters and a global network of 27 national organisations, 5 associates and 21 program offices. For more information, see *www.panda.org*.

15 For detailed account of the Ok Tedi environmental disaster, see also Banks & Ballard (1997).

16 BIAC is an advisory committee of the OECD representing business and industry associations in all OECD countries.

17 It is interesting to note that UNICE later changed its position and expressed its support for WTO investment agenda during the Seattle Ministerial Conference in November 1999 (Chapter Ten).

18 Speech made by Dr. R.D. Rauschenbah, member of BIAC's Committee on International Investment and Multinational Enterprises, at OECD/DNME/ Workshop on FDI held in Hong Kong on 26-27 March, 1996.

Chapter 8

International Organisations

The preceding three Chapters discussed the perspective and strategies of developed and developing countries, as well as key international NGOs for global investment rules. The discussion revealed the similarities in some respects and divergences in others of these international players in their perspective and strategies. This Chapter discusses the roles of the major inter-governmental organisations in the rule making process. The organisations covered are the United Nations, the World Trade Organisation, the World Bank and regional economic groupings such as APEC.

The United Nations

The United Nations has played significant role in the debate about global investment rules. The UN was involved in facilitating the drafting of such rules until the early 1990s. Since then, it has also been active in the debate through UNCTAD. The next part of the Chapter discusses the role played by the UN in this process. In the first section, we will discuss the draft UN Code of Conduct for Transnational Corporation. We will examine briefly its historical background, its contents and the reasons that led to its collapse. Then, we will discuss UN's activities after the collapse of the Code.

The UN Code of Conduct for Transnational Corporations

Background In July 1972, at the meeting of the UN Economic and Social Council (ECOSOC), a Chilean diplomat charged the International Telephone and Telegraph Company (ITT) with interference in the domestic political affairs of his country (Crough and Wheelwright, 1982: 72-73). This incident prompted ECOSOC to request the UN Secretary-General to establish a Group of Eminent Persons to study the effects of multinational corporations (MNCs) on world development and international relations (ECOSOC Res. 1721). The Group recommended the creation of a commission attached to ECOSOC that would work, *inter alia,* to develop both specific and more general arrangements dealing with MNCs, including formulating a code of conduct for MNCs (Report of the Group of Eminent Persons, 1974). The UN Commission on Transnational Corporations (CTC) was then formed in 1975 consisting of 48 members[1] (ECOSOC Res. 1913). This incident formally marked the beginning of the effort by the UN to develop rules on the conduct of MNCs.

At its second session in 1976, the Commission solicited lists of areas of concern and issues to be considered in Code negotiations (CTC, 1976). A year later the Inter-governmental Working Group on a Code of Conduct was established by the Commission. The Working Group submitted its report to the Commission in 1982, containing negotiated texts of all substantive parts of the Code. Although the Working Group had reached tentative agreements on most of the provisions of the Code, it was unable to resolve a number of key outstanding issues (Draft UN Code of Conduct, 1982).

Member countries were basically divided in two main opposing groups. The main objective for developing and socialist countries in the negotiation of the Code was the establishment of international standards for the conduct of MNCs, particularly in areas of corporate conduct, adequate disclosure of information, and environmental and consumer protection. For Western countries, who were never enthusiastic about the whole initiative, the main objective was the establishment of a regime of minimum standards for the security of investment and the treatment of MNCs. In light of these objectives, the Code was meant to minimise any negative effects associated with the activities of MNCs and provide a stable, predictable and transparent framework that would facilitate the flow of foreign investment across boundaries. Its dual focus on the conduct of MNCs and their treatment by Governments was intended to meet the concerns of host and home countries, as well as MNCs.

Structure and Content of the Draft Code The provisions of the draft Code were structured around six main Chapters.[2] The first Chapter dealt with issues related to the activities of MNCs. The provisions set out basic ground rules relating to the exercise of sovereignty and the rights of states to regulate economic activity within their territories in accordance with their national objectives and priorities. The specific issues dealt with included national sovereignty, economic goals and development objectives, renegotiation of contracts, socio-cultural objectives and values, human rights and fundamental freedoms, non-collaboration with the apartheid regime of South Africa, non-interference in internal political affairs, non-interference in inter-governmental relations, and abstention from corrupt practices. The basic principle underlying this Chapter, national sovereignty, which was generally agreed upon by all parties, urged MNCs to respect the national sovereignty of host countries, including the right of each State to regulate and monitor the activities of MNCs within its territories (paragraphs 6-8 and 47).

The draft Code had a provision on transfer pricing calling for the avoidance of pricing policies that are not based on market prices or on the arm's length principle, in transactions between MNCs or their subsidiaries (Paragraph 34). It also made a cross-reference to the Multilaterally Agreed Equitable

Principles and Rules for the Control of Restrictive Business Practices (Paragraph 35) and to the UNCTAD draft International Code of Conduct on the Transfer of Technology (Paragraph 36).

Provisions on consumer and environmental protection were included in the draft code requiring MNCs to observe national laws and policies, as well as international standards on consumer protection (Paragraph 37) and to disclose information on the hazardous effects of products, processes and services (Paragraphs 41-43).

The draft Code also required MNCs to disclose to host countries information on their structure, policies and activities as a whole, as well as financial and non-financial information (Paragraph 44). In return, host countries were required to protect the confidentiality of business secrets (Paragraph 51).

The clauses on the treatment of MNCs were probably among the most important as well as most contentious in the draft Code. They covered fair and equitable treatment of MNCs, respect by governments for international obligations, non-discrimination between foreign and domestic investors and transparency and predictability of national laws (Paragraphs 47-51). The standard of "fair and equitable treatment" for MNCs was agreed upon by almost all parties (UNCTC, 1988: 18). National treatment post-establishment was agreed upon in principle, but with qualifications: it would be subject to national requirements to maintain public order and protecting national security, should be in conformity with national constitutions, and should be without prejudice to measures specified in legislation relating to declared development objectives of the developing countries. Developed countries argued that the provision should be flexible enough to allow preferential treatment for MNCs if the host country deemed it appropriate. Developing countries argued that, while the question of preferential treatment for MNCs was within the sovereign discretion of host countries, it should not be made a general international standard (UNCTC, 1988: 18).

Another contentious issue during the negotiations referred to the transfer of funds by foreign investors from the host country (Paragraph 53). Developing countries opposed the inclusion in the draft Code of a clause on the free transfer of funds arguing that such transfers should be subject to domestic laws and regulations. Developed countries, on the other hand, wanted the inclusion in the Code of a provision on the transfer of funds, but were willing to accept a general qualification that such transfers should be subject to the right of host countries to apply restrictions for a limited period in times of exceptional balance-of-payments difficulties (UNCTC, 1988: 19).

The draft Code attempted to address the issue of expropriation and compensation (Paragraph 54). There was agreement among all parties that States had a right to expropriate properties of foreign investors with the payment of compensation. There was disagreement on whether the standard of compensation should be specified in the Code and whether international law governs the payment of compensation for expropriated property. Developed countries maintained that the right to expropriate and the duty to pay compensation should be specified in the Code as being subject to the requirements of international law. Developing countries and socialist countries, on the other hand, disputed the existence of generally accepted principles of international law in this area. In particular, they rejected the contention that international law required "prompt, adequate and effective" compensation (UNCTC, 1988: 20).

The Final Fate of the Code The debate on whether to have a Code of Conduct for MNCs was born in fiery oratory in the early 1970s. By the early 1990s, a draft text was nearly complete, waiting for agreement on only a few remaining issues. On the one hand, developed Western countries felt that insufficient protection was given to MNCs and to their investments, and too little understanding was shown of the necessities of conducting efficient worldwide business enterprises. On the other, developing and socialist countries felt that too little recognition was given to the host countries' right to make MNCs accountable to domestic laws (Rubin, 1990: 16).

By the early 1990s, the US Government started to question whether much of the sections of the Code on the activities of MNCs were consistent with the trend towards liberalisation after all. Most of these provisions were agreed *ad referendum* in the late 1970s. In her testimony to a Congressional Hearing on the Code, Ms Jane Becker, then Deputy Assistant Secretary of the US Department of State, stated:

> ...In our view, the draft Code has fallen behind the times. The draft's section on the activities of corporations is... somewhat at variance with positions of the United States in the Uruguay Round of Negotiations on Trade-Related Investment Measures (TRIMS), which distort trade and investment flows to the detriment of United States business.... Traditional United States investment policy is that ... foreign investors are entitled to:
>
> - fair, equitable and...non-discriminatory treatment;
> - ...prompt, adequate and effective compensation, in the event of expropriation;
> - the right to transfer profits and capital freely;
> - ...third-party settlement of disputes with Governments of host countries.
>
> The United States Government and the Governments of other developed countries believe that the UN Code of Conduct for Transnational Corporations must include these points... (Quoted in Kline, 1990: 4).

Those points of view, held by each negotiating side with the fervour of religious tenets, negated some of the optimism on the conclusion of a broadly acceptable and general Code (Rubin, 1990: 16). One may say that the excruciatingly slow and inept development of the Code was probably another victim of the Cold War; the final killing off of the Code was perhaps another victim of the ending of the Cold War.

At the 19th Commission Meeting in April 1993, Australia proposed a "fresh approach" for an "internationally agreed set of principles" or guidelines, as opposed to a Code of Conduct.[3] It proposed the following goals for the Guidelines (Asher and Hayes, 1993):

- to confirm a set of ethical principles for the conduct of global business activities;
- to express these principles as universal guidelines for good business behaviour;
- to recognise the need for fair a and equitable treatment of global business; and
- to foster cooperation between foreign investors and host countries.

The Australian proposal also suggested that materials forming part of the guidelines should, where possible, be drawn from existing multilaterally agreed instruments. Australia hoped for an informal drafting committee to be established prior to the convening of the 19th session. However, the proposal did not get off the ground because the US and a few other countries were strongly opposed to it (Asher and Hayes, 1993). This marked the end to the life of the draft Code.

United Nations Conference on Trade and Development (UNCTAD)

In 1996, UNCTAD held its ninth conference in Midrand, South Africa. At stake was the future direction of the Organisation. The US called for the reform and restructuring of UNCTAD without duplicating the work of the WTO and the Bretton Woods institutions, and focusing more on technical assistance on policies decided elsewhere (Raghavan, 1996: 2). The EU demanded that UNCTAD should focus on trade and development issues, supplementing but remaining distinct from the WTO and UN bodies such as regional economic commissions (Raghavan, 1996: 2). The EC Commissioner Joa de Deus Pinheiro further said that UNCTAD's main role should be to facilitate sustainable development through trade and investment and participation of developing countries in the international trading system, and pursue work in the more traditional areas (Raghavan, 1996: 2-3).

Most developing countries expressed views in support of expanding UNCTAD's role. For example, Amnuay Viravan, then Thailand's Deputy Prime Minister, said that the role and contribution of UNCTAD to economic development offered hope to billions of people. In a similar tone, the Argentine delegate stated that UNCTAD was the only instrument available for an integrated approach to development and it should focus on analysing policies, particularly those not covered by multilateral rules and disciplines, and concentrate on technical cooperation with developing countries (Raghavan, 1996: 3).

At its conclusion, the Conference mandated UNCTAD, among other things, to focus on:

> Identifying and analysing implications for development of issues relevant to a possible multilateral framework on investment, beginning with an examination and review of

> existing agreements, taking into account the interests of developing countries and bearing in mind the work undertaken by other organisations...(UN, TD/377, 24 May 1996).

UNCTAD has so far been given widespread recognition for its expertise in issues such as investment policy, technology transfer, restrictive business practices and competition policy. Its annual publications such as World Investment Report and Trade and Development Report are seen by many as top class publications. Moreover, many developing countries have faith in the workings of UNCTAD and see the organisation's views on many contentious issues as balanced. They would therefore like UNCTAD to host negotiations for global investment rules, should that happen at a future time (Chapter Six).

While emphasising the benefits of FDI, UNCTAD consistently argued in its publications that a complete liberalisation of investment rules may not necessarily be beneficial for host countries. The following arguments taken from World Investment Report (WIR) 1999 highlight the organisations position on FDI and FDI regulation:

- Market failures characterise the MNC investment process in its relationship to developing countries. The first arises from information or coordination failures in the investment process, which can lead a country to attract insufficient FDI, or the wrong quality of FDI. The second arises when private interests of investors diverge from the economic interests of host countries (UNCTAD, 1999: xxv).
- The key benefits which developing countries are likely to get from FDI and MNCs involve dynamic effects of upgrading which occur over time and which might not happen automatically without significant government intervention (UNCTAD, 1999: 313-26).
- In the short term, MNCs might crowd out more dynamically productive local businesses that cannot compete with MNCs for labour, finance and/or markets. Therefore, opening up to MNCs without some support or protection for domestic firms may be unwarranted (UNCTAD, 1999: 171-195).
- To overcome market failures, host country governments must be able to guide and regulate MNCs in varying ways and to various degrees depending on the particular situation facing those countries and governments (UNCTAD, 1999: 323).
- A substantial share of recent FDI has taken the form of mergers and acquisitions rather than new investment. But mergers and acquisitions are much less likely to contribute toward economic development than are new investments (UNCTAD, 1999: 321).

At a press conference made to release the World Investment Report 1999, UNCTAD Secretary-General, Rubens Ricupero, said he would be opposed to any international agreement that would reduce the flexibility of choice of policies by host countries. He emphatically said "I am against it, and will be against it in the future". Such remarks by UNCTAD and its officials undoubtedly have been a source of confidence for many developing countries in the organisation's work and integrity.

The World Trade Organisation (WTO)

Background

The WTO came into existence in 1995 as a product of the Uruguay Round of GATT negotiations that started in 1986 at Punta del Este and finished on 14 April 1994 in Marrakesh. The WTO replaces GATT, which ceased to exist on 12 December 1994 as a trade organisation. It provides an organisational mechanism for administering trade relationships[4] by:

- administering trade agreements;
- acting as a forum for trade negotiations;
- settling trade disputes;
- reviewing national trade policies;
- providing technical assistance and training programs to developing countries; and
- cooperation with other international organisations.

The WTO system was developed through a series of trade negotiations under GATT in which the 1986-94 Uruguay Round negotiations led to the WTO's creation. Some negotiations, however, continued after the end of the Uruguay Round. In 1996, the WTO held its first Ministerial Conference in Singapore, the second in Geneva in 1998, and the third in Seattle in 1999.

Numerous specialised committees, working groups and working parties deal with individual agreements the WTO oversees and other areas such as the environment, development, membership applications and regional trade agreements. The Singapore Ministerial Conference added three new working groups that deal with the relationship between trade and investment, the interaction between trade and competition policy and transparency in government. At the second Ministerial Conference in Geneva, ministers decided that the WTO would also study the area of electronic commerce (see WTO Internet site).

According to Braithwaite and Drahos (2000: 184), the elaborate structure of the WTO is somewhat deceiving, in that the real work is normally done through informal negotiations between the key players such as "the Quad, the Cairns Group, EC members, the 'Boeuf Rouge' Group of like minded states who meet at Geneva restaurants...". Braithwaite and Drahos (2000: 184) further state that:

> Members of the Secretariat [then] draft a text, then invite one or six key states with different views on the text to thrash out a compromise, then widen this to the ten most consequential states for that particular issue or a ten-plus-ten meeting (ten developed and ten developing states)....Issues move between narrower and wider groupings until there is a

> consensus that the secretariat, consulting with the strong states, can make the weaker states agree to....The least developed countries do not get a seat at any of the meetings that matter, so they are often opponents to the end....

Trade Related Investment Measures (TRIMS)

TRIMS is one of the inherent agreements attached to the WTO Agreement.[5] It deals with trade-related measures that have prohibitive effects upon trade in goods. The United States was the key player in listing TRIMs as one of the issues to be negotiated in the Uruguay Round in 1986. According to Mo (1996: 95), it took the US more than ten years to "convince" GATT Members that foreign investment law and policy are related to trade in goods covered by the GATT.[6] The US approached the issue by identifying a number of areas that it believed had distorting or prohibitive effects on investment, such as (Christy, 1991: 779-780):[7]

- local content requirements;
- export performance requirements;
- trade balancing requirements;
- requirements for supplying specified markets;
- domestic sale requirements;
- restrictions on local manufacturing;
- technology transfer requirements;
- requirements for transfer by licensing only;
- remittance restrictions;
- local equity requirements;
- exchange restrictions; and
- incentives based on the acceptance of other TRIMs.

The list, obviously, covered measures that were beyond the scope of the GATT. Measures such as technology transfer requirements, remittance restrictions and local equity requirements were not necessarily related to trade in goods. Many countries, developed and developing alike, opposed the US approach (Mo, 1996: 96). By 1990, the Negotiating Group's views were divided across three options (Jackson, 1996):

- investment measures discriminating and restricting trade in goods should be prohibited or discouraged. This constituted the majority view.
- investment measures that do not directly relate to trade in goods should also be prohibited. This was the US view.
- the prohibition should be restricted to only those measures that are directly related to GATT principles, and should not exceed the scope of GATT.

The Group finally reached consensus in 1991 adopting the present approach (Jackson, 1996). The TRIMs Agreement expressly states in Article 1 that it "applies to investment measures related to trade in goods only", thus limiting the scope of its application to GATT principles. It also means that the Agreement does not apply to trade in services.

TRIMs are meant to be those investment measures that contravene the principles of Articles III (national treatment of imported products) or XI (prohibition of quantitative restrictions on imports or exports) of the GATT (Article 2, Agreement on TRIMs). An Illustrative List annexed to the TRIMs Agreement lists measures that are inconsistent with Articles III and XI. The Illustrative List covers:

- local content requirements;
- trade balancing measures;
- restriction of imports in the form of foreign exchange balancing requirements;
- restrictions on the export of or sale for export by an enterprise.[8]

The Agreement focuses on discriminatory treatment of imported products and does not govern the issue of entry and treatment of foreign investment. Therefore, the fact that there is no discrimination between domestic and foreign investors in the imposition of the requirement is irrelevant under TRIMs as long as there is discriminatory treatment of imported goods in favour of domestic products. The TRIMs Agreement also does not cover export incentives and export performance requirements.

Article 7 of the TRIMs Agreement establishes a Committee on TRIMs as a forum to examine the implementation operation of the Agreement. The Committee is required to meet at least twice a year. The Agreement also obliges member countries to eliminate TRIMs that have been notified to the Council for Trade in Goods. The elimination was to take place within two years after the entry into force of the WTO Agreement in the case of developed countries, within five years in the case of developing countries, and within seven years in the case of least developed countries (Article 5, Agreement on TRIMs).

Article 9 of the TRIMs Agreement stipulated that, no later than five years after the date of entry into force of the Agreement, the Council for Trade in Goods shall review the operation of the TRIMs Agreement. In the review, consideration was to be given as to whether the Agreement should be complemented with provisions on investment policy and competition policy. Although it is now more than five years since the Agreement came into force, no such review has taken place to date.

The Singapore Ministerial Conference

The Singapore Ministerial Conference of December 1996 was the first serious test of the WTO's cohesiveness and ability to lay down solid foundations of trade liberalisation. Many contentious items were on the agenda, including "new issues" such as investment, competition policy, labour and environmental issues.

Several weeks before the Conference, Indonesia presented to the Heads of Delegations of countries at the WTO Headquarters a joint statement of eight developing countries[9] opposing the start of any discussion of investment issues within the WTO (Khor, 1996: 1). The joint statement pointed out that the WTO already had sufficient rules to deal with aspects of investment that have direct and distorting effects on trade and cause material injury to trading partners. It also stated that the first WTO Ministerial Conference would not be an appropriate occasion for introducing the issues of trade and investment that lack consensus (Khor, 1996: 1). At the same meeting, another joint statement was presented by another group of countries, spearheaded by Canada and Japan, arguing that it would be useful for the WTO to take up the investment issue.[10] The group also lodged a "draft decision" for the ministers to adopt in Singapore. It called for the setting up of a working party on trade and investment to look into the barriers to investment, existing international investment agreements, and to identify key issues on rights and obligations in the area of investment (Khor, 1996: 1).

When the Singapore Ministerial Conference was started, it was apparent that member countries were divided along the above two lines. Ambassador Charlene Barshefsky of the US stated in her speech at the Conference that the US was prepared to consider whether the WTO should begin careful examination of new issues. She also acknowledged that it was not easy to find the right balance of interests, and that the US was "willing to go along with others who wish to begin a modest work program in the areas of investment and competition, as part of a balanced overall agenda for the WTO". Mr. Tungky Ariwibowo of Indonesia, on the other hand, said in his speech:

> With respect to trade and investment, we believe that the issue of a multilateral framework for investment is essentially outside the scope and competence of the WTO… the International Community has already mandated UNCTAD to thoroughly study the issue, and we do not see any justified reason for the WTO to duplicate the work of UNCTAD in this area.

Malaysia, India and Philippines too were opposed to negotiating investment rules within the framework of the WTO.

As the debate went on, a meeting of a small group of countries was called on the fringes of the Conference by then WTO Director-General Renato Ruggiero and Conference Chairman Yeo Cheow Tong (which was later dubbed by some the Yeo-Ruggiero process.[11] In the meeting, Director-General Ruggiero proposed that the Conference Declaration would recognise that the investment and competition policy issues were inter-linked, and that an educational study process should begin in the WTO, but that this process would not move forward to negotiations unless there is explicit consensus (The WTO Trade-off, 1996: 3).

The Conference finally agreed, among other things, to form a Working Group on Trade and Investment (WGTI), with the task of making an exploratory study of a number of issues and submit its report within two years (WTO, 1996). The issues to be covered in the study included:

- the implications of the relationship between trade and investment for development and economic growth;

- the economic relationship between trade and investment;
- the stocktaking and analysis of existing international instruments and activities regarding trade and investment; and
- on the basis of the work on the above issues;
- the identification of common features and differences as well as possible gaps in existing international instruments;
- advantages and disadvantages of entering into international agreements;
- rights and obligations of home and host countries and of investors and host countries; and
- relationship between existing and possible future international cooperation on investment policy and existing and possible future international cooperation on competition policy.

The Ministerial Declaration also made it clear that "future negotiations, if any, regarding multilateral disciplines... will take place only after an explicit consensus decision is taken among WTO Members regarding such negotiations" (WTO, 1996).

The Working Group held seven formal meetings in the two years ending in December 1998 and invited several international organisations and countries to make written contributions on the issues under study. Contributions were submitted by the OECD, UNCTAD, World Bank, IMF and UNIDO (WTO, 1997). Written or oral contributions were also made by countries including Japan, Poland, Korea, the United States, Hong Kong (WTO, 1997a), Costa Rica, Australia, India, Indonesia, Egypt and Tanzania (WTO, 1998).[12] At the end of the two-year period, the WGTI submitted a report to the General Council recommending that the Working Group continue its study, as it was not able to deliver a final report (WTO, 1998). Its mandate was therefore extended for one more year to coincide with the Seattle Ministerial Conference in 1999 (WTO, 1998a: 52).

The Seattle Ministerial Conference (Nov/Dec 1999)

The Seattle Ministerial Conference started in an atmosphere of NGO protests around the world and deep divisions on key issues between member countries. Protests were organised by NGOs in many European cities and some major cities in other parts of the world against the WTO and the Millennium Round trade negotiation that was expected by some to be launched at the Conference. Many of the protestors demanded a moratorium on new WTO negotiations until stock was taken of the WTO and its management radically changed (Singh, 1999: 1). The biggest of all the protests was held in Seattle, where the Conference took place. Thousands of protestors, many with contradictory aims, blocked the roads leading to the Conference venue, forcing the abandonment of the opening ceremonies on 30 November 1999. Police had to fire rubber bullets and use tear gas and pepper spray on the demonstrators blocking access roads, to enable delegates get access to the Conference centre. Riots, looting and arson by some groups ultimately resulted in a declaration of civil emergency, street curfew and the calling out of the National Guard.

The Conference finally met in the afternoon, combining the opening and plenary session, where it heard some ministerial statements, and established five working groups to negotiate the text of a ministerial declaration. Discussions on "new issues" covering, *inter alia*, investment and trade started on December 2, with most countries sticking to their former positions. The same line of division that was apparent during the MAI negotiations and the Singapore Ministerial Conference was generally maintained in Seattle. Several delegations, particularly the EC, Switzerland, Japan and other OECD countries, with the exception of the US, called for negotiations on an agreement for investment to be launched at the Seattle meeting. There was however a noticeable change in the way these countries wanted the issue to be addressed. There was more recognition for the role of "civil society". The need to address the concerns of some developing countries vis-à-vis MNCs was also recognised. In its communication to the General Council of the WTO, the EC for example stated:

> International rules on foreign direct investment protection contribute to create a favourable investment climate that benefits both international investors and host countries. Further reflection is needed on the question of investment protection rules... Thus, international rules on FDI, while aimed at encouraging FDI flows, should preserve the ability of all host countries to regulate, in accordance with basic WTO principles, the exercise of basic economic activity in their territory. These rules must respond to the concerns expressed by civil society concerning their impact on the environment and labour conditions (WTO, 1999).

A statement sent to the WTO General Council by the Japanese Government before the Seattle Conference also had a similar tone:

> ...The next WTO negotiations, therefore, should include a multilateral rule-making on investment. The objective of a WTO agreement on investment rules should be to promote foreign direct investment by providing disciplines for governmental measures on such investment, and priority should be given on improving the transparency and stability of the legal systems in host countries. While the rules need to substantially contribute to the promotion of foreign direct investment, consideration should be given to providing an appropriate balance with the development needs of developing country members (WTO, 1999).

The US, which in the past had been the main proponent of a comprehensive set of international investment rule (Chapter Five), appeared not interested in an investment agreement during the Seattle Ministerial Conference (Das, 1: 1999). Changed domestic political realities that had been fomented by United States NGOs seemed to be the explanation.

This apparent change in approach by the proponents of a multilateral investment framework did not, however, cool the strong opposition to such an agreement by developing countries and public interest groups. Some of the developing countries that opposed the starting of investment negotiation were ASEAN countries, Egypt, Jamaica, India and Pakistan (Das, 1: 1999). According to Das:

> The main concern of the developing countries is that the proposed negotiation is not about enhancing investment, but for ensuring freedom of operation of foreign investors and protecting their rights. Any such agreement in the WTO, they fear, is likely to constrain the role of the host countries in channelling investment in priority sectors, in appropriate regions and for activities beneficial for their development process. Also it may restrict their discretion to put conditions on foreign investors in respect of dissemination of technology, linkages with domestic economic activities and transfer of funds (Das, 1: 1999).

The business community was, as always, supportive of multilateral investment rules while most NGOs opposed such a move. The ICC, for example, urged WTO members "to seize the opportunity of the new round to push forward the process of creating within the WTO high-standard multilateral rules to protect and liberalise foreign investment..." (ICC, 1999:4). On the other hand, a joint NGO statement, endorsed by over 1,200 NGOs outlined their objection to the Millennium Round, calling for a moratorium on new issues or further negotiations in the WTO. The statement further said there should be a comprehensive and in-depth review and assessment of the existing WTO agreements before embarking on to any new negotiations (Oh, 1999: 1). The following table summarises the positions taken by different countries/groups.

The Conference ended after four days with a decision to suspend the discussions and to restart them again at WTO headquarters in Geneva at a date to be determined later (WTO, 1999a). For those who opposed the conference, it was definitely a moment of celebration.

Table 8:1 Positions taken by Some Countries/Groups at the WTO Seattle Ministerial Conference

Country/Group	Position Taken
United States	♦ Would respond to other submissions ♦ Favours expansion of TRIMS and work/study program
Canada	♦ Supports negotiations
EU	♦ Favours a new multilateral agreement ♦ Bottom-up approach ♦ Investor protection ♦ Transparency
Switzerland	♦ Negotiate investment agreement under broad, open mandate
Japan	♦ Supports multilateral investment rules ♦ Transparency and stability of legal systems in host countries ♦ National Treatment and MFN ♦ Abolish performance requirements ♦ No investor-state dispute settlement mechanism
Korea	♦ Supports negotiation ♦ Bottom-up approach ♦ No investor-state dispute settlement mechanism
India	♦ Oppose new investment agreement ♦ TRIMS should be revised allowing developing countries to impose domestic content and export requirements past 2000 phase out date
Uganda	♦ Opposes starting investment agreement
Argentina	♦ Willing to negotiate investment agreement
Chile	♦ Willing to negotiate investment agreement
Mexico	♦ Willing to negotiate an investment agreement
ASEAN	♦ Opposes investment negotiation
Malaysia	♦ Opposes investment negotiations
Egypt	♦ Opposes investment negotiations
ICC	♦ Supports high standard, liberal, multilateral investment rules
UNICE[13]	♦ Supports a global regime for foreign investment to be included in the WTO agenda

Sources Positions on a New Round of WTO Negotiations, *http://www.foe.org/international/wto/govt/htm*, accessed on 1 December 1999.

Update of Government Positions, *http://193.6.128.150/consumers/trade/government/update-government.htm*, accessed on 3 December 1999.

UNICE, UNICE Sets out New WTO Priorities, Press Release, 22 April 1999.

What went wrong in Seattle? Although Ambassador Barshevsky blamed Conference participants for being "not quite willing to make the political decisions" needed to reach a compromise (Pruzin, Yerkey & Felsenthal, 1999: 1), the complexity of the issues and the sheer volume of the negotiations that were to be completed within a short period of time undoubtedly contributed a great deal to the failure of the Conference. This was apparently clear for some governments, including the US, even before the conference started, but they hoped the problem could be resolved as the Conference date approached. President Clinton's chief economic adviser Gene Sperling said "over a period of many months there proved to be a high degree of intractability among a diversity of many countries who had very legitimate domestic demands, and there was perhaps a faith that somehow that intractability might melt away under the pressure of seeking a launch over a four day period" (Pruzin, Yerkey & Felsenthal, 1999: 2). Barshevsky herself, in her closing statement, said that "as time passed...divergences of opinion remained that would not be overcome rapidly" (WTO, 1999B). She went even further to say "the WTO has outgrown the process appropriate to an earlier time" and acknowledged that the organisation needed "a process which had a greater degree of internal transparency and inclusion to accommodate a larger and more diverse membership".

The WTO Secretariat in Geneva and the US Administration were also blamed by many for the failure. The Secretariat's inability to narrow the gaps between members' positions before the Conference started, a perceived conflict of interest in Barshevsky's role as Conference Chairperson and chief US trade negotiator, and President Clinton's remark regarding the need for trade sanctions against countries that violate core labour standards apparently contributed to the collapse of the conference (Pruzin, Yerkey & Felsenthal, 1999: 2). Clinton's remarks were not, however, totally unexpected given that the year was to be a presidential election in the US where his party needed NGO support, especially that of unions.

Heightened participation and influence on the part of developing countries too was among the factors. Just as had happened in Singapore in 1996, there was an attempt to hammer out differences between "key" players by holding a "green room" meeting, that is, a mini-conference of the "key" players on the side of the main Conference. This did not work this time round. A Pakistani delegate, from one of the small group of countries invited to the "green room" meeting, said "we had about 30 countries in the green room process. A hundred were waiting outside. We can't conclude [an agreement] without talking to the hundred outside" (Pruzin, Yerkey & Felsenthal, 1999: 2). Frederico Camilo of the Dominican Republic said the breakdown of the Seattle talks "will serve as an important lesson in humility for the small group of countries who think [the WTO] is their club" (Pruzin, Yerkey & Felsenthal, 1999: 2). The Organisation of African Unity also said in its statement:

> We wish to express our disappointment and disagreement with the way in which the negotiations are being conducted at this Third Ministerial Conference. There is no transparency in the proceedings and African countries are being marginalised and generally excluded on issues of vital importance for our peoples and their future....We reject the approach that is being employed and we must point out that under the present circumstances, we will not be able to join the consensus required to meet the objectives of the Ministerial Conference...(Raghavan, 1999: 2).

Similar disappointments were expressed by the Latin American and Carribean group of countries through their organisation GRULAC (Raghavan, 1999: 2).

Shortly after the collapse of the Conference, activities were started by WTO to try to narrow the differences between members' positions and call another conference in Geneva. The organisation, however, needs to make significant changes in its approach to the issues before that can happen. First, it needs to win the trust of developing countries, which make up two-thirds of the membership. Some of these countries see the WTO as a club of rich countries and lacking transparency. The WTO may need institutional reform if it is to remain credible as a multilateral organisation. This trust has been lacking so far, as was vividly witnessed in Seattle. Secondly, it needs to consult with the key NGOs in a meaningful way at all stages of the process. Some of these NGOs already play big roles in shaping public opinion and influencing government policy in many countries. In some instances, they even formally advise governments in areas of their concern. Not involving them in a meaningful way, as was the case in the past, would have a negative impact in consensus building efforts of the organisation. Thirdly, issues such as investment regulation, on which there is a very slim chance of acquiring consensus, may have to be dropped off the agenda altogether.

The World Bank

One of the purposes of the World Bank as enshrined in its Article of Agreement is "to promote private foreign investment".[14] Three other institutions created under the Bank's auspices complement its operations in support of the promotion of foreign investment. These institutions are the International Finance Corporation (IFC), the International Centre for the Settlement of Investment Disputes (ICSID), the Multilateral Investment Guarantee Agency (MIGA). Much of the Bank's lending program at present focuses on building an environment conducive to private investment, such as financing infrastructure projects and other basic services that facilitate new investment (Shihata, 1992: 499).

The International Finance Corporation (IFC)

The IFC provides loans to and takes equity participation in privately financed projects in developing countries. It also offers advisory services to international investors and governments in mobilising both domestic and foreign private capital for investment purposes. IFC is designed to play an important catalytic role in attracting FDI to developing countries. While it previously offered advice only in connection with projects financed by it, it now offers its consultant services independently of project financing (Shihata, 1992: 500).

The Multilateral Investment Guarantee Agency (MIGA)

The MIGA was formed in 1988 to complement the World Bank's private sector efforts in the reduction or elimination of non-commercial deterrents to FDI, especially political risks (MIGA Convention). It is an autonomous organisation within the World Bank Group whose objective is to encourage the flow of investments for productive purposes among member countries, in particular to developing member countries through the issuance of guarantees against non-commercial risks in respect of investments that flow from one member country to another (MIGA Convention, Article 2).

Every member country is required to subscribe to the Agency's capital stock. Subscriptions of original members are at par to the number of shares of capital stock set forth for them in Schedule A to the Convention, while the subscriptions of acceding members have to be determined by the Agency's Council ((MIGA Convention, Article 6). The details of each guarantee operation and the mutual rights and obligations of both parties are to be set forth in the contract of guarantee concluded between MIGA and the investor. The guarantee provided by MIGA is limited to investments made in the territory of a "developing member country" of the Agency (MIGA Convention, Article 14).

The type of investments eligible for cover by the Agency are defined under Article 12 of the Convention. Any form of equity investments, different forms of direct investments, and medium- or long-term loans made or guaranteed by owners of equity in the enterprise concerned are envisaged as eligible for cover. Moreover, guarantees can be extended to transfers of foreign exchange and to the use of earnings from existing investments which would otherwise be transferred outside the host country. The Agency's cover is limited to those investments which are believed to be sound, contribute to the economic and social development of the host country, comply with the host county's laws and regulations, and are consistent with the country's declared development objectives (MIGA Convention, Article 12).

Article 11 of the Convention specifies four types of non-commercial risks eligible for cover. They are currency transfer, expropriation and similar measures, breach of contract, and war and civil disturbance.

The International Centre for the Settlement of Investment Disputes (ICSID)

The ICSID is another autonomous organisation within the World Bank Group, established by a multilateral agreement of states in 1966. It provides international facilities for the conciliation and arbitration of investment disputes between Contracting States and nationals of other Contracting states (ICSID Convention). Like MIGA, ICSID is intended to complement the work of the Bank in reducing non-commercial deterrents to foreign investment. It has an Administrative Council and a Secretariat. The Administrative Council is chaired by the World Bank's President and consists of one representative of each State which has ratified the Convention. The expenses of the ICSID Secretariat are financed out of the Bank's budget, although the costs of individual proceedings are borne by the parties involved. As of 1st of October 1999, 147 Countries signed the Convention.[15]

Recourse to ICSID conciliation and arbitration is voluntary. However, once the parties have consented to arbitration under the ICSID Convention, they cannot unilaterally withdraw its consent. The parties are also bound to carry out their undertaking and, in the case of arbitration, to abide by the award as binding. Moreover, all ICSID Contracting States, whether or not parties to the dispute, are required to recognise and enforce ICSID arbitral awards as binding and to enforce the pecuniary obligations imposed thereby. Awards are not subject to any appeal or other remedy except those which are provided for in the Convention.

Since 1978, the Centre has had a set of Additional Facility Rules authorising the ICSID Secretariat to administer certain types of proceedings between States and foreign nationals which fall outside the scope of the Convention, such as the conciliation and arbitration proceedings where either the State party or the home State of the foreign national is not a member of ICSID, and fact-finding proceedings to which any State and foreign national may have recourse if they wish to institute an inquiry "to examine and report on facts".

A third activity of ICSID in the field of the settlement of disputes has consisted in the Secretary-General of ICSID accepting to act as the appointing authority of arbitrators for ad hoc (that is, non-institutional) arbitration proceedings. This is most commonly done in the context of arrangements for arbitration under the Arbitration Rules of the United Nations Commission on International Trade Law (UNCITRAL), which are specially designed for ad hoc proceedings.

ICSID maintains broad panels of conciliators and arbitrators. Each contracting state of ICSID can designate up to four members to these panels. Panellists are typically distinguished experts in international trade and investment law.

A relatively small number of cases have been registered by ICSID so far, but the number of cases has increased significantly in recent years. Thirty-eight cases have been concluded so far and there are another thirty pending cases. These include cases brought under the ICSID Convention as well as under the ICSID Additional Facility Rules. Although the number of actual cases registered by the Centre are relatively low, the presence in many investment agreements of ICSID clauses may have served as an incentive to avoid disputes or to settle them amicably.

In addition to its dispute settlement activities, ICSID carries out advisory and research and publishing[16] activities relevant to its objectives.

The World Bank Guidelines on the Treatment of FDI

In 1992, the World Bank adopted a set of Guidelines for the treatment of FDI.[17] The Guidelines do not purport to regulate the activities of investors, nor are they binding on member states, but attempt to guide government behaviour toward foreign investment. They cover the admission (Clause II), treatment (Clause III) and expropriation (Clause IV) of foreign investments and the settlement of disputes between governments and foreign investors (Clause V).

The Guidelines urge host countries to encourage foreign investment as a matter of principle and "avoid over-regulation...and unnecessary bureaucratic obstacles to admission". They also prohibit the usage of performance requirements as conditions of admission of foreign investment. However, host countries would be allowed to exclude from their territories foreign investments that threaten their "national security" under clearly defined requirements. They can also exclude foreign investment from areas/sectors reserved by the law of the host country to its nationals on account of the host country's economic development objectives or national interest requirements. Other grounds of exclusion include fundamental values of society as defined in the host country's laws and judicial practice, environmental protection and public health (Clause II of the Guidelines).

The treatment provision of the Guidelines cover the establishment and various aspects of operations of the foreign investor. Foreign investors would be given national treatment to the extent that the circumstances of the two groups are similar, implying that foreigners may be treated more favourably when the circumstances of the two groups are different. Foreign investors would also be granted MFN treatment. The Guidelines also stipulate labour market flexibility, emphasising in particular the investor's freedom to fill top management positions regardless of nationality. The transfer of funds abroad with minimal restrictions is stipulated (Clause III of the Guidelines).

Host countries may not expropriate or "take measures which have similar effects, except where this is done in accordance with applicable legal procedures, in pursuance of a public purpose, without discrimination on the basis of nationality and against the payment of appropriate compensation" (Clause IV of the Guidelines). The Guidelines do not explain what measures having similar effects to expropriation would mean, but the explanatory notes refer to bilateral investment treaties and other multilateral agreements that have similar provisions. Compensation is deemed to be appropriate if it is "adequate, prompt and effective" (Clause IV of the Guidelines). The Guidelines also prescribe the ICSID facilities for the resolution of investment disputes (Clause V of the Guidelines).

Regional Economic Groupings

The crucial role of the EU has already been extensively canvassed in this book (see Chapter Five). At different points we have also discussed the role of ASEAN (Chapters Six and Eight), GRULAC (Chapter Eight) and NAFTA (Chapter Three). There are dozens of these regional economic groupings and investment agreements are often among their most important functions. I have chosen APEC as case study to illustrate the role regional bodies play, partly because of its importance, the comparatively newness of its impact on the international scene, and ease of access to information about its operation.

APEC was established in 1989[18] the largest regional economic grouping in the world, in terms of both economic and population sizes. Its 21 member economies had a combined GDP of over US$16 trillion in 1998 as well as 42 per cent of global trade. In 1994, the APEC Ministers and Leader meeting adopted a vision for an "open and free trade and investment in the Asia-Pacific by 2010 for developed member economies and 2020 for developing ones". This vision was further adopted in the subsequent yearly meeting of leaders.

In 1993, APEC Ministers adopted a Declaration on a Trade and Investment Framework. Based on the Declaration, Ministers formed the Committee on Trade and Investment (CTI), which would aim to create an APEC perspective on trade and investment issues and to pursue liberalisation and facilitation initiatives.

The APEC Principles on foreign investment are a set of non-binding guidelines for the treatment of foreign investment in the Asia-Pacific region. They were adopted at the APEC Conference held in Bogor, Indonesia, in November 1994. The drafting of such Principles had been recommended in the report of a group of eminent persons to the 1993 APEC Ministerial meeting, which pointed out that FDI was one of the leading elements in the market-driven economic interdependence and that the countries of the region should encourage the inflow of foreign investment (APEC, 1993). The report argued that since the existing system of bilateral investment treaties was unsatisfactory, a region-wide investment code was the answer:

At the meeting, the Ministers agreed to make FDI policy a priority for work by a newly created Trade and Investment Committee. This was further amplified in the "vision statement of the APEC Heads of State meeting" held on Blake Island following the Ministerial, wherein the Heads of State "ask APEC to undertake work aimed at deepening and broadening the outcome of the Uruguay Round, strengthening trade and investment liberalisation in the region...." (Graham, 1993: 1). It was agreed that part of this work would include the development of a non-binding Asia-Pacific Investment Code (APIC), to be presented at the APEC ministerial meeting to be held in Indonesia in October 1994.

The non-binding nature of the principles was important to obtain the agreement of the parties. The language used was aspirational in character and non-legalistic. The principles do not require immediate changes to the policies or practices of members but are simply agreed objectives. Also it was necessary to include numerous exceptions.

The US first objected to the Code at the 1994 APEC Senior Officials Meeting in Bogor on the ground that the language used in the Code was not strong enough. The American strategy was that, since the Code was to be non-binding, it was best to go for the highest possible standard of treatment for foreign investment from the outset (Song, 1994).

The APEC Non-Binding Principles consist of twelve provisions. The first provision covers transparency. Several members were concerned at the potential extent of the reach of this provision. The view finally taken was, however, that the provision was aspirational and to be applied not legalistically but in a pragmatic way, allowing members to decide for themselves how far it was practicable to achieve it (Hyde, 1995). The second provision requires members not to discriminate between foreign investors from any economy in relation to the establishment, expansion and operation of their investments. There is also a provision for national treatment, but it is subject to exceptions set out in the domestic laws of each host country (Article 3).

The provision on investment incentives refers to not relaxing health, safety and environment regulations as an incentive to encourage foreign investment (Article 4). Apparently members were not able to agree on any wider formulation limiting the use of investment incentives, but they did accept that the topic was an important one.

Performance requirements are another issue covered by the Investment Principles (Article 5). Members have agreed only to minimise the use of performance requirements that distort or limit expansion of trade and investment, not to eliminate them. One reason for such a formulation could be that the economies of the region are at different levels of development and not all of them can be expected to conform with definite standards in this regard. Some may think that performance requirements may be the only way through which they could ensure that their development objectives could be achieved. That being the case, it is unlikely that a Code containing definite programs for the elimination of performance standards would prove to be acceptable to many of these countries.

The Non-Binding Principles also contain a provision relating to expropriation and compensation. Expropriation may not take place except for a public purpose, on non-discriminatory basis, and "in accordance with the laws of each economy and principles of international law". Compensation is guaranteed on the "Hull formula" (Article 6).

In settling disputes between the parties, priority would be given to settlement through consultation and negotiation between the parties. Failing that, resort may be had to arbitration, either in accordance with international commitments or through other procedures acceptable to the parties (Article 8). Investor-State dispute is not covered by the Principles.

The Principles also contain statements of concerns of many developing countries. There is a provision which states that the foreign investor should abide by the host country's laws (Article 11). The reference to this principle stems from the idea that the regulatory mechanisms devised by the State for foreign investment is respected.

Conclusion

International organisations play significant roles in shaping the global regulatory regime. Although some success has been seen at regional levels, none of the global organisations have so far succeeded in developing a comprehensive global investment regime acceptable to all countries. As the discussion in this and previous Chapters revealed, several attempts to develop such a regime in the past have failed. It is however striking to note that most of the sticking issues were similar in all of the attempts and no significantly new approach has been taken to resolve them. The same mistrust between developed and developing countries that was apparent during the negotiations for the UN Code of Conduct was seen during the recent WTO Ministerial Conference in Seattle. The treatment of foreign investors was an issue in the 1970's, as it is now. So is the settlement of disputes between foreign investors and host countries.

As was seen during the Seattle Ministerial Conference as well as during the MAI negotiations, exclusion of some major international players from the real process of rule making may not be helpful in overcoming the stalemate. An inclusive and transparent process seems to be a necessary starting point. The concerns of all countries and key civil society representatives should be addressed in a meaningful way. Moreover, organisations that have already been seen as partisan by some groups may not be the appropriate venues for developing and administering such a regime. In general, a fresh approach is needed to overcome the current stalemate and develop a global investment regime.

Geopolitically, the draft MAI and WTO were forged in a post-cold war climate where developing countries had completely lost confidence in their capacity to influence events. During the Cold War, developing countries could use incidents like ITT's intervention in Chile's military coup to forge alliances with the Soviet block to initiate processes such as that for the UN Code of Conduct on TNCs. A coalition of developing countries and the Soviet block could in certain limited contexts prevail over the West. Post-MAI, post-Seattle, a new more complex coalition reality prevails that is giving developing countries a new confidence within international organisations like the WTO. This is a veto coalition of developing countries and NGOs in developed countries. A conclusion of this book is that the existence of this veto coalition has created the geopolitical context where regulated openness is the realpolitic of international investment.

Notes

1 Thirty-three were from Latin America, Africa and Asia; ten from Western Europe and "other states"; and five from Eastern bloc countries.

2 The Chapters were preamble and objectives, definitions and scope of application, activities and conduct of MNCs, inter-governmental cooperation, and implementation.

3 The Australian position was that, although the goals of the Code of Conduct remained relevant and useful, much of its language and content was outdated.

4 The GATT, initially, was a Protocol of Provisional applications, but gradually evolved as an elaborate system of agreements on world trade (Braithwaite and Drahos, 2000:

177; Jackson: 1990). At present, the GATT is one of the international agreements within the WTO. For a detailed account of WTO's history and activities, see the organisation's Internet site at *www.wto.org*, accessed 10 June 2000.

5 The documents made in the Uruguay Round are divided into two categories, according to their effects: inherent agreements and plurilateral agreements. An inherent agreement becomes effective as soon as a country has ratified the WTO Agreement. A plurilateral agreement applies only to those Members which have expressly ratified it. TRIMS automatically applies to all Members of the WTO because it is inherent.

6 The link between foreign investment law and policy and trade in goods gave GATT the right to deal with the issue.

7 See also Markus & Eby (1991: 449-69).

8 Article 4 of the TRIMs Agreement allows developing countries to deviate temporarily from the obligations of the TRIMs Agreement, as provided for in Article XVIII of GATT and related WTO provisions on safeguard measures for balance-of-payments difficulties.

9 The countries were Malaysia, India, Egypt, Tanzania, Ghana, Uganda, Haiti and Indonesia itself. These countries were later joined by others.

10 The other countries in the group were Bolivia, Chile, Costa Rica, the Czech Republic, Hungary, Iceland, Madagascar, Morocco, Norway, Peru, Slovak Republic and Switzerland.

11 The countries invited for the meeting included the US, EU, Japan, Canada, Australia, South Korea, India, Indonesia, Malaysia, Pakistan, Egypt, South Africa, Tanzania, Morocco, Chile, Brazil, Hong Kong and Mexico.

12 For the summary of the contributions received by the Working Group, see the WGTI 1998 Report (WT/WGTI/2).

13 In the past, UNICE opposed the inclusion of investment rules in the WTO agenda (see Chapter Five).

14 The name "World Bank" is often used to denote the International Bank for Reconstruction and Development (IBRD) together with the International Development Association (IDA). IDA is established under the IBRD's auspices to assist the less developed members on concessional loan. But, unlike the IBRD, it does not have an explicit mandate in its Articles of Agreement with regard to foreign investment.

15 For details about ICSID, see the organisation's Internet site at *www.worldbank.org.icsid*, accessed on 15 April 2000.

16 The publications of the Centre include multi-volume collections of Investment Laws of the World and of Investment Treaties, which are periodically updated by ICSID staff. Since April 1986, the Centre has published a semi-annual law journal entitled ICSID Review-Foreign Investment Law Journal. The journal was recently rated as one of the top 20 international and comparative law journals in the United States.

17 The Guidelines are reproduced in 31 International Legal Materials 1363 (1992).

18 APEC member countries are Australia, Chile, Indonesia, Malaysia, Papua New Guinea, Russia, Thailand, Brunei Darussalam, China, Japan, Mexico, Peru, Singapore, United States, Canada, Hong Kong, Korea, New Zealand, Philippines, Taiwan and Vietnam. For detailed information about APEC, see the organisation's web page at *www.apecsec.org.sg*, accessed on 13 May 2000.

Part III

Evaluation:
Towards Regulated Openness

Chapter 9

Evaluation of the Strategies

As demonstrated in Part II, the debate by the key players on a global regulatory framework for FDI is centred on two themes: more openness (full liberalisation) or more regulation. Developed countries, the multilateral financial institutions like the IMF and World Bank, business groups and some developing countries advance the idea of having a more liberal regime at both global and national levels. Most developing countries and various NGOs, such as consumer organisations, environmental activists and the labour movement, on the other hand see danger in an extensive liberalisation of investment rules and mostly argue that what is needed is regulation. This chapter evaluates the strategies and two positions of the key players. Also, the implications of the Multilateral Agreement on Investment (MAI) will be discussed.

Liberalisation

A liberal investment regime is one which government intervention by laws, regulations, policies or practices is kept to the minimum or is non-existent (Clairmont, 1996). Under a liberal investment regime, the investor is largely free to decide for itself where, when and how to set up or expand its business operations. If it is a foreign investor, governments may not have the power to subject it to screening procedures where the host country authorities may pick and choose among investment proposals, or to performance requirements where the investor would be required to promote some economic and social objectives of the host government (Clairmont, 1996).

As has been discussed in Chapter Five, liberalisation was one of the core objectives of the MAI. The National Treatment, MFN, and Performance Requirement clauses of the Agreement, together with the "stand-still" and "roll-back" provisions, were intended to dismantle barriers to and restrictions on FDI, and give foreign investors greater market access. An OECD official told me that "since trade and FDI are intertwined, the liberalisation of trade rules which has been taking place for some time has to be accompanied by the liberalisation of FDI rules" (see also discussion in Chapter Five). Hence the next logical step after trade liberalisation would be FDI liberalisation. It is also argued that a liberal FDI regime, together with free trade, generates more investment, leads to a better allocation of resources, brings greater economic efficiency, and accelerates economic growth. It is often said that the benefits of FDI are best achieved under a liberal investment regime (Ley, 1996: 69).

The historical relationship between FDI and trade "has been characterised by linear, step-by-step sequential process of internationalisation, running from trade to FDI or from FDI to trade" (UNCTAD, 1996: 10). In the manufacturing sector, for example, companies may begin with domestic production and sale, and then internationalise gradually through exports, licensing and other contractual arrangements and by establishing foreign trading affiliates (UNCTAD, 1996: 10). As a final stage, they may invest abroad directly. Companies may also opt to invest abroad directly when they seek low-cost inputs (UNCTAD, 1996: 10). With natural resources companies may begin either with imports followed by FDI, or may undertake FDI and proceed to export from the host country (UNCTAD, 1996: 10).

According to a study by UNCTAD, the environment for FDI and trade has changed significantly since the mid-1980s (UNCTAD, 1996: 13). The reduction in technological and policy-related barriers to the movement of goods, services, capital and skilled workers has apparently given companies more freedom to choose either to produce at home and export, or produce in a foreign country for local sale or export. This means that any part of the value added chain can be located wherever it contributes most to a company's overall performance (UNCTAD, 1996: 13). Consequently, the flows of FDI and trade are determined simultaneously, making the issue of whether trade leads FDI or vice versa or whether FDI substitutes for trade or vise versa, or whether they complement each other largely irrelevant. What is more important for foreign investors is how they can get market access. Therefore, business groups pressure governments to liberalise their investment regimes.

To the extent that FDI and trade are linked, there may well be a need to harmonise trade and FDI policies and laws. Hence, most restrictions and controls on FDI and trade have disappeared in almost all developed countries and are also being gradually abolished in many developing countries. Host countries also give foreign investors legal protection and guarantees against non-commercial risks (Chapter Three). On the other hand, the flourishing of FDI and trade is not an end by itself. Countries, particularly developing countries, wish to increase the flow and activities of FDI and trade in their territories mainly because they want to use it as a tool for speeding up their growth and development. Governments may not see any advantage in the liberalisation of FDI regimes unless the latter result in more inflows of FDI.

Experience shows that liberalisation does not necessarily result in the increased inflow of FDI. For example, China has been the largest recipient of FDI in the developing world since 1992 (UNCTAD, 1999: 22) despite its restrictive investment regime, whereas many African countries receive little or no FDI (UNCTAD, 1999: 18) even though their investment regimes are far more liberal than that of China. Countries like Malaysia and Thailand have more strict regulations towards FDI than Latin American countries, but they receive more FDI than the latter (UNCTAD, 1997: 18).

There are normally extra costs and risks involved, at least initially, when companies invest in a country where they are not familiar. Despite these costs and risks, firms still invest abroad. This could be so because of factors such as ownership advantage (Hymer, 1960), locational advantage (Vernon, 1966), and internationalisation advantages (Buckley and Casson, 1976). These theories, together with other theories such as oligopolistic rivalry between firms at the global level, the empire building motive of managers, and the desire to build overseas capacity in order to stop potential rivals from entering any specific market or markets[1] attempt to encompass most of the practical reasons why firms prefer to invest abroad. If these theories are correct, it is open to question if adopting a liberal regime alone really makes a big difference in attracting FDI to a particular country.

FDI has certainly become a major source of funding development projects for many developing countries. This situation has given rise to both the temptation and pressure to fully liberalise FDI regimes. Despite this fact, however, the performance of the economy with respect to certain vital indicators in industrial countries, where the liberalisation process has gone furthest, is significantly worse now than it was in 1970. In 1970 the average unemployment rate for OECD countries was 3% (OECD, 1994); in February 2000, it rose to 6.6%. Similarly, the trend rate of growth of production as well as productivity in the 1990s have been half of what they were in the 1960s (South Centre, 1997: 57). Therefore, the more dynamic period in industrial countries was the period prior to their extensive liberalisation of internal and external markets. In view of this poor record in developed countries in the last two decades, a degree of caution and scepticism with respect to extensive liberalisation would appear to be appropriate.

There are both important benefits and costs associated with FDI (Chapter Six). Whether or not the benefits that result from certain types of FDI projects or FDI collectively would outweigh the costs is a relevant issue to be considered when a country forms its FDI policies. Moreover, traditionally FDI was seen as a form of long-term, stable capital inflow because, unlike portfolio investment, it usually requires a long-term commitment on the part of the investor. This situation has changed with the liberalisation of financial markets.

The other factors on the cost side of FDI include transfer pricing and certain types of advertising which may give rise to economically and socially distorting patterns of consumption. These types of advertising can sometimes have far-reaching effects, such as when more costly foreign foods replace local and more nutritious food products as a result of the advertising or when drug addiction is promoted by the advertising of tobacco or alcohol. A liberal FDI regime in the media and entertainment field could also pose the risk of cultural hegemony. This is particularly so in developing countries where funds for local production of films and other entertainment materials are scarce. FDI in the media sector could also have the danger of facilitating political influence, both through the world views conveyed and by attitudes adopted towards domestic issues.

Therefore, it may not be correct to presume that the net impact of FDI in all circumstances will be positive. A review carried out in the United Nations University concludes that FDI promises more than it delivers and the diverging experiences of countries with respect to host country gains from MNE entry could probably result from different policy packages adopted by different countries (Kumar, 1996, 45).

For many countries, a regime of unrestricted FDI entry may be inappropriate, as it will not allow the host country to determine the optimum level and type of FDI suitable for the country concerned. The experience of East Asian countries is consistent with this interpretation. It can be said that these countries achieved high growth mainly by getting the fundamentals right. On the other hand, in all of these countries, except Hong Kong, the government intervened systematically and through multiple channels, to foster development, and in some cases the development of specific industries (Patel, 1996: 33; see also Westphal, 1990; Jomo, 1996; World Bank, 1993). If one takes the South Korean experience as an example, since the early 1960s Korean industrial policy has had two main objectives: encouraging exports and promoting infant industries (Westphal, 1990). The government intervened selectively to achieve these objectives.

To sum up, it is obvious that FDI is becoming a major influence in the social and political life of many countries, and is defining national models of development in many developing countries. On the other hand, a fully liberalised regime may not necessarily promote widespread development and growth. In order to realise the full potential of FDI, therefore, it may be necessary for any government to have a policy that is selective with respect to projects and the volume and timing of FDI inflows. Liberalisation should also be seen as a continuous movement, rather than a one-off radical measure. The pace of the movement could vary from country to country. Governments should be able to examine their policies and laws on FDI on a regular basis in order to decide if new circumstances would necessitate change in their current policies and laws. As a result of such evaluations, the number of restrictions on FDI could be reduced, or new restrictions might be introduced if aspects of liberalisation proved counter-productive.

The Multilateral Agreement on Investment (MAI)

One of the shortcomings of the MAI was the exclusiveness of the negotiation process. There was not a meaningful consultation with the various stakeholders, except with representatives of the business community and the labour movement through BIAC and TUAC respectively. Both BIAC and TUAC are advisory bodies to the OECD Secretariat, and their constituency does not extend beyond the OECD member countries. Neither developing countries nor NGOs participated in the negotiations. The preparation of an agreement such as the MAI should have involved at least the concerned key international players. It should also have been transparent.

The MAI contained no binding and enforceable obligation for corporate conduct. But history has taught us the MNCs are not always law-abiding, responsible citizens. They sometimes disregard not only the laws of host countries, but also the laws of their home countries. The UN Code of Conduct for MNCs was initiated mainly because of the conduct of MNCs (see Chapter Eight). More than two decades later, similar problems are being witnessed in many parts of the world, as demonstrated by the behaviour of the French multinational company Elf Aquitaine.

A television documentary[2] in Australia recently exposed how Elf Aquitaine corrupted politicians in developed and developing countries, how it interfered in the internal politics of host countries, how it served France to perpetuate its influence on its former colonies in Africa, and how it undermined the French Government's activities. According to the documentary, each time the company won big contracts overseas (often through corrupt practices), a certain amount of the "money was creamed off the top to illegally fund French politicians". In Congo (Brazzaville), Elf Aquitaine seems to play the role of a kingmaker. The former president of Congo, Patrice Lissouba, said in the documentary that:

> Over time Elf became in the Congo, as well as elsewhere, a great power. An energy power, of course, but also a financial power, political power, and a politicians' power as well. Elf became power. Espionage with police powers.

And he went on accusing the company for his overthrow from power:

> It was Elf that made the choice. Sometimes of those people who are not wanted, they don't even bother to eliminate them. I left. They could have chosen not to get rid of me. I could have been simply eliminated. If I left it was because Elf wanted Mr Sassou to come back.[3]

These are indeed very serious allegations. But Elf Aquitaine had its own espionage network, and did even interfere in the activities of its own home state, France. Mr. Pierre Marion, the former Head of the French secret service, DGSE, said in the documentary:

> The people from Elf were interfering in our activities… we are quite often in a confrontational situation.
>
> **Q:** So, Elf would deliberately interfere with the French state?
>
> **A:** Deliberately. And because they were very strongly enmeshed in the same area as me, but without the same objectives.

Elf Aquitaine was founded by Charles De Gaulle as a fully state-owned oil company in the early 1960s. One of the objectives of its foundation was to serve as a tool to cement French power in the newly independent African colonies. Valerie Lescable, who wrote a book on Elf Aquitaine, said in the documentary:

> He (De Gaulle) gave them (former African colonies) independence, but after independence, he thought a big oil company was a way France could have economic, not just political power and have these countries working for France.

Although similar stories have been heard from time to time around the world, the strongest provisions in the MAI were those that would protect the rights of the foreign investor including some which are not available to the domestic investor. Moreover, the MAI was designed to reduce significantly the ability of governments to set national objectives and regulate MNCs accordingly. The expropriation provision was perhaps one of the serious threats to governmental regulatory power. This has already happened in Canada where the Parliament banned the production and transportation of a toxic gasoline additive (MMT) in the country. Ethyl Corporation, which had been affected by the new law, sued the Canadian government under the provisions of NAFTA, which happens to be similar to those of the MAI, for damages worth $C250 million. The National Treatment and Performance Requirement provisions too seriously limit the ability of governments to design their national priorities and regulate the inflow of FDI. More importantly, the standstill provision limits the government's ability to introduce in the future any laws and policies that are contrary to liberalisation.

To conclude, the MAI was a liberalisation agreement designed to dismantle regulation. As such, it predominantly represented the interests of business groups, ignoring the interests of the poor and economically weak. It failed to balance the granting of investor rights with responsibilities for social improvement, human rights, environmental protection and consumer safety. It also seriously limited the ability of governments to control FDI in the public interest.

Regulation

The demand for regulation is mostly heard from a number of developing countries like China and India, and NGOs from the consumer movement, environmentalists, and labour unions. All of these groups advocate regulation of FDI in one form or another, for different reasons. The reasons for the position taken by one group do not always coincide with those of the other. In the following section, the positions of each group will be evaluated.

Developing Countries

As the discussion in Chapter Six shows, developing countries' positions on the regulation of FDI are divided. There are countries that have already liberalised their investment regimes extensively, and others with stricter regimes. Those with stricter regimes oppose liberalisation measures through an international framework like the MAI. They claim that they do so mainly for two reasons: 1) preservation of sovereignty, and 2) their desire to fully control and direct the inflow of FDI. They argue that unrestricted entry of FDI into their territories could be a threat to their national sovereignty and the independent development of their social and cultural life. Most of these countries have a favourable attitude towards FDI. One may, therefore, ask that why they appear to be so sensitive about the issue of sovereignty. It could well be that they just want to use it as leverage to negotiate the best terms of FDI regulation.

Erosion of Sovereignty The claim that the profound transformation currently taking place globally and within nation states is undermining the sovereignty of states has been advanced from different angles. During my discussion with developing country diplomats in Geneva, it was put to me that:

- states can no longer pretend to be autonomous or to exercise a monopoly on the legitimate use of their powers in their respective territories;
- the most important things that affect people's lives today are global in scale and consequences; and
- states can no longer deal even with their national security by their own. The need to cooperate has in return limited the sovereign prerogatives of states.

These claims have some truth in them. The interdependence of states and its consequent impact on the exercise of sovereignty, however, does not signal the end of sovereignty. Sovereignty has always been an ambiguous and flexible concept, and it has always been interpreted in relative terms.

The origin and history of the concept of sovereignty is closely related to the nature, origin, and evolution of the state, and in particular to the development of centralised authority and an administrative system of political control (Hinsley, 1966: 1). But the term state itself had different meanings at different times. For sixteenth and seventeenth century theorists like Bodin and Hobbes, the state represented the highest power in the land, acting as a court of last resort and holding an effective monopoly on the use of force (Bodin, 1606). Accordingly, sovereignty lies in the highest body of the land that has the power to make, administer and enforce laws. To others like Rousseau and Hegel the state represented not the institution of government, but the politically organised society, the community of free people (Rousseau, 1950). Hence, sovereignty lies in the people. So what is sovereignty? Is there a limit to it? The answers that will be given to these questions can at the same time address the validity of the concerns of those groups that argue that multilateral, liberal FDI rules erode sovereignty.

In the sixteenth century John Bodin believed that sovereignty was "supreme power over citizens and subjects unrestricted by law" (Bodin, 1606: 84) and therefore unlimited in extension and duration. The supreme power of the ruler was subordinate only to the "law of nature and God". Later in eighteenth century, Jean-Jacques Rousseau argued that sovereignty was unlimited and indivisible, but that the state was the result of a contract in which all individuals had agreed to submit to its will (Hinsley, 1966: 153). He further argued that the state represented the "general will" of the community, and hence popular sovereignty was the basis of state sovereignty (Rousseau, 1950: 31). For John Austin in the nineteenth century, on the other hand, the state was a legal order in which a specific authority is the unlimited source of power, and this authority is the sovereign power in the state. Its authority is unlimited, and its legal authority derives from its supreme coercive power.

Although all the above approaches to the issue of defining sovereignty and state are vastly different from each other, that of Karl Marx was revolutionary. For Marx, although the state presents itself as a sovereign and guardian of the general interest of society, this is largely an illusion. He argued that the state represents the interests of the dominant social order and in the case of a capitalist society, the bourgeois class, or the free movement of private interests (Miliband, 1983: 6).

To put the above discussion in a nutshell, the theory and practice of sovereignty as it evolved in the past five hundred years was a reflection of the socio-politico-economic pre-occupation of the era. Sovereignty as conceived by Bodin was based on the necessity of an absolutist state that could impose order in a Europe that had experienced the disintegration of the feudal system and prolonged conflict and civil war. The more democratic version of state sovereignty offered by Rousseau and others reflected both the experience of a more benign Swiss society and the emergence of a new economic class. The theory and practice of sovereignty evolving in the eighteenth century and after also reflected a rapidly changing economic and political environment.

Following the French revolution, national sovereignty as a principle continued to be applied in the external conduct of states. Increasingly the world was seen as comprising social units (states), each with a supreme authority enjoying the allegiance of citizens within their territories. Outside their boundaries, these units acted with restraint, but in no circumstance did they acknowledge an external authority higher than their own.[4]

It is arguable if state sovereignty has ever been exercised without any limitations, either internal or external. This is certainly not so since the first treaties were signed. With the expansion of international law and international organisations, the environment under which nation states operate has become very complex. Regardless of how treaties, agreements or conventions arise, the rapidly developing international legal order both reflects the inadequacy of states as self-contained units of decision-making and restricts their freedom of action. In these circumstances, it has become progressively difficult to demonstrate the primacy of domestic law over international law. The exercise of sovereignty is also limited by the realities of power between states. To the extent that the international system normally comprises a few powerful and many weaker states, there inevitably arises a hierarchy of relations that does not easily correspond with the theoretical equality of all sovereign states.

Unprecedented proliferation of international organisations has occurred after World War II. They range from global organisations like the UN and WTO to regional organisations like the OAU and APEC; from entities concerned with a broad range of issues, such as the World Bank, to those with limited and specific functions such as WIPO. Their activities vary from attempts by states to extend their jurisdiction (which may imply an extension of sovereignty beyond their territory) to the development of higher institutionalised schemes for cooperation and integration (which has a tendency to diffuse national power and limit sovereignty).

International organisations such as the World Bank, IMF, WTO, FAO, ILO and other United Nations agencies have become important elements of an emerging global structure which facilitates multilateral monetary and trade transactions, the flow of technical and managerial expertise, taxation agreements and so on. The debt problem and the recent Asian crisis, for example, have propelled the IMF to the forefront of international decision making. Both developing countries and Eastern European nations with sizeable debt problems have almost without exception had to rely on IMF emergency relief. To gain such relief and have their creditworthiness restored, however, these countries are required to accept the IMF's tough conditionalities. In the process, and by virtue of their global reach, organisational strength, professional expertise and close connections with important governments and private banks and corporations, institutions such as the IMF and the World Bank have acquired authoritative status within the world economy.

The trend towards internationalisation and globalisation is the other factor that compounds the already considerable ambiguity surrounding the principle of sovereignty. Rapid technological change and expanding trade are perhaps the key for the process of global integration that is taking place. Innovation in transport and communication, coupled with the computerisation of knowledge, has enabled large multinational corporations to move capital and labour at lower cost and at an increased speed. The reproduction of capital now occurs primarily through global rather than purely local or national strategies. There is a world market for goods, capital and labour, and this market connects cities, countries and regions.

The fusion of industrial and financial capital could have the effect of reinforcing the global integration of economies. Multinational corporations have accumulated large stocks in banks, insurance and investment companies. For their part, banks control an increasing proportion of the world's largest corporations. As a result, the capacity of financial institutions to link diverse and distant markets could be expanded, thereby reinforcing the globalisation of capital, trade and production.

As a consequence of this, governments now can do very little to influence the global market, and local and national institutions are under severe constraints when confronted with global market forces. The bond market can, for example, pronounce instant judgement on national economic capacities and policies and compel interest rate adjustments. Unilateral decision of the value of one's money is also no longer possible.

Another illustration of the effect of international finance on sovereignty is the debt structure of many developing countries. The total external debt of all developing countries and countries in transition reached $2.2 trillion at the end of 1997 (UN, 1998: 3). Most of these states have little option but to comply with IMF conditions in order to continue receiving funds from abroad. They have to devalue their currencies, cut back on social programs, privatise public enterprises, introduce high taxes and interest rates, and so on. Failure to comply with IMF conditions would result in accumulating arrears, a drastic fall in their credit rating and the drying up of new loans from both bilateral and multilateral private and official sources. To this extent, at least, the international mobility of capital has challenged state authority, a key for the theory and practice of sovereignty.

All the above discussion should not suggest that the state is not powerful or functional. Rather it is to suggest that the state can no longer perform its functions single-handedly, and this inevitably weakens its claim for sovereignty. However, this is not necessarily a bad thing. The cooperation of states to manage transnational activities is much more a matter of pursuing national interests by cooperative methods. The state's sovereign right either to participate or not to participate in any international arrangement is always intact and the ultimate decision remains national. More importantly the enforcement of any international cooperation by and large remains national. Moreover, governments accept multilateral rules in large part in order to constrain the activities of other members of the group or to create a common set of regulatory conditions which would benefit the domestic constituency. By giving up some power of command in some areas of policy, they can effectively use their resources and increase their total command over certain other areas or national affairs in general.

To sum up, it is not therefore enough to say that multilateralisation of investment rules or liberalisation policies erode sovereignty. As the above discussion shows, firstly sovereignty has had several meanings, and secondly the process of international cooperation between states and globalisation has been eroding it for some time. Instead, it is necessary to rethink the meaning of sovereignty in the contemporary world, to what extent nation states may sacrifice their sovereign rights, and under what conditions. Giving away some sovereign rights could have both positive and negative implications for the country concerned, and hence each country needs to examine its particular situation and national priority before embarking on such judgments. They have to weigh carefully what they get from any international arrangement in return for a limited loss of sovereignty.

The Development Issue As the discussion in Chapter Six shows, some developing countries believe that FDI can contribute to their economic development only when they are capable of determining FDI's entry and conditions of operation in their countries. Some of their reasons for such a belief include the following.

- Local firms in most countries could be too weak in some sectors to compete with large foreign firms. Giving unrestricted access to foreign investors in these sectors would drive many of such local firms out of business.
- Removing the host country's ability to treat domestic investors more favourably than foreign investors would have a negative effect on domestic enterprises and perpetuate or worsen dependence on foreign firms.
- In order to avoid problems in balance-of-payments, host governments should have the ability to limit the share of foreign ownership (so that some of the

profits will be locally owned and retained) and regulate repatriation of profits (so that there will be a sizeable reinvestment of profits).

- In order to retain a meaningful measure of sovereignty over natural resources and economic activity, host countries should retain the ability to limit the degree of foreign ownership in crucial resources such as land. Land and natural resources have been seen in many countries as belonging to the citizens as a whole, and to future generations. From this perspective, the sale of land and natural resources to foreigners may be seen as the sale of the country's heritage.
- In many countries ownership of natural resources and wealth is an important political issue. If foreign investors own most of the key industries, services, infrastructure and natural resources in the country, that could give rise to public reaction which endangers domestic stability.
- Foreign ownership of the media and communications and related services is likely to lead to domination by the norms and images of other cultures and undermine the cultural identity of the host country.
- Some foreign investors may use transfer pricing manipulation which may minimise the tax revenues of the host country.

The interests of foreign investors and host developing countries do not always coincide, although they are not necessarily incompatible. While the foreign investor's primary interest is the maximisation of profits, the host country is usually interested in the development of its services and infrastructure, production of exportable goods, and continuous technological development in its industrial production and services. The removal of the government's power to screen and select FDI proposals may result in increased flow of FDI into a country. But the increase may not be in sectors to which the host country would like the investment to go. It could even be in sectors where foreign investment is not needed.

Developing countries may therefore need to retain a certain amount of power to determine the entry and conditions of operation of FDI in their territories. This does not mean that all such restrictive measures against FDI are always proper and without risk. Experience in many developing countries has shown that excessive regulation may sometimes lead to arbitrariness, incompetence and corruption (see the discussion in Chapter Two). Strict regulatory regimes could also become non-transparent. The net effect of these would be underdevelopment and poverty, rather than development and prosperity. Such regulatory powers should therefore be used with caution and transparency. It is important to recognise the positive role FDI can play in a country's development process, and hence foreign investors should be made partners of development. A country's economic development and prosperity is to the benefit of not only the citizens of that particular country, but also of foreign investors, because more economic development usually leads to more investment and profit.

On the other hand, developing countries can achieve at least some of their objectives listed above by using alternative methods rather than restricting the entry of FDI. Using these alternative methods is particularly important because they can both achieve their objectives and gain all the benefits FDI brings with it. Some of these alternative methods include the following:

- Governments can directly assist domestic enterprises to grow and become competitive. They can, for example, direct their embassies and consulates around the world to assist their domestic investors in finding markets for their exports. In this way, even a small business can link with potential customers and distribution networks around the world.
- Governments can also apply lower tax and other fiscal incentives for small domestic firms at least until they become competitive, rather than prohibiting FDI from areas where small businesses have traditionally been prominent. This will strengthen small businesses in their competition with large, often foreign owned companies, while at the same time giving them opportunity to learn from the business practices of such companies.
- Stock markets can serve as an important mechanism for diluting foreign ownership and control. Governments can require foreign investors to list in domestic stock markets. Domestic investors can then buy shares, provided that the listed shares have good earnings, thereby stopping some of the company's earnings from being repatriated. Another arrangement is that an agreement between the government and the foreign company can include a right for the government to have a "golden share" and attach certain specific rights to the government's "golden share". Such specific rights could include the right of government intervention in certain kinds of decisions by the company.
- In areas where foreign ownership is not desired for sovereignty and other reasons, like in natural resources, FDI can still be permitted through lease arrangements. Since leases introduce a time profile, eventual ownership will revert to domestic owners or the government. Other mechanisms such as production sharing contracts, exploration and development contracts, and management contracts can also be used to allow foreign investors to operate without owning the resources.
- Governments can also pass regulations which focus on specific matters that may be seen as the unwanted consequences of FDI, instead of prohibiting FDI altogether. They can, for example, regulate the appropriateness and accuracy of domestic advertising and marketing programs, consumer health and safety, environmental standards, and so on. A wide range of externalities can be directly regulated instead of imposing entry restrictions on FDI.

Generally, governments need to be open minded in their quest for ways through which they can achieve their objectives. For example, in addition to the above, they can leave some matters for firms themselves to self-regulate either voluntarily or compulsorily, with the prerogative to revert to direct regulation if firms do not live up to their expectations.[5] They can also involve NGOs in the regulatory process, especially in the preparation of guidelines for self-regulation and supervision of their execution.

Non-Governmental Organisations (NGOs)

The key international NGOs that have been playing significant roles in the debate about global regulation of FDI are the labour movement, and various environmental groups such as the World Wide Fund for nature (WWF), Friends of the Earth and Greenpeace International, and the consumer groups through Consumers International. Although the priorities of each of these groups are different, most of them seem to agree on the need for some form of global FDI regime. The following section evaluates the positions of these three players.

The Labour Movement The strategy of the international trade union movement, as manifested by the Trade Union Advisory Committee (TUAC) in their proposal to the negotiators of the MAI, is focused on ensuring universal respect for some fundamental worker's rights and improving labour standards. The rights selected as the most important are seven ILO *core* Conventions (Chapter Seven). The labour movement argues that universal respect for these seven *core* labour standards would prevent the most extreme forms of exploitation (Chapter Seven).

As the discussion in Chapter Seven shows, these rights are not fully observed by every country. In some countries workers are not allowed to form free trade unions and bargain collectively. In many developing countries, children join the work force at an early age, and they receive very little payment even when they work the same or even longer hours than adults. And of course, women are discriminated against in many parts of the world.

Having said this, the question of labour standards has been a long-standing concern in some quarters (for its history see Hanson, 1983; Alam, 1992; Charnovitz, 1987), and has both ethical and economic dimensions. The ethical argument is that "certain basic human rights are universal to mankind, and that governments everywhere should therefore be urged or may be even coerced to institute measures that will insure that these rights are available to their citizens" (Brown, 1996: 229). The economic argument says that "countries which do not guarantee and enforce these rights domestically may have an undue cost advantage in their export trade" (Brown, 1996: 230-31). Since many developing countries have lower labour standards than those prevailing in developed countries, domestic companies in the wealthy countries argue that they cannot compete effectively against imports from countries with lower labour standards. Exporters too argue that they cannot compete effectively in third markets against firms whose costs are low because of the low labour standards in the countries they produce their products (Brown, 1996: 230). This situation may force such firms to lower their costs by either substituting capital for labour, or depressing wages (depending on their market power), or relocating some of their production to countries with lower labour standards, or convincing their governments to weaken the labour standard in their countries. All of these measures could have serious political, economic and social consequences to the countries concerned.

The issue can also become complex if it is recognised that the choice of labour standards may depend on a country's stage of development and the weight attached to the different labour standards in individual countries. To avoid all this, it seems appealing to urge or require that an international minimum labour standard be set, and those countries with lower standards raise their standards to the international minimum. The real problem with such a proposal, however, is how to get consensus among the international community. Whether a substantive consensus on anything except broad principles could be achieved is therefore highly dubious.

The diversity of labour standards, to some extent at least, may be a reflection of diversity of cultural values, economic conditions, and theories concerning the moral consequences of specific labour standards. As a result, different countries may give different emphasis to different labour rights. For example, worker participation in decision-making on the plant level is more widespread in Europe than in the United States, and migrant workers are "ill-treated in United States agriculture due to grossly inadequate and corrupt enforcement" (Bhagwati, 1995: 745). Children under a certain age are not allowed to work in all developed countries, and the right to form unions is protected. On the other hand, many families in developing countries have little choice but to allow their children to work at an early age in order to survive. In some cases children make a large contribution to the family income, particularly in households facing extreme poverty and in single parent families where the mother is the sole breadwinner. Many in these countries feel that children's work is unavoidable in the face of poverty and when the alternative to it is starvation. Whether child labour should be altogether prohibited in a poor country is therefore questionable. One should also ask whether protecting children from hazardous and oppressive working conditions is perhaps more important than banning them from working altogether.

A Chinese diplomat in Geneva was among those who told me that some developing countries suspect the demand for an international minimum labour standard derives from the desire of labour unions in developed countries to protect their jobs by protecting the industries that face competition from the poor countries where labour and other production costs are cheaper. This suspicion is reinforced by the fact that none of the major OECD countries supporting the demands of the international labour movement[6] expect to be defendants in labour standard related disputes. It is therefore argued that the choice of some standards as *core* is biased against developing countries since none of the problems where many of the developed countries would be found in violation, such as worker participation in management, rights of migrants, etc. are considered as major problems (Bhagwati, 1995: 756).

The labour movement is therefore at loggerheads with both developing countries and the multinational companies that invest in those countries. Developing countries do not wish to address *core* labour standards because they fear that if they do they will lose their competitiveness in trade. MNCs do not support anything that may increase their cost of production. That is why BIAC and the powerful US Council for International Business have vigorously opposed the inclusion in the MAI of any clause on labour standards (Chapter Five). The labour movement has gained cautious support from the United States, France and other developed countries except Australia and New Zealand.

To sum up, it appears that by selecting certain ILO Conventions as *core*, the labour movement has antagonised business groups and developing countries. Given the influence business groups have on the OECD and its member governments, it was difficult to get consensus on labour standards within the OECD during the MAI negotiations. The same would be true in the WTO where developing countries oppose any such move, as evidenced at the Ministerial Conferences in Singapore and Seattle. However, these standards are issues of fundamental human rights. A formula needs to be developed to address them satisfactorily if the world is to become a fairer place to live in for all.

The Environment Movement Environmentalists worry that the increasing integration of world capital markets and the ability of investors to freely locate their capital in the region where it can earn the highest return may cause the relocation of "dirty" industries from strictly controlled countries to those with few or no environmental standards. Extensive relocation might create substantial adjustment costs for countries losing production, and environmental abuse and social costs in countries attracting polluting industries. Countries with stricter environmental standards will then have to lower their environmental standards in order to protect their competitive edge and retain investment capital, thereby resulting in a "race to the bottom". Hence, a multilateral investment agreement should address the issue of establishing international minimum environmental standards (see Chapter Seven)

Whether or not such a "race to the bottom" actually exists is contentious as we will see. But even if one assumes that there indeed exists a "race to the bottom", and hence a need for an international minimum standard, it is not clear what such a standard should be. Certainly, most developing countries will be required to introduce higher environmental standards since they are the ones with lax or no environmental control laws. But how high should they go? Even within developed countries, one does not find uniform environmental standards everywhere, and how is this going to be addressed?

Environmental standards may take many forms: standards specifying permissible levels of pollution (for example, nitrogen oxide levels in urban areas); environmentally related product standards (for example pesticide residue levels for food products); emission and effluent standards specifying permissible discharge levels for economic activity, and so on (Pearson, 1987: 114). A global investment agreement will then have to set not only one standard but many standards for the various environmental concerns. On the other hand, countries naturally have differences in the priorities they attach to the kind of environmental problem they wish to attack, arising from their particular circumstances. Mexicans may want to worry more about clean water than their richer American neighbours who may want to spend their money on clean air. Hence, finding the right formulae to address these issues is not an easy task, and the environmentalists do not provide one.

For the argument about the "race to the bottom" to hold, it is essential that the empirical evidence shows that (a) FDI is in fact responsive to the difference in environmental standards between countries and (b) different countries actually compete to attract FDI by lowering their environmental standards. Without the presence of empirical evidence proving the existence of these two, the argument about the "race to the bottom" will only be theoretical.

Examination of the available literature does not provide strong empirical evidence proving such a "race to the bottom". Duerksen and Leonard (1980: 52-58) examined United States trade and investment data to determine if environmental factors have influenced investment decisions. Their findings were that:

a) US foreign investment in pollution-intensive industries grew no more rapidly than for all manufacturing industries;
b) Host countries that received most of the FDI in pollution-prone industries such as chemicals, paper, metals, and petroleum refining were other industrial countries, not developing countries;
c) US import of products manufactured by pollution-intensive industries grew at about the same rate as total imports.

They therefore concluded that there is no credible evidence that strict environmental regulations have caused widespread relocation of United States industries to countries where environmental regulations are lax or non-existent. They however found that environmental regulations may have motivated relocation in those industries producing highly toxic products such as, asbestos, benzidine dyes, and a few pesticides and those processing copper, zinc and lead.

A survey by the United States General Accounting Office (Levinson, 1996: 234), which reported on the relocation of wood-furniture firms from Los Angeles to Mexico, however, had a different finding. It found that, of those wood-furniture manufacturers that relocated to Mexico from 1988 to 1991, 83% identified labour costs as a significant factor, while 78% identified pollution control costs. Stafford and his colleagues also analysed relocation of investments within the United States. Their conclusion was that environmental factors were more important in the 1980s than the 1970s but were still not major location determinants, that the speed and efficiency of the permit-granting process is important, and that environmental factors may influence siting within a region (Cited in Pearson, 1987: 122).

In another study, Knodgen (1987) examined the relationship between environmental laws and industrial siting, with a view to identifying relocation of West German FDI in developing countries. Her findings indicated that there was no evidence that West German firms have reallocated production in any major way to developing countries with lax or no environmental regulation. In response to an open ended question as to the companies' investment motives, only one company (a chemical manufacturer) responded that environmental regulations played a role, but only as the least important of the seven considerations it mentioned (Cited in Pearson, 1987: 122-23).

UNCTAD surveyed 794 companies with sales of over $1 billion during the summer of 1990. According to the survey, differences across plants in their environmental practices seem to be affected more by home-country regulations than host-country regulations. "Many of the companies surveyed claimed that they would not only comply with all local laws, but would write their own company policies if local laws were thought to be inadequate" (Levinson, 1996: 435).

To sum up, there is very little evidence showing a systematic tendency of governments lowering environmental standards in order to attract or retain investment capital and foreign companies responding positively. It is true that countries, or even state governments in federal arrangements, provide various sorts of incentives to investors in their attempt to outbid their competitors in attracting investors. But this game is almost universally played, not by allowing firms to pollute freely, but instead through tax breaks and holidays, and other grants (see Chapter Three for the various types of incentives provided to investors).

The Consumer Movement Consumers International, has proposed that an international investment agreement should:

- commit states to adopt and/or effectively apply national competition laws along the lines of UNCTAD's Set of Multilaterally Agreed Equitable Principles and Rules for Control of Restrictive Business Practices,
- encourage governments to target investment incentives and avoid competitive bidding for investment through the provision of excessive incentives,
- incorporate binding provisions ensuring domestic health, safety, labour and environmental standards will not be lowered in order to attract or retain FDI,
- respect the right of developing countries to screen and select FDI proposals.

Parallel to this, it encouraged companies to adopt its voluntary Consumer Charter for Global Business. The main areas Consumers International wants the international agreement to address are competition policy, corporate practice, and consumer protection.

Most of the problems raised by the consumer groups can be and are being addressed by national laws. Many developing countries do not still have competition policies, but the trend is that more and more countries are adopting such policies with the technical assistance they get from UNCTAD (Chapter Seven).

An international agreement controlling international Mergers and Acquisitions (M&A), international cartels, and strategic alliances is among the priorities for CI. These activities are not internationally banned, and countries have different national laws controlling these activities. Given the diversity of national approaches to competition policy appropriate to different types of economies, harmonisation on anything more than extremely broad principles seems unlikely and undesirable.

The free flow of FDI can act as an effective device for ensuring competition. It can create welfare gains to the domestic consumer by acting against entrenched monopolies and lowering prices. It can also have the potential of replacing one monopolistic firm by another. This situation can easily be avoided by introducing competition laws and effectively implementing them, without retaining restrictive investment laws.

Conclusion

The debate on the global regulation of FDI has been hot particularly in the past five years. Most of the key international players give their support for some sort of a global framework. None have however come up with a formula that has general support.

The discussion throughout the book demonstrates that the positions of each of the key players have their own limitations. Developed countries would argue for a liberalised global investment regime. But there does not seem to exist a consensus among themselves to how far the liberalisation should go. The fallout from the MAI negotiations has clearly shown this. Some developing countries oppose extensive liberalisation, others do not. They know that the alternative to extensive liberalisation is not extensive regulation, but they are not sure to what extent they should deregulate. The NGOs too do not have a consensus position on the key issues. They do not like the push for extensive liberalisation, but they do not have an alternative model.

While in the 1960s and 1970s attitudes towards FDI in most countries were hostile or sceptical, these attitudes have largely changed since the 1980s. Countries have become increasingly appreciative of the benefits that can be gained from FDI. This situation would suggest that there is a better chance now than ever before for the realisation of a global investment regime. Despite this, however, there are still serious differences between the major international players. Differences arise both on the process of negotiating the agreement and on its substantive content.

The MAI negotiation process excluded most of the key stakeholders. Unless the major stakeholders are involved in such a process, it is unlikely that any such agreement would become workable. The participation of the major stakeholders in the process brings the opportunity to address the main concerns associated with FDI and build widespread support for the agreement. In this regard, an agreement whose main pre-occupation is liberalisation may not be the answer. Similarly, a regime that gives extensive regulatory powers to states may not build economies.

Neither liberalisation nor regulation may be a solution for the economic and social problems of a country. It cannot be assumed that either liberalisation or regulation is necessarily good or bad for growth and development, for all countries, under all circumstances, conditions and levels of development. Both liberalisation and regulation can have positive and negative aspects. Hence, a county's FDI regime should be designed to meet its peculiar needs at any particular time. As the needs of the country concerned change, so should its policies and laws.

A balance needs to be struck between regulation and liberalisation. This book describes the balanced option as "regulated openness" at both the global and national level. What is meant by regulated openness and how it might work will be the subject of discussion in the next Chapter.

Notes

1 For a review of these theories, see Pitelis (1996).
2 The documentary entitled "ELF Oil" was broadcast on SBS Channel (Special Broadcasting Service) on 12 April 200, at 8:30 pm.
3 Mr Sassou Nguessou is the person who overthrew Mr Lissouba in a bloody coup d'etat.
4 For more discussion on this, see Wight (1979); Morgenthau (1978).
5 The next Chapter discusses how this works.
6 During the MAI negotiations, only Australia, New Zealand and Mexico opposed TUAC's proposal.

Chapter 10

Regulated Openness

In the previous Chapter, the positions of each major international player on global regulation of FDI have been analysed. The analysis has revealed that some actors advocate a liberal investment regime while others see stricter rules as better. The analysis has also revealed that both liberal and restrictive investment regimes have their own serious shortcomings, and that none of them, taken separately, may be the best way of regulating FDI globally. The purpose of this Chapter is to explore an alternative approach in the regulation of FDI, called "regulated openness", which seeks to preserve the strengths and cover the shortcomings we have uncovered in each model.

As revealed in Chapter Five (in relation to the MAI) and in Chapter Eight (in relation to the now defunct UN Code of Conduct for Multinational Enterprises), the current approach in attempting to formulate an international regime for FDI has serious flaws, both in the manner the negotiations are conducted and the substantive content of the rules. Regarding the manner of the negotiations, both the MAI and the UN Code of Conduct have to some extent excluded major international players from participating in the negotiations, although it was more so in the MAI than in the UN Code of Conduct. Regarding the substantive content of the rules, both are similar in attempting to create comprehensive rules. But the MAI was seen by developing countries and most NGOs as too liberal, while the UN Code of Conduct was seen by major capital exporting countries such as the US as too restrictive. "Regulated openness" is a hybrid position where the interests and concerns of all major international players might be accommodated in a balanced and pragmatic way, both regarding the manner in which the negotiations would be conducted and the substantive content of the rules.

The Chapter consists of two major parts. The first discusses the structure of the rules both at the international and national levels, and the content of the rules at the international level. The second part covers the process of negotiating the international agreement, venue, and implementation of the rules. Before embarking on these two major parts, we consider the definition of "regulated openness".

Definition

Regulated openness has a substantive and a procedural dimension. Substantively, regulated openness means an investment regime which seeks to allow both regulation and openness co-exist in a balanced and pragmatic manner. It implies a balance between regulation and liberalisation in the major issues of investment regulation. Procedurally, it is a process where all major stakeholders would have an input and role in the preparation and implementation of FDI laws.

The effort to devise a global investment agreement has stimulated discussion and heated debate ever since the failure of the International Trade Organisation in 1948 (Braithwaite & Drahos, 2000) and other related proposals. In Chapter Eight we said that there have been a number of sticking points in the discussions. Critical among them has been, should the rules be binding or voluntary? What should be the substantive content of the rules? How comprehensive should they be? Who should make the rules? Where should the rules be made? And who will be the enforcement agency at the international level?

Under "regulated openness", the proposed solution to the above problems is as follows. Regarding the structure of the rules, a binding international framework agreement on principles is a more pragmatic solution than comprehensive rules. Once the framework agreement of core principles has been formed, each country would have its own detailed rules consistent with the internationally agreed principles and the priorities of individual countries. These national and self-regulatory initiatives would be subject to reporting to ICSID and periodic review by a committee of experts to evaluate compliance with the investment principles. At the national level, self-regulation by business would be encouraged except in those activities where the government decides to have direct regulation. The international negotiation of the principles would have been conducted by governments, but key non-governmental international players should be consulted and given opportunities to contribute to the formulation of the principles. At the national level, too, committees consisting of representatives from business, communities and government might be formed with a task of evaluating and approving self-regulation rules prepared by firms. It is proposed to hold the negotiation of the international agreement within the framework of UNCTAD and entrust the implementation of it to ICSID. All these features will be discussed in more detail in the following sections of the Chapter.

Structure and Substantive Content of the Rules

Core International Principles, not Comprehensive Rules

One of the lessons one learns from past negotiations on comprehensive international investment regimes is that it is practically impossible to reconcile the conflicting interests of the major international players. The most recent example is the collapse of the MAI negotiations (see discussion in Chapter Five). A new approach is therefore needed. The principles that are considered very important by all major stakeholders would be put on the negotiating table, and those *core* principles on which agreement can be reached could form the international regime. Then each country would be empowered to introduce its own rules that elaborate those principles depending on its particular situation and priorities.

The main advantage of an international regime of principles rather than detailed rules is that it would give flexibility to individual countries to manage their own affairs based on their priorities and economic and social objectives, while at the same time seeking some form of internationally agreed framework, thereby giving certainty to investors. The certainty arises at two levels – at the level of national rules, and at the level of certainty that national rules cannot be changed to flout the principles in the international agreement. Moreover, as the global agreement would be less detailed, the likelihood of countries agreeing to sign increases, further increasing rather than decreasing certainty for investors.

A global regime of core principles facilitates the recognition of the need for economic pluralism in international economic agreements. A tolerance for economic pluralism requires the recognition that different goals, economic conditions and cultures throughout the world require different solutions to problems. One system will not serve the needs of all people in all circumstances. An attempt to impose uniform economic and social policy worldwide creates impossible positions for people in countries that have vastly different problems and resources, in addition to different values and goals. For example, the competition policy needed for a large economy with many strong competitors is very different from that required in a small economy with few strong firms. Even within large developed economies there are different models of successful capitalism which require very different competition policies. For example, Soskice's (1999) comparative capitalism project shows how business-coordinated market economies (e.g. Germany, Switzerland, Japan) require a different kind of competition policy from liberal market economies (e.g. US, UK, Ireland). If, on the other hand, the global agreement is based on principles, and detailed rules are left for each country to make in line with the principles, particular solutions can often be found for the particular regulatory problems of each country.

Commercial and technological realities change very rapidly in today's world, and economic entities have to continually adapt to such changes. In this regard, comprehensive global investment rules could inhibit change, for legal institutions are designed to be stable and predictable. An agreement on principles rather than comprehensive rules would avoid this problem, for it could leave room for flexibility by the regulators and the regulated.

One of the serious deficiencies of the MAI was that it assumed a liberal investment regime is beneficial to all countries, at all times, and at any level of economic development. Chapters Five, Nine and Ten concluded that this is not correct, and a liberal model of investment rules is just one model. A global regime of core principles rather than detailed rules can solve the problem of choosing either a more restrictive or a more open investment regime. It gives opportunity for every country to decide for themselves on the extent of restrictiveness or openness of the rules they want to have in their own respective territories.

Core Principles for the Major Players There are certain issues that each of the players wants addressed in a global investment agreement (see Chapters Five, Six and Seven for details). These issues are being summarised in table 10:1. One can see from the table that only on the issue of MFN have all the players taken a common position. For most of the issues, developing countries and NGOs take similar positions while business representatives and developed countries form a united front.

National Treatment

The granting of National Treatment to foreign investors is a great worry for many developing countries and NGOs. This is not, however, because these groups are against the principle of liberalisation, but because they believe that hasty and excessive liberalisation could result in a total loss of control on the activities of foreign investors, most of whom are big multinational corporations. Developing countries want foreign investment to contribute to their development endeavours. A Chinese diplomat in Geneva told me "any FDI agreement must be one that takes into account the developmental dimension. It should be one that makes contributions to the development of developing countries" (see Chapter Six). These countries believe that this can only be done if they retain the power to select among investment proposals and channel FDI according to their developmental priorities. They recognise the benefits of FDI, but then they also do not want to lose their ability to control and direct it. This includes the ability to introduce new policies and laws when the need arises. Hence, their strong opposition to the standstill and rollback approach of the MAI.

The environmentalists too believe that hasty liberalisation may result in the environment being damaged by some irresponsible investors. Consumer advocates believe that liberalisation could result in more competition, more choices to consumers, and cheaper prices. But they also believe that liberalisation could endanger consumer safety if it is not accompanied by appropriate consumer safety regulations. Hence, what all of these groups say is a cautious approach to liberalisation is preferable to hasty liberalisation.

Table 10:1 Issues to be Addressed in a Global Investment Agreement and the Respective Positions of the Key Players

	BL	Dev'ed Countries	Dev'ing Countries	LM	EM	CI
National Treatment	For	For	Against	---------	Against	Against
MFN*	For	For	For	For	For	For
No Performance Requirements	For	For	Against	--------	Against	Against
Labour Standards	Against	Mixed	Against	For	For	-------
Environmenta l Standards	Against	Mixed	Against	For	For	For
Investor-State Dispute Settlement Procedure	For	For	Against	Against	Against	Against
Standstill	For	For	Against	Against	Against	Against
Rollback	For	Mixed	Against	Against	Against	Against
Broad Def. of Expropriation	For	For	Against	Against	Against	Against
Human Rights	Against	Mixed	Against	For	For	For
Consumer Protection	Against	Against	---------	For	For	For
Competition Policy	Against	Against	--------	For	For	For
Corporate Conduct	Against	Against	For	For	For	For
Transfer Pricing	Against	Against	For	For	For	For
Technology Transfer	Against	Against	For	For	For	For
Unrestricted Movement of Key personnel	For	For	Against	---------	Against	For
No Restriction on Currency Transfer	For	For	Against	--------	---------	Against

***MFN** = Most-Favoured-Nation Treatment

Keys: BL = Business Lobby; LM = Labour Movement; EM = Environment Movement; CI = Consumers International

Consensus Issues:

- free transfer of funds, except in circumstances where there is a balance-of-payments problem;
- no expropriation, except for the public purpose and against the payment of prompt, adequate and effective compensation.

Performance Requirements

The abolition of performance requirements is the other issue that has polarised the major players. This is again because developing countries and the NGOs believe that it would limit the host country's ability to make the most out of FDI, namely the transfer of technology and knowhow, employment generation, and so on. Furthermore, environmentalists and consumer advocates see the need to impose environmental and consumer safety standards, respectively, on investors, whether domestic or foreign. Similarly, labour groups want to respect core labour standards. There seems to be no opposition if certain performance requirements, such as the ones addressed under the Trade Related Investment Measures (TRIMs) or the WTO, be abolished, but complete abolition of them is not acceptable to these groups.

Labour, Environmental and Human Rights Standards

Interestingly, developing countries and business representatives have a common position on issues of labour standards, environmental standards, and human rights. Developing countries reject the inclusion of these three issues in a global investment agreement mainly on grounds of maintaining their comparative advantage as providers of cheaper labour. Business representatives, such as the Business and Industry Advisory Council of the OECD (BIAC), believe that the observance of basic human rights and improvement of working conditions around the world can best be achieved by encouraging the flow of goods and services to facilitate economic growth (see Chapter Seven). Moreover, although the ILO, the Trade Union Advisory Council of the OECD (TUAC) and the International Confederation of Free Trade Unions (ICFTU) have selected seven ILO Conventions as *core* (see Chapter Seven), business representatives argue that it would be very difficult, if not impossible, to define a set of international labour standards which would be acceptable to all countries. This is particularly true with the abolition of child labour. Hence, business representatives suggest that progress in improvement in working conditions must be determined in accordance with the economic development in each country, and must respect the right of countries to decide when and how to apply labour standards (see Chapter Seven). On the other hand, while developed countries have a somewhat united position on human rights, they seem to be divided on the issue of labour standards and the environment.

Consumer Protection

Most countries, particularly developed countries, have laws on consumer protection. However, developed countries and business representatives are opposed to the idea of addressing consumer protection issues in investment agreements. Their usual argument is that an agreement on investment cannot be expected to address every issue connected to investment; consumer protection should be in the domain of national sovereignty.

Effective Dispute Settlement

The procedure of settling investment-related disputes is the other polarising issue, as is the issue of corporate conduct. Developing countries and NGOs reject the idea of binding investor-state dispute settlement by an international tribunal, mainly on the ground of national sovereignty. Business representatives, on the other hand complain that some countries do not have an impartial, reliable and efficient court system, which is true in the case of many developing countries. While developed countries and business representatives oppose incorporating binding clauses in the agreement on corporate conduct, developing countries and NGOs insist this is essential on the ground that any corporate rights and privileges the agreement provides should be matched by corporate obligations.

Consensus Issues

Some of the issues are less controversial than others. There is, for instance, agreement on the free transfer of funds, except in circumstances where there are balance-of-payments constraints, in which case a temporary halt may be permitted. There is also consensus on the principle of not expropriating private property except in certain internationally recognised circumstances and against the payment of compensation. There is however disagreement on the appropriate wording of the expropriation provision.

Core Principles under Regulated Openness

As has been said earlier, one of the problems in reaching agreement on global investment lies inn the detailed nature of the draft agreement. Under regulated openness, it is suggested that all the issues listed above, and more, could be covered by the following six core principles. These are:

- Sustainable development
- Investment security
- Core Labour standards
- Consumer Protection and Business Ethics
- Good governance
- Effective dispute settlement

The following section will elaborate how regulated openness works against these core principles, addressing the concerns of each player in a quest for balance and pragmatism and a framework that enables the analytic weaknesses of one position to be covered with the strength of another.

Sustainable Development

The right to development is a right recognised as one aspect of human rights. Article 1 of the UN Declaration on the Right to Development (1986) states that:

> The right to development is an inalienable human right by virtue of which every human person and all peoples are entitled to participate in, contribute to, and enjoy economic, social, cultural and political development, in which all human rights and fundamental freedoms can be fully realised.

The Declaration also states that "states have the right and the duty to formulate appropriate national development policies" (Art. 2(3)) and that "sustained action is required to promote rapid development of developing countries" (Art. 3(1)). It is therefore essential to address this right in any investment agreement.

Foreign Direct Investment can play a key role in the development of a country. It can also damage a country in many ways. This is the least disputed fact. The fundamental question is, however, whether or not countries should retain the right and power to restrict the entry of certain types of investments into their markets and, once the investments have been allowed to enter, should they impose performance requirements on the investor.

A focus on sustainable development would emphasise the importance of country-specific, rather than universal, policy packages and rules. In contrast to one particular model of policy or rule, such as liberalisation or excessive regulation, sustainable development should be based on achieving multiple, interacting objectives, including sustainable resource use, technology transfer, employment generation, income growth, human resource development and social cohesion. Every type of FDI may not be useful for this purpose, and countries should have the right and power to screen investment proposals; encourage investment that will contribute to sustainable development, transferring technology, generating employment; and refuse entry to investments that are likely to harm local communities and destroy the environment.

Sustainable development is a consensus international principle that critics could say is vague. This vagueness is a virtue in context where what is needed is a framework of principles that allow nation by nation adoption of the principle, yet which also allows more specificity of content to be injected into the principle over time. We conclude this section suggesting that a protocol might ultimately be fleshed out to list forms of restrictions on investment that are arbitrary in the sense of not capable of being defended in terms of the principle of sustainable development. The list would expand over time but would never expand so far as for example to prevent a poor country from imposing a technology transfer performance requirement as a condition of a particular investment. The idea is to give business and developed countries what they want in terms of the liberalisation of investment, but gradually, in a way that enables developing countries incrementally to learn where they can throw the door open and how they can gradually narrow their selectivity of intervention in the interests of both their own people and the interests of foreign investors.

Recent history has seen that successive theories on the most appropriate policies for development have been adopted and abandoned. Development theory has embraced approaches such as import substitution, state ownership, socialism, endogenous growth, export-led growth, infant-industry protection, liberalisation, and so on. Yet the MAI attempted to lock signatories to a particular model of development. It prohibits the adoption of policies to protect national economies from possible instabilities that may follow capital liberalisation, as has been seen in the Asian financial crisis. Most developing countries do not have the protection afforded by a large economy or powerful common currency area. Therefore, in order to sustain their development, it is absolutely essential for developing countries to retain the power to introduce responsive measures when the need arises.

Sustainable development would embrace many of the prescriptions of current structural adjustment, including abandonment of resource depleting input and output measures and innovation through liberalisation measures. However, it would add regulatory policies that internalise environmental costs in market prices and that manage production processes within ecological limits. To ensure that economic growth stays within ecological limits, enforceable environmental management policies must be in place in step with liberalisation. In short, sustainable development should be seen as a way of optimising maximum economic growth with ecological and environmental constraints.

Sustainable development requires greater attention to the improvement of internal capacity. Foreign investment should not be taken as a substitute for developing a base for domestically owned business enterprises. Development can be sustained when foreign investment complements indigenous industries. Host countries, therefore, have to be able to select the type of foreign investment that is suitable to their development objectives and priorities at any given period of time. It is hard to see how the contextual optimisation of sustainable development could be attained without imposing performance requirements on investors, such as technology transfer, environmental standards and employment conditions.

Such restrictions, however, can and should be the exceptions rather than the rule. Regulated openness implies that countries should endeavour to liberalise their investment regime, since the positives of FDI outweigh its negatives. National Treatment and MFN would be the rule rather than the exception. In other words, the presumption should be that host country investment regimes are open, not restrictive. However, it is a presumption whose effects on sustainable development should be monitored and can be restricted if it militates against sustainable development. Therefore, save for the purpose of sustainable development (and a few other reasons discussed later), host countries would generally maintain an open investment regime.

A country's development policy and laws could change with time. The international trend suggests that the more countries develop the more they liberalise their investment laws. Hence, host countries should endeavour to continuously improve their openness policies. As their domestic capabilities improve, they should open their markets for more competition. Improvement in domestic capability should lead to the gradual abolition of restrictions on foreign investment.

This arrangement creates a win-win situation for all the major stakeholders. Developing countries and NGOs get what they want, that is, the right of host countries to regulate FDI and use it for their development. Foreign investors too win from this arrangement because they will not be discriminated against for being a foreigner. If the restriction placed on them were arbitrary and not related to sustainable development (and the limited list of reasons discussed later), that action by the host country could be challenged through the dispute settlement mechanism. An optional protocol listing actions that may be acceptable on the ground of sustainable development may be attached to the Agreement. If that is done, any host country regulation that is against the protocol or its spirit may be taken as a breach of the Agreement. Moreover, since countries could be required to gradually abolish restrictions as their development progresses, any current restrictions could only be temporary.

Investment Security

No investor is willing to invest in a place where the security of its investment is in danger. Lack of a clear set of rules governing the security of a firm's investment once it is made raises the cost of investment through, among other things, raising the risk premium. It can also lead to misunderstandings between the foreign investor and the host government, which may discourage future investments.

There appears to exist a consensus among the major players on the need to provide adequate security to foreign investment. All of the bilateral investment treaties, which number over one thousand, contain provisions on investment protection (security). All the major stakeholders interviewed for this research agree on the need to address this issue in a global investment agreement. The disagreement, however, lies in the wording for best addressing the problem.

The clause on investment security would oblige host countries not to expropriate private property, except for a public purpose, on a non-discriminatory basis, and against the payment of prompt, adequate and effective compensation. Expropriation could be "direct" or "indirect". "Direct" expropriation means the taking of property by the government through explicitly declared expropriatory measures. "Indirect" expropriation refers to the taking of property through all those measures whose undeclared purpose is expropriation. Although what constitutes "indirect" expropriation is sometimes controversial, there are already some judgements made by international tribunals (such as the US-Iran Claims Tribunal) that help clarify it.

The NAFTA and MAI attempt to expand the meaning of expropriation beyond the traditional dichotomy of "direct" and "indirect" expropriation. Under these two Agreements, "any measure or measures having the equivalent effect" of direct or indirect expropriation would be considered as expropriation. The test here is the "effect" of the measure, not its intended purpose. This dramatically expands the scope of the term, and its ramifications could be enormous. For example, a regulatory measure whose effect is the reduction of the value of the property of a foreign investor or its income, however unintended that may be, could give rise to a claim for compensation on the ground of expropriation. This has already happened in Canada when the parliament of that country enacted a law banning the production and transportation of a gasoline additive called MMT on health grounds. Ethyl corporation, which was apparently affected by this new law, sued the Canadian government for damages worth $C250 million, on the ground that the introduction of the new law had the equivalent effect of expropriation.

Governments may attempt to expropriate private property through various indirect ways such as through discriminatory and excessive taxation. Such measures could, however, be covered by the term "indirect" expropriation. The elastic phrase "measures having equivalent effect..." would not clarify the term, but it complicates the issue further. It also significantly limits governments' regulatory power. As a result, most governments, particularly in the developing world, would not be willing to sign an agreement with such an open-ended clause on expropriation.

The investment security provision needs to guarantee the repatriation of funds from the host country. This guarantee, however, cannot be absolute in the sense that whenever there is a balance-of-payments crisis, a temporary halt of such transfers may be needed. This is quite a reasonable position especially in light of recurrent financial turmoil around many parts of the world. Investment security should also include the protection of the property of investors from armed conflict and civil disturbances and other similar events. The approach adopted here would enable an agreement which would substantially increase investment security, dramatically reducing the cost of insurance against the residual risks, without opening up new litigation exposures which may entail unsustainable costs for many developing countries.

Core Labour Standards

There is increasing competition between countries to attract foreign investment. Trade unions fear that this international competition could lead to increasing downward pressure on wages, working conditions and labour standards. Some call this "the race to the bottom" (see Chapter Seven).

Employment is among the most important issues connected with FDI. It is therefore essential that a global investment agreement addresses the concerns of the labour movement. However, there is a problem in defining a set of international labour standards that would be acceptable to all countries and be practical to implement. As the table on page 197 shows, developing countries, supported by business representatives, are not prepared to sign an agreement that sets minimum labour standards (see also Chapter Six). In the negotiation for the MAI, the issue of labour standards was discussed in conjunction with environmental standards. Some OECD countries want to separate the two and, if possible, ignore labour standards altogether (see Chapter Five). On the other hand, the labour movement has selected seven ILO Conventions as *core* and seeks an international investment agreement to address them.

Some of these standards are more controversial than others (Chapter Nine). Many countries therefore don't seem to be ready to bind themselves to implement these standards. It is however possible to take these core labour standards as principles and allow countries to translate them into law based on their particular situations. This can be done in three ways. Firstly, each country could make a binding undertaking not to lower its labour standards below those that prevail at the signing of the agreement. This would help stop any perceived "race to the bottom". Secondly, countries may be allowed to reject investment proposals made by firms that are known for breaching the seven core labour standards in another country. In other words, national treatment, which will be a presumption in the agreement, becomes a privilege that may be denied for those firms who do not respect the core labour standards. The fact that a host country can deny a foreign firm entry into its territory for breach of these standards elsewhere might encourage investors to become cautious in their workplace practices. Thirdly, countries would be asked to undertake to continuously improve their labour standards with the aim of achieving the full implementation of the seven core labour standards. Each year, signatories would be required to ratchet their standards a little higher that in the previous year. The international trend shows that labour standards improve as a country's economic development improves. Workers in economically advanced countries have more rights and higher payments than those in economically less advanced countries.

One of the fears most countries have is that setting binding minimum labour standards amounts to the global harmonisation of labour laws. Approaching the issue in the way proposed above would alleviate this fear. It would also eliminate the fear of the "race to the bottom". The simultaneous application of the continuous improvement principle and the host country's right to discriminate against those firms which breach these standards elsewhere might ensure long run meaningful compliance. This is a win-win situation for developed and developing nations, though it is win-lose for long-run redistribution from owners of business to labour. The combination of a right to prohibit investor entry for violation of labour standards and capacity building for monitoring continuous improvement would deliver labour movement objections without allowing trade sanctions against countries that allowed child labour to sustain poor families or that had very low minimum wages.

Consumer Protection and Business Ethics

Consumer advocates under the umbrella of Consumers International argue that any global investment agreement needs to address the issues of consumer protection, competition and the conduct of multinational firms (see Chapter Seven). It seems just that universal access of investors to the world's consumers should result in universal obligations for minimum protection for consumers. Poor nations that cannot afford adequate consumer protection should not have to expose their consumers to dumping of unsafe products banned by wealthier states as a result of signing the agreement. Nor is it just that consumers be exposed to monopoly power as a result of liberalisation that opens the door to monopolisation by global investors.

Many countries around the globe have consumer protection and competition laws. Despite this fact, however, a number of countries are not interested in addressing the issue in an international investment agreement. The usual argument is that an investment agreement cannot address everything connected to an investment, and that consumer protection and competition issues are better addressed by national laws. However, there are many countries that do not yet have such laws. Secondly, even in countries where such laws exist, often times their implementation is extremely limited. An investment agreement could address these problems in two ways. Firstly, signatories could be required to make a binding undertaking to introduce national consumer protection and competition laws. This should not create much of a problem, for many countries already have such laws. Secondly, countries bound by the treaty could also be required to make an undertaking to continuously improve their national consumer protection and competition laws. It is also possible to attach to the agreement the UN Guidelines for Consumer Protection and the UN Rules on Restrictive Business Practices to serve as guidance in their effort to improve their consumer protection and competition laws. Moreover, third parties such as consumer advocates and NGOs need to be given the right to bring to task those firms that violate such laws. This could ensure that the laws were implemented effectively, even when governments are reluctant to implement them. NGOs do not usually have the resources to take to court or an international tribunal every foreign investor that infringes these laws. However, the existence of the right alone could deter investors from violating the laws.

The issue of business ethics is stickier. As table 10:1 shows, both developed countries and business representatives are strongly opposed to including any binding clause in an investment agreement. Under the current circumstances, it appears the chance of states signing a binding agreement with clauses on business ethics in it is extremely slim.

On the other hand, it has been demonstrated on various occasions that domestic laws alone, particularly in developing countries, may sometimes become ineffective in regulating the conduct of multinational companies (see Chapters Six and Seven). The argument for the international regulation of corporate conduct therefore has strong validity, at least for weaker nations. Given the current diametrically opposite positions of countries on whether and how to regulate corporate conduct, one pragmatic compromise position would be the following. The compromise starts from the assumption that it is not feasible to have a binding clause on corporate conduct in the investment agreement. Instead, a protocol on a minimum standard of corporate conduct (such as the OECD Guidelines for Multinational Enterprises) could be attached to the agreement. Secondly, it could allow states to discriminate against the investment proposals of those firms that are known or proved not to satisfy those minimum standards. Thirdly, third parties such as consumer, environmental or other NGOs could be allowed to bring action against both states and/or firms when states fail to take action against irresponsible firms.

Such an arrangement could make firms behave responsibly without the need to impose on them any binding international obligation regarding their conduct. At the same time, it gives power to states to address the issue of corporate conduct. If and when states fail to exercise this power for whatever reason, NGOs can intervene and bring both states and firms to task. This would discourage firms from trying to convince states through corruption or other means not to exercise their power.[1] Moreover, attaching to the agreement a separate non-binding protocol on agreed minimum standards of corporate conduct would prevent states from setting arbitrary standards just for the sake of discriminating against foreign investors. Both protectionist abuse of state power in the interests of domestic firms and captured or corrupt abuse of state power in the interests of multinationals would be contestable under an appropriate dispute resolution mechanism for the treaty.

Good Governance

Good governance is increasingly becoming the buzzword in various international fora. It is now manifestly present in bilateral and multilateral development cooperation agreements between developed and developing countries, and the donor community is showing a growing interest in the principles of good governance. In 1991, the European Community adopted a resolution that stipulates four pre-requisites for achieving balanced and sustainable development in developing countries.[2] One of the pre-requisites is good governance, the others being human rights, democracy and reduction of excessive military spending. The World Bank too has made it one of the factors it considers when approving development loans. On the other hand, good governance still does not have a universally accepted meaning. It addresses the quality of government covering social policy, democracy, transparency, creation of a market friendly environment, combating corruption, and human rights.[3] We now address each of these in turn.

Social Policy

Social policy affects the well being of individuals and it is not something that must be left to the market. The UN Declaration on Social Progress and Development states:

> Each government has the primary role and ultimate responsibility of ensuring the social progress and well-being of its people, of planning social development measures as part of comprehensive development plans, of encouraging and coordinating or integrating all national efforts towards

> this end and of introducing necessary changes in the social structure...(UN General Assembly Resolution XXIV, 11 December, 1969).

International collaboration could contribute to the promotion of social policy. Parties to the Lome IV Convention, for example, have agreed that structural adjustment support should, *inter alia*, "improve the social and economic well-being of the population as a whole" (Art.243 of Lome IV Convention).[4]

Democracy

A large number of authoritarian regimes have introduced some form of democratic institutions in their nations after the collapse of the cold war. Since democracy is a process, it will take time before these become fully-fledged democratic nations. It is, however, important to make sure that there is always a step forward, not backward, in the democratic process in those countries. One way of doing this is making good governance an internationally recognised duty of states.

Corruption

Corruption seriously undermines sustainable economic development because it favours inefficient economic decision-making and enhances unequal distribution of development gains. Foreign aid structural adjustment plans imposed by donors on developing countries fail to alleviate poverty partly because corruption has invaded the economic and political decision-making process of those countries. Many countries have declared corruption illegal and have set up institutions to control and combat corruption. However, these institutions themselves are not sometimes immune from corruption. This is particularly so in a large number of developing countries.

The experience of some countries such as Singapore shows that it is possible to remove at least the backbone of corruption even in the most unpromising situation. To effect this, political leaders cultivate good governance through:

- accountability of government officials and bureaucrats for public funds and exercise of power;
- transparency in procedures, investment decisions, contracts and appointments;
- rule of law.

Corruption is not a national issue only, but is also an international issue. Multinational corporations offer bribes or use other corrupt means to win valuable contracts. Because of lack of effective anti-corruption agencies in many developing countries, much of the corruptly acquired money could fly out of those countries to be deposited safely in banks in other countries. It is therefore important to form an effective international system that monitors corrupt international business practice, both at the MNC level and the level of States.

Human Rights Human rights is one of the most controversial issues in international fora. There are many developing countries that see the concept of human rights as an arrogant attempt by the West to impose Western values and culture on their societies. For example, the debate at the tenth Non-Aligned Movement Summit, held in Jakarta in 1992 on human rights was focused, almost entirely, on formulating a strategy and rationale for resisting pressure for human rights improvement. In his opening address to the Summit, President Suharto, the former President of Indonesia, stated:

> Each nation has its own culture, economic system, norms, and the right to maintain and implement its own definition of rights.

Human rights is a legal concept recognised by international law. Consequently, the rules of international law do address the correlation between human rights and other concepts of international law, such as sovereignty.[5] This puts legal limits to what a state can and cannot do to its own citizens in respect of human rights, and it may not be possible to argue that human rights is essentially within the jurisdiction of states. Under contemporary international law, state sovereignty is not absolute (see Chapter Nine), and states are duty bound to respect the universally recognised human rights.

Multinational corporations are often accused of violating human rights, or collaborating with governments that violate human rights, particularly in developing countries (see Chapter Nine). In relation to this, it is sometimes asked whether it might be desirable to impose on multinationals the legal, or at least ethical, duty and obligation to protect human rights. This does not seem to be feasible in the current circumstances for the reasons discussed earlier. However, some prominent multinational corporations have, in the past few years, been taking unilateral, but significant, measures which may contribute to the improvement of human rights in host countries. In 1992, Sears, Roebuck and Co. announced that it would not import products produced by prison or other involuntary labour in China, and established a monitoring procedure to ensure compliance with its policy (Steiner and Alston, 1996: 871). In the same year, Reebok adopted a human rights code of conduct governing workplace conditions in all of its overseas operations (Steiner and Alston, 1996: 871). Levi-Strauss and Co. and the Timberland Company apply human rights criteria in their selection of business partners, and avoid investing at all in countries where there is serious violation of human rights.

Companies such as the above are the exception. However, there appears to exist an emerging trend in that direction. Perhaps, the investment agreement might allow host countries to discriminate in favour of companies with good human rights records, when approving investment proposals. One path to accomplishing this would be attaching the OECD Code of Conduct for Multinational Enterprises to the investment agreement and allowing denial of access to markets on grounds that a MNC had failed to meet its human rights requirements.

Effective Dispute Settlement

The proposed investment agreement creates both rights and duties to both governments and foreign investors. Such a network of rights and duties would occasionally produce disputes between governments, and between host governments and foreign investors. Hence, the agreement needs to provide an effective mechanism of settling investment-related disputes. A rule-driven means of settling such disputes lies at the core of the utility of such an agreement. Moreover, a significant growth in the number of unresolved investment disputes could be highly detrimental to the future of FDI flows throughout the world, and such disputes could also cause strains in diplomatic relations between governments.

The MAI prescribed two separate procedures for settling investment-related disputes, depending whether the disputes are between states or between foreign investors and states. In the case of state-state disputes, it prescribes a procedure already widely applied in many bilateral investment treaties and regional treaties, that is, consultation, conciliation, and mediation before going to arbitration by an international tribunal (see Chapter Five for details). In the case of investor-state disputes, the MAI gives the foreign investor an absolute right to decide where to lodge its complaints. The investor could choose to go to the courts or tribunals of the host country, or it may choose to ignore the domestic judicial system and go to an international tribunal (see Chapter Five for details).

Although international arbitration of disputes between foreign investors and host countries is not new, it is normally done with the consent of both parties and after exhausting local remedies. The MAI allowed the foreign investor to take its complaint to an international tribunal without the need to exhaust local remedies and seek the consent of the host country. This could have serious negative consequences for many smaller nations.

It is essential that foreign investors be given the right to take their case to an international tribunal, even without the consent of host countries, because a country which knows that it has breached its treaty obligations may not always consent to go to an international trial or panel. Moreover, there are so many countries around the world where the judiciary is not free and independent from the executive arm of the state. This is the negative side of national sovereignty – sovereignty of national executives over the judiciary – crushing a just separation of powers. It will be unjust to deny foreign investors operating in such countries the pursuit of justice in an international tribunal. However, there are many countries that have competent, free and independent judicial systems. It would be equally unjust to deny such countries the exercise of their sovereign rights, when it is possible that justice can be done in their domestic judicial bodies. Regulated openness proposes that foreign investors need to be given a right to take their complaint to an international tribunal, but only after exhausting all available local remedies. This includes consultation and conciliation measures, as well as making formal complaints in administrative and judicial bodies of the host country. The exhaustion of all these local avenues should entitle the foreign investor to take its complaint to an international tribunal, without the need for consent of the host country. The decision of the international tribunal should be final and binding. But it should operate on the basis of reluctance to trump domestic justice by agreeing to hear cases – a principle of subsidiarity in justice unless justice transparently cannot be done domestically.

This approach would address the concerns of both parties. It alleviates the fears of nations regarding loss of sovereignty, because they can still exercise their judicial power as long as it serves justice. It alleviates the fear of foreign investors that justice would not be expected to be served in some countries, because they would still have the right to go to an international tribunal if they do not get justice from local judicial bodies. On the other hand, the knowledge that the foreign investor could finally go to an international tribunal in the absence of fair treatment in the host country, could encourage host countries to obey their treaty obligations and treat foreign investors accordingly. This is a win-win situation for both the host country and the foreign investor. Again, it covers the weakness of a position that allows MNC forum-shopping with the strength of subsidiarity and it covers the weakness of local judicial corruption and injustice with the strength of international contestability.

There are a number of international arbitration centres for the settlement of investment disputes. One of them is the International Centre for the Settlement of Investment Disputes (ICSID), which was created within the World Bank Group in 1965. Most bilateral investment treaties designate it as the prospective arbitration Centre for disputes, refer to it as an appointing authority, or indicate that its rules would be applicable in ad hoc arbitration. There are now over 100 national parties to ICSID, and its principles are widely accepted by both developed and developing countries (Paulson, 1991: 380). Given the long experience and legitimacy it has in handling investor-state disputes, ICSID seems to be the most appropriate international arbitration body for investment disputes. Other international bodies include the International Court of Arbitration (of the International Chamber of Commerce), the London Court of International Arbitration, the World Intellectual Property Organisation, the European Convention on International Commercial Arbitration. These arbitration organisations are mainly concerned with firm-firm disputes, although the ICC sometimes handles firm-state disputes as well (see Chapter Eight).

The MAI v Regulated Openness

As the discussion in Chapters Five and Nine shows, the approach taken by the MAI to address investment issues has proved to be controversial. It has generated opposition from the wide spectrum of the population around the world and from many developing countries. Most importantly, it could not secure the agreement of the OECD countries themselves on many issues. Deadline after deadline had been broken, before the negotiations were suspended indefinitely. Regulated openness attempts to address the same issues the MAI raised and more, but in a cautious, hedged and pragmatic manner. The following table compares the approach taken by the two models on addressing the major issues.

Table 10:2 Comparison of the MAI and Regulated Openness

The MAI	Regulated Openness
A. Liberalisation through: ▪ national treatment, pre- and post-establishment (with very few exceptions) ▪ MFN ▪ Standstill and Rollback ▪ Abolition of Performance Requirements	A. Presumption of openness. National treatment and MFN apply pre- and post-establishment, but openness may be restricted temporarily for specific reasons, namely: ▪ sustainable development ▪ consumer protection ▪ encouraging firms with good corporate ethics ▪ good governance Performance requirements are allowed in certain circumstances. Obligation of continuous improvement.
B. Investment Protection ▪ no expropriation except for the public purpose, and against the payment prompt, adequate and effective compensation ▪ the meaning of "expropriation" includes any government measures having "effects similar to expropriation" ▪ due process of law	B. Investment Security ▪ no expropriation except for the public purpose, and against the payment of prompt, adequate and effective compensation ▪ in the case of "indirect" expropriation, both the purpose and effect of the act should be considered to conclude whether or not it is an " expropriation" ▪ due process of law
C. Binding Dispute Settlement Mechanism i) State-State dispute ▪ consultation, conciliation, mediation, and arbitration ii) Investor-State dispute ▪ local courts or international tribunal, at the choice of the investor	C. Binding Dispute Settlement Mechanism i) State-State dispute ▪ consultation, conciliation, mediation, and arbitration ii) Investor-State dispute ▪ exhaustion of local remedies before going to an international tribunal. Once the local remedies are exhausted, the investor would not need the consent of the host state to take its case to an international tribunal ▪ presumption of subsidiarity in agreeing to hear disputes internationally

	D. Core Labour Standards Continuous improvement in: ▪ Freedom of association ▪ Freedom of collective bargaining ▪ Discrimination in employment ▪ Equal pay for equal work of equal value ▪ Minimum working age ▪ Abolition of forced labour ▪ Consumer Protection and Business Ethics ▪ A binding undertaking to introduce national consumer protection and competition laws ▪ An undertaking to continuously improve consumer protection and competition laws ▪ Public interest groups will have the right to take companies to court if the consumer protection and competition laws are violated. ▪ A protocol on minimum standard of corporate conduct
	E. Good Governance ▪ Social policy ▪ Democratisation ▪ Anti-corruption measures ▪ Protection of human rights

Binding v Voluntary Rules The basic problem facing the proponents of a binding global investment agreement is the simple but basic fact that major differences in aims and interests exist in the world of sovereign nation-states. Substantively divergent interests and objectives can block the formulation of a common basis for harmonised international binding rules. Moreover, such binding rules may restrict the freedom of action of national governments vis-à-vis foreign investors in areas covered by the agreement. As Cynthia Wallace puts it:

> A certain loss of sovereignty is necessarily involved in the application of any binding agreement enforced by an international or even a regional body. Those states must realise that international regulations can be as much of a compromise of sovereignty – or more so – as the commercial activities of multinationals, which at least are subject to national regulation (Wallace, 1983: 304).

On the other hand, unlike voluntary rules, binding rules enjoy the advantage of certainty and predictability. The rights and obligations of each party are clearly spelt out, and failure to comply with them risks sanctions.

Most voluntary rules take the form of a code of conduct. Governments may negotiate an international code, similar to the OECD Guidelines for Multinational Corporations. Companies, too, may create their own codes of conduct which can serve them as a galvanising device for internal policy reviews and as initial vehicle for corporate communication with the general public and authorities. At the international level, organisations such as the International Chamber of Commerce (ICC) and the International Federation of Pharmaceutical Manufacturers Associations (IFPMA) have codes for business practice. However, neither governments nor international investors nor the association that formulated them are under any legal obligation to implement these codes.

The dilemma is therefore this: one cannot reach an agreement on a binding comprehensive agreement because of the diversity of interests of individual countries and its sovereignty implications; it may be possible to agree on a comprehensive voluntary code of conduct, but such an agreement may not have any significant relevance. This dilemma can however be solved if the agreement is on binding principles rather than comprehensive international rules. Investors will get the certainty of national rules, and governments will retain as much sovereignty as they need to design their own national rules.

Detailed Rules at the National Level

Once the core principles have been laid down at the international level, each government would be able to introduce national laws consistent with the international core principles. The national laws themselves could be constrained by the principles from attempting to elaborately regulate each and every activity of foreign investors. Instead, they would give a clearer interpretation of the core international principles in light of the country's particular situation, lay down the administrative framework, and define the structure of the national regulatory framework. At the national level, regulation of the activities of firms may take two forms: self-regulation and direct regulation. Most activities of firms could be left for self-regulation. In activities of greater importance for the government or where firms are not in a position to self-regulate, direct regulation may be used. The national law should define the activities for which firms are obliged to make their own rules (enforced self-regulation)[6] and those for which self-regulation is totally voluntary.

Self-Regulation Self-regulation is normally defined as the concept of leaving the control of business in the hands of business itself. The term is applied in situations where there are recognised sets of rules in accordance with which the activity is regulated (Cane, 1987: 324). Moreover, self-regulation is normally conducted as a complement to direct governmental regulation, not in the absence of external control (Cane, 1987: 326).

Self-regulation has a number of advantages over direct governmental regulation. One is it costs the government and taxpayers less (Cane, 1987: 328). Allowing firms to self-regulate internalises the costs of regulation to the regulated industry, thereby sparing the government from incurring the costs of drafting codes and establishing and running the regulatory machinery. Self-regulation is also said to produce greater flexibility in the creation, interpretation and application of rules than direct governmental regulation (Cane, 1987: 331). In self-regulation, rules can be made and changed more easily and flexibly than in direct governmental regulation where changes of rules are subject to more cumbersome procedures (Cane, 1987: 331).

Self-regulation allows firms to adapt quickly to changing commercial and technological realities (Ayres and Braithwaite, 1992: 110). Direct governmental rules, on the other hand, are meant to apply to a range of industries, and hence, they cannot change as quickly as the circumstances of particular industries change. Ayres and Braithwaite conclude found out that the main reason why law fails to control corporate crime is "because legal institutions are made to last, whereas economic institutions are designed for rapid adaptation to changing economic and technological realities" (Ayres and Braithwaite, 1992: 110). As a result, lawmakers are usually very slow in enacting new regulations when they are needed and even slower at removing those laws that are no longer needed.

> When a new threat to the public interest is perceived (e.g. research discovers a new industrial carcinogen), years of delay can be expected as universalistic rules are drafted and redrafted to meet objections from the disparate types of industries that would be differentially affected by the proposed rule. Lengthy consideration must be given to the now almost inevitable pleas by some firms that they would be forced out of business by the new rules (Ayres and Braithwaite, 1992: 111).

Self-regulation can be one of the solutions for such problems. Particularly under compulsory self-regulation, firms would be obliged to take swift measures when the threat is perceived, if not for any other reason, for fear of sanctions.

A deal of research also suggests that self-regulation can have a much wider coverage than direct governmental regulation (see Clifford & Braithwaite, 1981; Fisse & Braithwaite, 1983; Braithwaite, 1984, 1985).

> While large companies manage to write rules regulating a substantial proportion of the most serious harms or wrongs that could occur in their business, governments simply do not. They fail to do so because they lack the time, research resources, and political will necessary to build consensus around a comprehensive set of rules (Ayres & Braithwaite, 1992: 112).

Allowing firms to make their own rules can therefore broaden the law to cover a wider range of activities, which otherwise may be overlooked by direct governmental regulation.

Another factor that makes self-regulation important is it creates a sense of responsibility in the firms themselves. In a system where regulation is conducted solely by the government, firms may become unconcerned about malpractice that government inspectors may not discover. Ayres and Braithwaite have found that "irresponsible companies are frequently pleased to hand over incomplete facts to facilitate the government's regulatory decision; if the agency gives them a green light, they delightedly claim 'It's within the rules, so let's go ahead'" (Ayres & Braithwaite, 1992: 113). If, on the other hand, firms were allowed/required to write their own laws, this abdication of responsibility by firms would be minimised.

The type of self-regulation proposed here is both compulsory and voluntary. It will be up to each country to decide which activities should fall under compulsory self-regulation and which fall under the jurisdiction of voluntary self-regulation. Because of differences in priorities, level of economic development, strength of regulatory agencies and cultures the arrangement may differ from country to country.

One may find it naïve to trust firms to regulate themselves effectively. Often it is. This problem, however, can be overcome in many contexts by subjecting the rules firms make to approval by a committee of stakeholders consisting of representatives from NGOs, business associations, and government. Hence, any rules firms write for themselves will have to 1) meet the minimum requirement broadly stipulated in the national legislation, and 2) the committee has to be satisfied that the rules are up to the standard. The committee may develop, based on the national legislation and the internationally agreed upon principles, a checklist of issues that firms could use in developing their own rules. If the independent body is not satisfied of the standard of the rules, the firm will have to write another rule or negotiate with the body and reach a compromise.

In making their own rules, firms may have a number of sources of reference to choose from. There are a variety of rules of company conduct around the world prepared by industry and business associations, NGOs, UN agencies, and so on. Firms may wish to adopt such rules. However, these various international rules of conduct may not sometimes be totally appropriate for a particular firm. They can provide important guidelines, but may not necessarily satisfy the firms' requirements.

> Attempts...to formulate a set of guidelines applicable to all companies and industries...run into the problem of the great diversity of enterprises. MNCs cover a wide spectrum of countries and include industry sectors, ranging from extractive to manufacturing to service industries. They use various kinds and levels of technology and have complex requirements, quite apart from the differences in their business practices and corporate philosophies (USA-BIAC, 1975: 19).

Therefore, the best approach would probably be to encourage individual firms to write their own individual rules, if need be, taking some of the concepts from the international codes.

Direct Regulation Centralised, detailed and direct regulation could be a powerful social instrument, but it is not necessarily the most efficient. By requiring firms to take a prescribed set of rules, direct regulation assumes a certain uniformity in problems to be solved. However, the causes of problems are not entirely predictable, risks may arise in different degrees, and hence uniform solutions cannot be given to different problems. When the rule lacks flexibility to apply in diverse situations, the result will be unreasonableness and unresponsiveness.

Direct regulation runs the risk of underestimating the diversity of the ways in which things can go wrong. The following description by Bacow may clarify this:

> Millions of products are marketed in the United States by thousands of different producers. The risk associated with each product varies with its design; the quality of the materials and the workmanship; the direction provided to the users; the user's skill, judgment and caution; the age of the product; whether the product is being used for its intended purpose; the way the product has been maintained; and the extent to which the product is used with other products (Bacow: 6, cited in Bardach & Kagan, 1982: 58-59).

In such circumstances, direct regulation relying on particular solutions may be appropriate for some products and users, but may needlessly be cumbersome, costly and ineffective for others (Bardach & Kagan, 1982: 59).

In many areas of regulation, voluntary compliance by firms is achieved because of economic pressures and legal sanctions that result from non-compliance. Companies that produce chemicals, for example, are well aware of multimillion-dollar damage awards for personal injury or environmental damage. Compliance with applicable regulations can limit liability and mitigate damages. Sometimes enlightened self-interest might make firms comply with regulations, even when compliance increases costs to the firm. They sense that the long-term gains of retaining a reputation as law-abiding corporate citizen may outweigh the short-term gains from regulatory non-compliance (Bardach and Kagan, 1982: 61). Moreover, many large corporations now have specialist staff whose duty is to ascertain regulatory compliance by subsidiary companies. Although these specialists are employees of the companies, and therefore interested in the companies' balance sheets, they can also have loyalty to the standards of their profession. A corporate environmental engineer told Bardach and Kagan (1982: 62) "I am a licensed engineer. I am not going to risk my license by lying to an agency". Bardach and Kagan also found that "some of [company specialist staff] have worked for regulatory agencies...and their job is to keep their company out of legal and political trouble, and in many corporations, compliance or some approximation thereof, not outright evasion, is the predominant strategy for keeping out of trouble".

Despite this general fact, however, there are still firms that try to evade regulations that they feel are unreasonable, or because they think they can get away with it. Moreover, firms may vary in their capacity to put in place their own rules of behaviour and comply with them. "A firm with greater financial depth, full-time environmental engineers, and an industrial hygienist usually is better able than is a small, financially hard-pressed firm" to formulate good standard rules of behaviour, monitor compliance, and invest in the latest control technologies (Bardach & Kagan, 19823: 62). It is not, therefore, possible to abolish direct regulation on a wide front and replace it by self-regulation. It is however possible to seed continuously to limit the role of unnecessary direct regulation. The proposal here is to keep direct regulation to the minimum necessary for effectiveness in a particular cultural context.

The Process of Negotiating and Implementing the Rules

Negotiating the Rules

One of the major lessons that could be learnt from the MAI negotiations is that a negotiation process that is more-or-less confined to a small group of like-minded countries could prove to be a source of great difficulty. The MAI negotiation failed partly because it was exclusive, and hence generated widespread opposition from non-OECD countries and NGOs around the world. A negotiation process such as the MAI needs to involve as many countries as possible, and address fully the concerns in civil society. NGOs need to be involved in a meaningful way in the negotiating process, as they are the main representatives of diversity in the world.

NGOs play roles that go far beyond political activism (Braithwaite & Drahos, 2000). Many are important deliverers of services, especially in developing countries. Some of them, such as CARE and Medecins Sans Frontieres, are primarily aid providers. Others such us Oxfam, are both aid providers and campaigners. Groups such as Greenpeace stick to campaigning (The Economist, 1999: 19).

The involvement of NGOs in international affairs has a long history. At the end of World War II, 1200 Organisations went to San Francisco to participate in the proceedings on the adoption of the United Nations Charter (Chayes & Chayes, 1995: 250). One of their main objectives was to ensure that the Charter would not be confined to international security matters, but would also include provisions dealing with economic, social and cultural issues (Chayes & Chayes, 1995: 250). With the adoption of the human rights Covenants in 1966, NGOs in that field began to proliferate. Similarly, environmental NGOs have grown spectacularly since the UN Conference on the Environment in Stockholm in 1972 (Chayes & Chayes, 1995: 250). Today, NGOs representing various sections of the society number in tens of thousands.

Although NGOs work usually with national governments and international organisations, they exert their major influence through the domestic political process. They mobilise voters, lobby legislators, disseminate information, bring lawsuits, launch petitions and so on. Even in countries without strong democratic traditions, domestic and international NGOs can mount significant pressure on governments through "shaming" campaigns organised around the norms of international agreements (Chayes & Chayes, 1995: 252). With the advent of the Internet, NGOs around the world have become ever more effective in coordinating their campaigns, and that is how they managed to paralyse the MAI negotiations. In relation to the their campaign on the Internet against the MAI, one Canadian newspaper wrote:

> High-powered politicians had reams of statistics and analysis on why a set of international investing rules would make the world a better place. They were no match, however, for a global band of grassroots organisations, which, with little more than computers and access to the Internet, helped derail a deal (Drohan, 1998).

NGOs are increasingly formidable international forces, and any negotiation that does not meaningfully involve them not only would be unfair, but also risks failure.

Many developing countries and a large number of NGOs have opposed the OECD Secretariat being the venue for the negotiation of the Agreement, and also the authority to monitor the implementation of the rules. This is because the OECD, being an Organisation consisting of developed countries, would not effectively address the interests of non-members (see Chapters Six & Seven). Unions admittedly like it, but only because it institutionalises an outdated Euro-tripartism that privileges unions, business and governments only. Some countries, mainly European, say that the WTO would be an appropriate venue for such an investment process (see Chapter Five). This is however rejected by many developing countries and NGOs (see Chapters Six and Seven).

The United Nations Conference on Trade and Development (UNCTAD) might be the best host of negotiations that aspire to regulated openness. UNCTAD has a number of advantages over the WTO or OECD to host such negotiations. Firstly, it is mandated to look into issues of both trade and development. This mandate was renewed by member countries, including the US and other major powers, in the conference held in Midrad, South Africa, in 1996 (called UNCTAD IX). Secondly, over the years, UNCTAD has accumulated enormous expertise on issues of trade and development, and its publications on such matters are ranked among the best. By holding the negotiations in UNCTAD, it is possible to make use of this expertise. Thirdly, because UNCTAD is not a rule-making body, the negotiators would feel relaxed in putting forward their proposals and making deals.

Implementation of the Rules

The fact that UNCTAD is not a rule-making body means that another Organisation is needed to monitor the implementation of the rules. This Organization could be the World Bank. Although the World Bank, in its original operational form, was not much concerned with FDI, over time FDI has become important to it through the activities of its several organisational components (Shihata, 1986: 13). The creation of the International Finance Corporation (IFC) in 1956 provided organisational mechanisms for involvement in FDI through equity participation with private investors and loans to private investors in FDI projects in developing countries. The Foreign Investment Advisory Service (FIAS) was created in 1986 as a part of the IFC to advise developing countries on their policies as hosts to FDI. The Multilateral Investment Guarantee Agency (MIGA) was created in 1988 to provide political risk insurance to foreign direct investors in developing countries (see Chapter Eight for details). The Banks new guarantee program, which insures private investors in major projects within developing countries against changes in government policies, was created to be more responsive to the role of private investment in the development process (Graham, 1994: 6). Its investment dispute settlement body, ICSID, as acceded to by a large number of countries around the world. The Bank also has introduced a non-binding code of Conduct for international investment. All these organisational structures and experience makes the Bank a competent authority to monitor the implementation of the investment agreement. The Bank has both clout and competence in investment matters.

Conclusion: The Path to Regulated Openness

I have argued that an agreement to liberalise investment could be a significant step for economic development in rich and poor countries alike. The benefits of this development, however, would disproportionately favour the rich, yet the risks would be disproportionately born by the powerless and the environment. Unregulated openness would therefore give us development without justice, unbalanced development, unsustainable development. Politically, all constituencies that represent the powerless – the labour, environment, consumer, womens' and development movements – should oppose the unregulated openness of the 1990s MAI draft, and have done so.

Development with justice, I have argued, first requires procedural justice – meaningful participation of those constituencies representing the powerless and credible dispute resolution. Substantively, it requires credible commitments to continuous improvement, not only of investment security, but also of environmental sustainability, core labour standards, consumer protection, business ethics and "good governance". An agreement that attends to all of these could promise both a wealthier and more just world. More than that, I cannot see any path to a global investment agreement that is environmentally and politically sustainable other than regulated openness.

In the 1970s and 1980s, we saw the political unsustainability of a global agreement for investment justice without convincing investment security or liberalisation – the UN Code of Conduct for MNC. In the 1990s, we saw the political unsustainability of its obverse (the MAI) – openness without regulation. Now in the new millennium, my claim is that the world will become ready for what is a more morally decent and economically sensible package – regulated openness. The political path to regulated openness is most likely to be cleared by the players which simultaneously have the global clout to do so, which have most to gain economically by a global investment agreement, and whose labour, environment and consumer movements have the greatest capabilities in their domestic politics for extracting concessions. These players are the US and the EU. In the course of the next decade, it seems likely they can and will clear a path in the direction of regulated openness. Chances are they will not support an agreement with an unbalanced privileging of openness over regulation. If they do, a coalition of developing countries and their own NGOs will defeat them again. The interests of their investors actually lie in balancing regulation and openness. Yet they must be careful to craft an agreement that is not so unbalanced that their own NGOs will scuttle it domestically. Leaders like Bill Clinton and Al Gore see the political cost of such a policy failure very clearly. Equally, the developing countries and the NGOs cannot hold out for their ideal of a perfect balance of regulation and openness. This is because the US and the EU hold the cards. These cards are the hundreds of existing bilateral investment agreements and the investment dollars. A continuation of the dominated, procedurally unjust openness of the network of bilateral treaties dictated by investor nations is not in the interests of developing countries and the global NGOs.

Pragmatism therefore dictates that both sides show some movement in the direction of a regulated openness package. How economically beneficial, sustainable and just this movement will be remains to be seen. My contention has been that the compromises are likely to be more decent if they are forged within a framework of principles that enable continuous improvement rather than rules that specify global performance standards. Not only would this make them more efficient and just compromises, a regime of principles with credible commitments to continuous improvement would make the compromises more likely to happen at all.

Notes

1 For both game theoretic and republican analysis of why this should be so, see Ayres & Braithwaite (1992: Chapter 3).
2 Resolution of the Council and of the Member States meeting in the Council on Human Rights, Democracy and Development.
3 See for instance the EC Resolution cited above.
4 Other international instruments which address this issue include the Universal Declaration of Human Rights, the Charter of Economic Rights and Duties of States, the Declaration of the Rights to Development, and so on.

5 Some of the international instruments that address human rights include the Universal Declaration of Human Rights, adopted by the UN General Assembly in 1948, and the two International Covenants on Civil and Political Rights and on Economic, Social and Cultural Rights.

6 For more discussion on enforced self-regulation, see Ayres & Braithwaite (1992: Chapter 4).

Chapter 11

Conclusion

This book has examined the issues surrounding the regulation of FDI. The theories that have had major influence in past decades on the formulation of investment rules and their shortcomings and strengths were found to be neo-classical economics, dependency theory and theories of State intervention in economic development (Chapter Two). The weaknesses of the current national and international rules on FDI have been described both in terms of these theories and in terms of the limitations of their coverage analysed (Chapter Two). The strategies of the key international players for global investment rules, their contradictions, and the main issues surrounding the debate have been scrutinised (Chapters Five to Nine). And finally, an alternative model for global regulation of FDI has been proposed (Chapter Ten).

By its nature, foreign investment falls within the jurisdiction of more than one country. More importantly, modern communications and financial integration have encouraged firms to operate on a regional or even global basis. Cross-border mergers and acquisitions (M&A) and other forms of strategic alliances have become widespread. In 1998, the absolute value of all cross-border M&A (sales and purchases) amounted to $544 billion, representing an increase of about 60 per cent over that of 1997 (UNCTAD, 1999: 18). This has enormous implications for national regulatory regimes.

The global expansion of FDI inevitably necessitates the transfer of tangible and intangible assets between parent companies and their foreign affiliates. How to establish prices for such cross-border transfers is a thorny issue for policy makers and regulators. The issue is even more pressing for developing countries, given the more limited resource and expertise of such countries in the field of transfer pricing. The problem is also aggravated by the absence of an international agreement on transfer pricing.

Globalisation of the world economy is said to have brought closer economic activities, such as trade and investment which, in the past, were treated as discrete (Fatouros, 1996: 59). Trade and investment increasingly intertwine to use inputs efficiently and sell outputs across borders. The successful conclusion of successive trade negotiations within the GATT/WTO framework also reduced trade barriers and stimulated global FDI flows. Such frameworks, however, do not address FDI in a satisfactory manner. Although BITs regulate FDI, they are limited in scope and geography and grapple with power imbalances between weak and strong states less adequately than the regulated openness proposed here.

The current regulatory framework for FDI is unsatisfactory on a number of grounds. Firstly, although BITs have so far played an important role in the expansion of the acceptance and application of certain standards, it is however doubtful if they are suitable for the increasingly globalised economy. BITs have limitations in scope. Besides, there is a risk that continued reliance on BITs would produce a wide range of non-uniform and inconsistent arrangements that could become increasingly inefficient, complex and non-transparent. Secondly, the few multilateral or sectoral or regional agreements we have (such as the EU, TRIMs, NAFTA, APEC) also have limitation either in scope or geographical coverage. Thirdly, national laws, too, although broader in scope, have geographical limitations in their applicability. Fourthly, the diversity of national and international legal regimes governing FDI introduces excessive distortions as between countries and sectors (Fatouros, 1996: 59). The emergence of global investment rules would, among other things, give coherence to the regulatory environment facing foreign investment.

The overall strategy of the OECD and its members on global investment rules has been greater liberalisation of investment rules and higher security for foreign investment around the world (Chapter Five). This was the project of the MAI, in which of the OECD and its members were enthusiastically supported by the business community (Chapter Seven). The majority of developing countries and key international public interest groups – notably the consumer, environment, development and labour movements opposed this strategy on the grounds that liberalisation may not necessarily be beneficial for the world community and the environment (Chapters Five, Six and Seven). Moreover, they believed that developed countries' preoccupation with liberalisation and protection of investor rights would mean that other issues of importance in FDI regulation would be ignored.

Although developing countries did not have a common strategy, issues of sovereignty and development have been central for most of them (Chapter Six). A liberal multilateral framework that would seriously limit the sovereign right of host countries' regulatory power was fiercely resisted. So also liberal multilateral rules that leave little room for host countries to manoeuvre their investment policies according to their development and social objectives and priorities (Chapter Six). Moreover, a global investment framework that would allow foreign investors to take the host country to an international tribunal without the latter's consent is seen as something that would seriously erode the sovereignty of a nation (Chapter Six). All of these positions are also held strongly by the public interest groups examined in the book (Chapter Seven). Where the public interest groups differ from the developing countries was on issues of environmental and core labour standards, as well as the protection of human rights. Developing countries oppose the inclusion of these in a global investment agreement.

Consumer advocates want competition policy (particularly rules on cross-border restrictive practices and M&A) and consumer protection to be part of a global investment framework (Chapter Seven). Environmental NGOs want environmental standards to be included, while labour unions want core labour standards to be part of any global investment agreement (Chapter Seven). There is opposition from developing countries and business on all these fronts (Chapters Five, Six and Seven). Developed countries are divided on labour and environmental standards, while uniformly oppose the inclusion of competition policy and consumer protection on the ground that consumer protection and competition policy should be the domain of national law (Chapters Seven and Ten).

Developing countries and the public interest groups consistently argued that any investment framework that would give rights and protection to foreign investors without corresponding obligation is, not only unacceptable, but also unjust and unbalanced (Chapters Six and Seven). This has been vehemently opposed by developed countries and the business community (Chapters Six and Seven). On the other hand, MNCs do not always behave in line with the host countries' wishes. In Chapter Nine, we used the example of the behaviour of Elf Aquitaine, a French MNC, in Congo and other countries where it has been accused of corrupting politicians in developed and developing countries, interfering in the internal politics of host countries, serving France to perpetuate its influence on its former colonies in Africa, and in other respects undermining the French Government's activities.

Where to negotiate a possible investment agreement, and who to mandate for its implementation has been discussed in Chapters Five, Six, Seven, Nine and Ten. This issue has become even more important after the MAI. While developed countries and the business community preferred the OECD or WTO (depending on who you ask and when) (Chapter Five), several developing countries and the public interest groups want neither of these organisations (Chapters Six and Seven).

The MAI was negotiated exclusively by OECD countries and largely in secrecy (Chapter Five). This was a fatal mistake. The longer the majority of developing countries and public interest groups were barred from participating in the negotiation, the stronger became their suspicion and opposition to it (Chapter Five). The exclusive nature of the negotiations meant that the Agreement was "being negotiated by the wrong group of nations" (Chapter Five). More importantly, however, the successful concerted opposition against it by developing countries and a global network of NGOs may have created a new chapter in the way multilateral treaties would be negotiated in the future. James Wolfensohn, President of the World Bank, realised this phenomenon a decade earlier and allowed more than 70 NGO specialists to work in the Bank's field operations. More than half of World Bank projects in 1998 involved NGOs (The Economist, 1999: 19). The fact that the WTO allowed some NGOs to participate in the Seattle Ministerial Conference was also a confirmation of the Bank's recognition of a new geo-political reality. This is one where developing countries can again flex some collective muscle to resist the West's plans for them. Prior to 1989, it was the support of the Soviet bloc that enabled them to do this at times. Post-MAI, developing countries can now see that they can foment a veto coalition with Western NGOs, even if they do not share most of their aspirations.

The discussion throughout the book demonstrates that the positions of each of the key international players have their own limitations. Much of the world wants a global investment agreement, but this can only be achieved if a balance can be struck between the positions of each key player. Drawing on the perspectives of all the key players studied, the book forged a balance described as "regulated openness" (Chapter Ten).

A liberal investment agreement could be a significant step for economic development in rich and poor countries alike. But this development may not necessarily be one with balance, sustainability and justice. FDI that replaces domestic capabilities, rather than complementing them, may not necessarily be a good thing for the host country. To address such problems, the host country may, for example, need to impose performance requirements on investors, or select the type of FDI it would allow into its territories in any particular time. For example, a developing country following Soskice's Liberal Market Economy model may want to seek a British or US partner in its telecommunications section while nations aspiring more in the direction a Business-Coordinated Market Economy may prefer a German or Japanese partner. An official of the South Centre told me:

> The cost of FDI could be very high. The foreign investor expects a very high return, and the money or profit has to be repatriated. That is why it is essential for a country to have the power to choose the kind of project it needs. FDI is productive if it contributes and links to the country's development. A hamburger shop or a supermarket may not be a productive foreign investment from the point of view of developing countries.

FDI could make significant additions to the foreign exchange supply of the host country in the initial phase of its entry. What happens after that largely depends on the type of investment products involved (Graham and Krugman, 1989). If the investment is export-oriented, its effect on balance-of-payments could be positive. If the investment is not export-oriented, its effect on balance-of-payments in the medium and longer term could be negative, particularly if it is a mere acquisition of a non-export oriented domestic company. The financial crisis in Asia and Mexico have demonstrated that indiscriminate inflow of foreign investment may not necessarily have a positive contribution to the balance-of-payments of the host country. Hence, Chile and Malaysia introduced capital control measures during their economic crises, which seem to have produced positive results (Chapter Six).

Through selective intervention by the State, FDI can be utilised to enhance the productive capacity of domestic enterprises and sustain development. This has been proven in South Korea and other South-East Asian countries (Chapter Six). Hence, regulated openness strives to achieve a balance between regulation and liberalisation in major issues of investment regulation (Chapter Ten).

Regulated openness has procedural and substantive dimensions. Procedurally, it is a process where all major stakeholders would have an input and role in the preparation and implementation of FDI laws. The international negotiation would be conducted by governments, but key non-governmental international players should be consulted and given the opportunity to contribute to the formulation of the principles. At the national level, too, a body consisting of representatives from business, public interest groups and government might be formed with a task of evaluating and approving self-regulation rules prepared by firms. Regulated openness proposes to hold the negotiation of the international agreement within the framework of UNCTAD and entrust the implementation of it to the World Bank. UNCTAD has a number of advantages over the WTO and OECD to host such negotiations. Firstly, it is mandated to look into issues of both trade and development. This mandate was renewed by member countries, including the US and other major powers, during UNCTAD IX Conference in 1996. Secondly, over the years, UNCTAD has accumulated enormous expertise on issues of trade and development, and has avoided extreme commitments to either neo-classicalism or dependency theory. By holding the negotiations in UNCTAD, it is possible to make use of this expertise. Thirdly, because UNCTAD is not a rule-making body, the negotiators would feel relaxed in putting forward their proposals and making deals. However, the fact that UNCTAD is not a rule-making body means that another organisation is needed to monitor the implementation of the Agreement. This organisation could be the World Bank. Although the World Bank, in its original operational form, was not much concerned with FDI, over time FDI has become important to it through the activities of its several organisational components such us the IFC and MIGA. Besides, it already has an investment dispute settlement body (ICSID).

A binding international framework agreement on principles is a more pragmatic solution than comprehensive rules. Once the framework agreement of core principles has been formed, each country would have its own detailed rules consistent with the internationally agreed principles and the priorities of individual countries. The national regulatory framework, consisting of direct regulation and self-regulatory initiatives, would be subject to reporting to ICSID and periodic review by a committee to evaluate compliance with the international principles and continuous improvement in terms of openness. Trade sanctions would not be needed to enforce this. Countries labelled by a respected ICSID Committee of Experts as slipping backwards in terms of openness would pay the penalty of reduced FDI flows.

Substantively, regulated openness means an investment regime where both regulation and openness co-exist in a balanced and pragmatic manner. One of the lessons learnt from past negotiations on comprehensive international investment regimes is that it is practically impossible to reconcile the conflicting interests of the major international players. The most recent example is the collapse of the MAI negotiations (see Chapter Five). Regulated openness would, therefore, be a break from these past experiences. Hence, it proposes an agreement on core principles rather than detailed comprehensive rules. The international core principles will be those principles which each major stakeholder would regard as paramount. However, this research has identified sustainable development, investment security, core labour standards, consumer protection and business ethics, good governance and effective dispute settlement as the issues that would form the international core principles (Chapter Ten). In addition, there would be a commitment for continuous improvement of national rules and self-regulatory outcomes under the agreed principles. Moreover, host countries would commit themselves to continuously improve their openness policies as their domestic capability improves. This would be underwritten by technical help from UNCTAD and the World Bank rather than by sanctions. Such commitments would more likely be honoured if they are forged within a framework of principles, rather than detailed international rules.

The main advantage of an international regime of principles rather than detailed rules is that it would give flexibility to individual countries to manage their own affairs based on their priorities and economic and social objectives, while at the same time seeking some form of internationally agreed framework, thereby giving certainty to investors. The certainty arises at two levels – at the level of national rules that are regularly reviewed by a Committee of Experts in terms of how well they deliver certainty, and at the level of certainty that national rules cannot be changed to flout the principles in the international agreement. Moreover, as the global agreement is less detailed, the likelihood of countries agreeing to sign increases, further increasing certainty for investors at the global level.

A global regime of core principles would facilitate the recognition of the need for economic pluralism in international economic agreements. A tolerance for economic pluralism requires the recognition that different goals, conditions and cultures throughout the world require different solutions to problems. One system will not serve the needs of all people in all circumstances. An attempt to impose a uniform economic and social policy worldwide creates impossible positions for people in countries that have vastly different problems and resources, in addition to different values and goals. If, on the other hand, the global agreement is based on principles, and detailed rules are left for each country to make in line with the principles, particular solutions can often be found for the particular regulatory problems of each country. It also leaves space for innovation in regulatory design, for regulatory competition in the crafting of a regulated openness that attracts FDI.

Commercial and technological realities change very rapidly in today's world, and economic entities have to continually adapt to such changes. In this regard, comprehensive global investment rules could inhibit change, for legal institutions are designed to be stable and predictable. An agreement on principles rather than comprehensive rules would avoid this problem, for it could leave room for flexibility by the regulators and the regulated.

One of the serious deficiencies of the MAI was that it assumed a liberal investment regime is beneficial to all countries, at all times, and at any level of economic development. But a radically liberal model of investment rules is just one model (see Chapter Ten). A global regime of core principles rather than detailed rules can solve the problem of choosing either a more selectively restrictive or a more open investment regime. It gives opportunity for every country to decide for themselves on the extent of restrictiveness or openness of the rules they want to have in their own respective territories.

Regulated openness aims at bringing development with justice. Development with justice requires both procedural justice and credible commitment to continuous improvement of investment policy, investment security, sustainable development, core labour standards, consumer protection, business ethics and good governance. Procedural justice, under regulated openness, can be achieved by making the rule-making process inclusive and transparent. The MAI failed partly because it was exclusive and not-transparent. It is essential for a global agreement such as the MAI to be negotiated by all stakeholders, and in a forum that would be acceptable to all. Liberalisation of investment policy, investment security, sustainable development, core labour standards, consumer protection, business ethics and good governance are the main concerns of the key international players. A commitment to continuously improve all these concerns could bring development with justice while creating a contracting space where all the key players that walked away from the MAI could see themselves on balance as better off.

In an ideal world, each nation would set the terms, conditions and standards for regulating FDI. Unfortunately this is not an ideal world. No country is capable is regulating MNCs on its own, not even powerful nations like the US. A global investment framework is an important way to improve this capability. As the discussion throughout the book showed, this has not been the case so far. On the other hand, the collapse of the MAI may have created the opportunity to approach the issue differently, and regulated openness could be an approach that commends consideration.

The past two WTO Ministerial Conferences have demonstrated that there is a desire by some countries to negotiate global investment rules, while other countries have shown some scepticism. The scepticism could be due to the fact that some countries and NGOs do not support the WTO's role in investment regulation. Regulated openness has suggested a possible solution for this problem. Future WTO Ministerial Conference could be opportunities for considering what is being proposed under regulated openness.

Yet this may be premature. This research has considerable limitations. I have only been able to consider the views and positions of major international players. There are other international, national and NGO players that have not been covered by the research. Exactly how the very little players on the Internet acted remains mysterious and inadequately analysed. To genuinely assess regulated openness we need rigorous empirical research that evaluates experiments in regulated openness. This book only takes us as far as an argument that regulated openness might be worth experimenting with. And that is not very far at all.

Bibliography

Afro-Asian Legal Consultative Committee Principles Concerning Admission and Treatment of Aliens, reproduced in F.V. Garcia-Amador, I. Shon and R.R. Baxter 1974 Recent Codification of the Law of State Responsibility for Injuries to Aliens. Dobbs Ferry, N.Y.: Oceana Publication.

Amerasinghe, C. 1967 State Responsibility for Injuries to Aliens. Oxford: Clarendon.

Amin, S. 1974 Accumulation on a World Scale: A Critique of the Theory of Underdevelopment. New York: Monthly Review Press.

Amin, S. 1976 Unequal Development: An Essay on the Social Formation of Peripheral Capitalism. Hassocks, Eng: Harvester Press.

Amsden, A. 1989 Asia's Next Giant: South Korea and Late Industrialisation. New York: Oxford University Press.

Amsden, A.H. 1992 "A Theory of Government Intervention in Late Industrialisation", in L. Putterman and D. Rueschemeyer (eds) State and Market in Development. Boulder: Lynn Reinner Publishers.

Antonelli, A. 1991 The Diffusion of Advanced Telecommunications in Developing Countries. Paris: Development Centre, Organisation for Economic Co-operation and Development.

APEC 1993 A vision for APEC: Towards an Asia-Pacific Economic Community: report of the Eminent Persons Group to APEC Ministers. Singapore: APEC Secretariat.

Ariyshi, A, K Habermeier, et al "Country Experiences with the Use and Liberalisation of Capital Controls". IMF Paper. January 2000. Available at *http://www.imf.org/external/pubs/ft/capcon/index.htm*, accessed on April 27, 2000.

Asher, A and E. Hayes Promoting Investment: Guidelines for Global Business Meeting Report. 19th Session of the United Nation's Commission on Transnational Corporations, 5-15 April, 1993.

Atkinson, J. 1995 APEC – Winners and Losers. Dossier 34. Canberra: Australian Council for Overseas Aid.

Australian Consumers Association (ACA) MAI Submission to the Commonwealth Treasury. Unpublished. September 1998.

Award in Dispute between Libyan American Oil Company (LIAMCO) and the Government of the Libyan Arab Republic relating to Petroleum Concession, April 12, 1977, p.168, reproduced in 20 ILM 1, (1981).

Ayres, I and J, Braithwaite 1992 Transcending the Deregulation Debate. New York: Oxford University Press.

Balassa, B. 1988 "The Lessons of East Asian Development: An Overview", Economic Development and Cultural Change 36: 273-96.

Balassa, B. 1991 Economic Policies in the Pacific Area Developing Countries. London: Macmillan.

Bale (Jr), H.E. 1990 "International Investment Policy: A View from the Private Sector", in C.D. Wallace (ed) Foreign Direct Investment in the 1990s: a New Climate in the Third World. Dordrecht, Boston: Martinus Nijhof.

Banks, G and C. Ballard (eds) 1997 The Ok Tedi Settlement: Issues, Outcomes and Implications. Canberra: National Centre for Development Studies, Research School of Pacific and Asian Studies, ANU and Research Management in Asia-Pacific and Asian Studies.

Baran, P. 1967 The Political Economy of Growth. N.Y.: Monthly Review Press.

Bardach, E and R.A. Kagan 1982 Going by the Book. Philadelphia: Temple University Press.

Basile, B. and D. Germidis 1984 Investing in Free Export Processing Zones. Paris: OECD.

Bennett, D. and K. Sharpe 1985 Transnational Corporations and the State. Sydney: Transnational Corporations Research Project, University of Sydney.

Bergten, C.F. et al. 1978 American Multinationals and American Interests. Washington: Brookings Institution.

Bhagwati, J. 1995 "Trade Liberalisation and 'Fair Trade' Demands: Addressing the Environment and Labor Standards Issues", World Economy 18: 745-759.

Biersteker, T.J. 1987 Multinationals, the State and the Control of the Nigerian Economy. Princeton, N.J.: Princeton University Press.

Billerback and Yasugi 1979 Private Direct Foreign Investment in Developing Countries, World Bank Staff Working Paper No.348. Washington, D.C.: World Bank.

Blaney, David L. 1992 "Equal Sovereignty and an African Statehood: Tragic Elements in the African Agenda in World Affairs", in L.C. Martha and Chih-yu Shih. (eds) Contending Dramas: A Cognitive Approach to International Organisations. N.Y: Praeger.

Blaxter, L., Hughes, C. and Tight, M. 1996 How to Research. Buckingham; Philadelphia: Open University Press.

Boadway, R. and A. Shah 1992 How Tax Incentives Affect Decisions to Invest in Developing Countries. World Bank Working Paper. WPS1011. Washington, D.C.: World Bank.

Bodin, J. 1962 The Six Bookes of a Commonweale. A facsimile reprint of the English translation of 1606, corrected and supplemented in the light of introduction, by K.D. McRae. Cambridge: Harvard University Press.

Brabowski, R. 1994 "The Successful Development of State: Where does it Come from?", World Development 22(3): 413-22.

Braithwaite, J. 1980 "Inegalitarian Consequences of Egaliatarian Reforms to Control Corporate Crime", Temple Law Quarterly 53: 1127-46.

Braithwaite J. and P. Drahos 2000 Global Business Regulation. Cambridge: Cambridge University Press.

Brierly, J. 1955 The Law of Nations. 5th ed. Ringwood, Vic: Penguin.

Broche, A. 1982 "Bilateral Investment Treaties and Arbitration in Dispute", in P. Sanders et al. (eds) The Art of Arbitration: Essays on International Arbitration: Liber Amicorum Pieter Sanders. Deventer, Netherlands; Boston: Kluwer Law and Taxation Publishers.

Brown, D.K. et al. 1996 "International Labor Standards and Trade: A Theoretical Analysis", in J. Bhagwati and R Hudec (eds) Fair Trade and Harmonisation. Cambridge, Mass: MIT.

Brownlie, I. 1990 Principles of Public International Law, 4th ed. Oxford: Clarendon Press.

Bruno, K. 1994 Screening Foreign Investments: an Environmental Guide for Policy Makers and NGOs. Penang: Third World Network.

Buckley P.J. and M.C. Casson 1976 The Future of Multinational Enterprises. London: Macmillan.

Buckley, Ross P 2000 "National Sovereignty in the Era of Hot Money: Strategic Options for Asian Countries", Unpublished Manuscript, Queensland University of Technology.

Bureau of Industry Economics 1993 Multinationals and Governments: Issues and Implications for Australia. Research Report 49. Canberra: Australian Government Publishing Service.

Bureau of Industry Economics 1995 Foreign Direct Investment in APEC: A Survey of the Issues. Report 95/21. Canberra: Australian Government Publishing Service, November.

Burgess, R. 1982 "The Unstructured Interview as a Conversation", in R. Burgess (ed) Field Research: A Sourcebook and Field Manual. London: Allen & Unwin.

Burstein, D. 1989 Yen! Japan's New Financial Empire and its Threat to America. New York: Simon and Schuster.

Business and Industry Advisory Council (BIAC), BIAC Statement on a Potential OECD Broader Investment Instrument. Paris. Unpublished. 1996a.

Business and Industry Advisory Council (BIAC), Environment, Labor and Consumer Matters and the Multilateral Agreement on Investment (MAI). Paris. Unpublished. 1996b.

Business and Industry Advisory Council (BIAC) 1995 The OECD Multilateral Investment Agreement – BIAC views on Specific Elements of an Eventual Instrument. Paris. Unpublished.

Cane, P. 1987 "Self-Regulation and Judicial Review", Civil Justice Quarterly 6: 324-47.

Castleman, Barry I. 1979 "The Export of Hazardous Factories to Developing Nations", International Journal of Health Services 9: 569-606.

Chang, Ha-joon and A. Singh 1999 "Lessons from the Asian Crisis and the New International Financial Architecture: a Developing Country Perspective", South Letter 1 &2(33): 5-8.

Chayes, A and A.H. Chayes 1995 The New Sovereignty. Cambridge, Mass: Harvard University Press.

Chen, E.K.Y. 1979 Hyper-Growth in Asian Economies. London: Macmillan.

Chomsky, N. 1998 "Power in the Global Arena", New Left Review, 230: 3-28.

Christy, P.B. 1991 "Negotiating Investment in the GATT: A Call for Functionalism", Michigan Journal of International Law 12: 743-798.

Chu, You-han 1989 "State Structure and Economic Adjustment of East Asian Newly Industrialised Countries", International Organisation 43: 647-72.

Chung, C., L. Chang, and Y. Zhing 1995 The Role of Foreign Direct Investment in China's Post-1978 E.C. Development, World Development Report 23: 691-703.

Claessens, S., M. Dooley, and A. Warner, World Bank Discussion Paper No. 228, 1993, quoted in UNCTAD 1996 World Investment Report: Overview. New York and Geneva: United Nations.

Clairmont, Frederic F. 1996 The Rise and Fall of Economic Liberalism: the Making of the Economic Gulag. Penang: Southbound and Third World Network.

Cohen, G. 1996 Nightmare and Hope in Bhopal. Available at *www.corpwatch.org/trac/bhopal/nightmare.html*, accessed on 15 May 1999.

Consumers International [July 1995] Promoting Best Practice: Transnational Corporations, Consumers and Codes of Conduct. Briefing Paper No.4. Available at *www.consumersinternational.org/campaigns/competition/html*, accessed on 11 May.

Consumers International, [September 1996] Competition in the Global Market: Making it Work for Consumers. Briefing Paper No.6. Available at *www.consumersinternational.org/campaigns/competition/html*, accessed on 11 May 2000.

Consumers International, [October 1997]. What Consumers Expect from International Rules on Investment. Available at *www.consumersinternational.org/campaigns/trade/ci-mai.html*, accessed on 11 May 2000.

Consumers International, [October 1997a] A Consumer Charter for Global Business. Available at *www.consumersinternational.org/campaign/trade/charter_en.html*, accessed on 11 May 2000.

Consumers International, Roads to Consumer Protection: Building Frameworks. Available at *www.consumersinternational.org/rightsday99/section1.html*, accessed on 15 April 1999.

Corporate Europe Observatory MAI: the Reality of Six Months of 'Consultation and Assessment'. Unpublished Manuscript. October 1998.

Crough, G.J and E.L. 1982 Wheelwright Australia: A Client State. Ringwood, Vic., Australia: Penguin Books Australia.

Cunningham, S.M. 1986 "Multinationals and Restructuring in Latin America", in C. Dixon, D. Drakakis-Smith and H. Wads (eds) Multinational Corporations and the Third World. Boulder, Colorado: Westview Press.

Das, B.L. [22 October 1999] New Initiatives on Investment at WTO. Available at *http://www.twnside.org.sg/south/twn/bldas2-cn.htm*, accessed on 15 December 1999.

Delupis, I. 1992 Finance and Protection of Investments in Developing Countries. Aldershot, Hants, England, Brookfield, Vt., U.S.A: Gower.

Denza, E. and S. Brooks. 1987 "Investment Protection Treaties: The United Kingdom Experience", International and Comparative Law Quarterly 36: 908-23.

Deyo, F. 1987 The Political Economy of the New Asian Industrialism. Ithaca, N.Y.: Cornell University Press.

Douglas, J.D. 1985 Creative Interviewing, Beverly Hills, CA: Sage.

Downer, A. 1998a "The Multilateral Agreement on Investment", Press Release, 31 March.

Downer, A 1998b Reply to a Question without Notice: Treaties, question tabled by Taylor, B., House of Representative (Australia), 5 March, p. 585.

Draft UN Code of Conduct on Transnational Corporations, UN Doc. E/C.10/1982/6 annex, 1982.

Drohan, M. "Grassrots Groups Used their Own Globalization to Derail Deal", The Globe and Mail. April 29, 1998.

Duerkesen, C. and H. Leonard 1980 "Environmental Regulations and the Location of Industries: an International Perspective", Columbia Journal of World Business 15: 35-50.

Dunning, J.H. 1993 Multinational Enterprises and the Global Economy. Wokingham, England: Reading, Mass, Addison-Wesley.

Eagle, A.M. and R.J. Higgins 1990 "Environmental Investigations of the Effects of the Ok Tedi Copper Mine in the Fly River System", in David Lawrence and Tim Cansfield-Smith (eds) Sustainable Development for Traditional Inhabitants of the Torres Strait Region: Proceedings of the Torres Strait Baseline Study Conference. Kewarra Beach, Cairns, Queensland, 19-23 November 1990, Workshop Series No.16, Great Barrier Reef Marine Park Authority, Townsville: 97-118.

ECOSOC Res. 1721, 53rd Session of the Council, 3-28 July 1972, (UN ESCOR, Supp. (No. I)), UN Doc. E/5209, 1972.

ECOSOC Res. 1913, 57th Session of the Council, (UN ESCOR, Supp. (No. IA)), UN Doc. E/5570/Add. I, 1975.

Edward, S. How effective are Capital Controls? NBER Working Paper No W7413. Available at *http://www.nber.org/papers/w7414*, accessed on 25 April 2000.

Elian, G. 1979 The Principle of Sovereignty over Natural Resources. Alphen Aan Den Rijn: Sijthoff & Noordhoff.

European Commission 1995 A Level Playing Field for Foreign Direct Investment World-Wide. COM(95) 42 Final. Brussels: Office for Official Publications of the European Communities.

European Commission 1996 Report on United States Barriers to Trade and Investment. Brussels: Services of the European Commission.

Evans, P. 1979 Dependent Development: The Alliance of Multinationals, State and Local Capital in Brazil. Princeton, Nj: Princeton University Press.

Evans, P. 1985 Bringing the State Back In. Cambridge; New York: Cambridge University Press.

"Explanatory Note to the 1961 Harvard Draft Convention", quoted in D. J. Harris 1991 Cases and Materials in International Law. 4th ed. London: Sweet Maxwell.

Eyre, J. 1997 "Ethnicity and Development in Malaysia", in Dixon, C and D.W Smith-Drakakis (eds) Uneven Development in South East Asia. Aldershot, Hants, England; Brookfield, Vt: Ashgate.

Faaland, J. et al 1990 Growth and Ethnic Inequality: Malaysia's New Economic Policy. London: Hurst.

Fachiri, Alexander P. 1925 "Expropriation and International Law", British Yearbook of International Law 6: 159

Fatouros, A.A. 1996 "Towards and Internatinal Agreement on Foreign Direct Investment", in OECD Towards Multilateral Investment Rules. Paris: Organisation for Economic Cooperation and Development.

Fisher, B.S. and J Turner 1983 Regulating the Multinational Enterprise: National and International Challenges. New York: Praeger.

Foighel, I. 1957 Nationalisation; a study in the protection of alien property in international law. London : Stevens.

Franz, D. and C. Collins 1989 Selling Out: How We are Letting Japan Buy Our Land, Our Industries, Our Financial Institutions, and Our Future. Chicago: Contemporary Books.

Friedman, M. and R. Friedman 1980 Free to Choose. New York: Harcourt Brace Jovanovich.

Friedman, S. 1953 Expropriation in International Law. London, Stevens: the London Institute of World Affairs.

Garcia-Amador, F. 1984 The Changing Law of International Claims, Vol. I. Dobbs Ferry, N.Y.: Oceana.

Ghandi, 1986 "Effects of Tax Incentives on Investment and Employment", in P. Shome (ed) Fiscal Issues in South-East Asia: Comparative Studies of Selected Economies. Singapore, New York: Oxford University Press.

Glaser, B. and Strauss, A. 1967 The Discovery of Grounded Theory: Strategies for Qualitative Research. Chicago: Aldine.

Glickman, N.J. and D.P. Woodward 1989 The New Competitors: How Foreign Investors are Changing the US Economy. New York: Basic Books Inc.

Goodman, J. 1999 "Stopping the Juggernaut: the Anti-MAI Campaign", in J. Goodman and P. Ranald (eds) Stopping the Juggernaut: Public Interest versus the Multilateral Agreement on Investment. Annandale (Australia): Pluto Press.

Gough, L. 1998 Asia meltdown The End of the Miracle? Oxford, U.K.: Capstone Pub.

Government of Malaysia 1971 Second Malaysia Plan 1971-1975. Kuala Lumpur: Government of Malaysia.

Government of Malaysia 1976 Third Malaysia Plan 1976-1980. Kuala Lumpur: Government of Malaysia.

Government of Malaysia 1991 The Second Outline Perspective Plan 1991-2000. Kuala Lumpur: Government of Malaysia.

Government of the Republic of Zimbabwe 1991 The Promotion of Investment: Policy and Regulation. Harare: The Government of Zimbabwe.

Graham, E.M, 1993 Towards an Asia-Pacific Investment Code, Working Paper No. 94(2). Washington, D.C.: Institute for International Economics.

Graham, E.M. and P.R. Krugman 1991 Foreign Direct Investment in the United States. Washington, D.C.: Institute for International Economics.

Graham, E.M., P.R. Krugman 1989 Foreign Investment in the United States: Initiatives for International Economies. Washington, D.C.: Institute for International Economics

Graham, G. "World Bank Backing for Investors." Financial Times (London), Sept. 13, 1994.

Graham, 1970 "The Calvo Clause: Its Current Status as a Contractual Renunciation of Diplomatic Protection", Texas International Law Forum 6: 289.

Greenberg, S.B 1980 Race and State in Capitalist Development. New Haven: Yale University Press.

Guisinger, S.E. and Associates 1985 Investment Incentives and Performance Requirement. New York: Praeger Publishers.

Harbison, J.R. 1996 Cross-Border Alliances in the Age of Collaboration. Available at ***http://www.bah.com/index.html***, accessed on 12 August 1999.

Heller, J. and K.M. Kauffman 1963 Tax Incentives for Industry in Less Developed Countries. Camb.: Law School of Harvard University.

Henderson, D 1999 The MAI Affair. A Story and its Lessons. London: Royal Institute of International Affairs.

Henkin, L. et al. 1980 International Law, Cases and Materials. St. Paul, Minn: West.

Hennings, K. and W. Samuels (eds) 1990 Neoclassical Economic Theory (1870-1930). Boston: Kluwer Academic Publishers.

Herzfeld, E.O and A. Wilson 1996 Joint ventures. Bristol : Jordans.

Hettne, B. 1990 Development Theory and the Three Worlds. Harlow, Essex, England: Longman Scientific & Technical; New York, N.Y.: Wiley.

Horst 1974 "The Theory of the Firm", in J. Dunning (ed) Economic Analysis and the Multinational Enterprise. London: Allen & Unwin.

Hymer, S.H. 1976 The International Operation of National Firms: A study of Direct Foreign Investment. Cambridge, Mass: MIT Press.

ICSID 1984 "Award on Jurisdiction in the Matter of the Arbitration between Amco Asia Corporation et al. and Indonesia", reproduced in International Legal Materials 23: 351-83.

ICSID 1997 Investment Laws of the World. Dobbs Ferry; New York: Oceana Publication.

ICSID 1998 Investment Treaties. Dobbs Ferr; New York: Oceana Publication.

IMF 1985 Foreign Private Investment in Developing Countries. Occasional Paper No. 33. Washington, D.C.: IMF.

IMF 1987 Annual Report of the Executive Board. Washington, D.C.: IMF.

Indian Council of Scientific and Industrial Research (ICSIR) 1985 "Report on Scientific Studies on the Release Factors Related to Bhopal Toxic Gas Leakage", cited in A.S. Kalelkar 1998 Investigation of Large-Magnitude Incidents: Bhopal as a Case Study. Available at *www.bhopal.com/CaseStudy.html*, accessed on 14 June 2000.

Industry Commission 1992 Review of Overseas Export Measures. Report 22, Appendix B. Canberra: Australian Government Publishing Service.

International Chamber of Commerce 1996 Multilateral Rules for Investment. Document No. 103/179 Rev., Paris: International Chamber of Commerce.

International Confederation of Free Trade Unions 1996a International Labour and Trade: an Anti-protectionist Mechanism for Promoting Basic Workers' Rights in the Global Market, ICFTU Discussion Paper. Brussels: ICFTU.

International Chamber of Commerce 1999 World Business Priorities for a New Round of Multilateral Trade Negotiations: Policy Statement. Paris: International Chamber of Commerce.

International Confederation of Free Trade Unions 1997 International Workers' Rights and Trade: the Need for Dialogue, ICFTU Discussion Paper. Brussels: ICFTU.

International Confederation of Free Trade Unions, Statement to the Ninth United Nations Conference on Trade and Development (UNCTAD IX), Midrand (South Africa), 27 April – 11 May 1996.

International Medical Commission on Bhopal (IMCP) 1996 Bhopal: a Tragic Model of an Industrially Induced Epidemic (Summary Statement). Available at *www.igc.org/trac/bhopal/icmb.html*, accessed on 14 June 2000.

Iran - United States Claims Tribunal 1986 "Interlocutory Award in Case Concerning SEDCO Inc. and National Iranian Oil Company and Iran, March 1986". Reproduced in International Legal Material 25: 629-49.

Irish Commission on Taxation, Direct Taxation 1984 "The Role of Incentives", cited in Y. Hadary 1990 "The Role of Tax Incentives in Attracting Foreign Investment in Selected Developing Countries and the Desirable Policy", International Lawyer 124(1): 121-52.

Jackson, John H 1990 Restructuring the GATT System, London: Pinter.

Jackson, J. 1996 GATT and the world trade organization. London : Pinter.

Jackson, Robert H. 1990 Quasi-States: Sovereignty, International Relations, and the Third World. Cambridge [England]; New York: Cambridge University Press.

Jain, S. 1983 Nationalisation of Foreign Property: a study in North-South dialogue. New Delhi : Deep & Deep.

Joint Statement of NGOs, October 1997, available at *www.mai.flora.org*, accessed on 12 Nivember 1997.

Jomo, K.S. 1996 "Lessons from Growth and Structural Change in the Second-tier East Asian Newly Industrialising Countries", in UNCTAD, East Asian Development: Lessons for a New Global Environment, Study No. 4. Geneva: United Nations.

Kalelkar, A.S. 1998 Investigation of Large-Magnitude Incidents: Bhopal as a Case Study. Available at *www.bhopal.com/CaseStudy.html*, accessed on 14 June 2000.

Kane, E. 1983 Doing your Own Research: Basic Descriptive Research in the Social Sciences and Humanities. Boublin: Turoe; London: Boyars.

Kang, C.S.E. 1997 "US Policies and Greater Regulation of Inward Foreign Direct Investment", International Organization 51(2): 301-33.

Katznelson, I. 1981 City Trenches: Urban Politics and the Patterning of Class in the United States. New York: Pantheon Books.

Kelsey, J. 1999 Reclaiming the Future. New Zealand: Bridget Williams Books.

Kennedy, C.R. 1992 "Relations between Transnational Corporations and Governments of Host Countries: a Look to the Future", Transnational Corporations 1(1): 67-91.

Khor, M, Vital Issues for WTO: Developed and Developing Nations Differ on Need to Discuss Investment Pact Now , The Business Times (Singapore), Friday, December 6, 1996a.

Khor, M, The Effects of FDI, the Need for National Investment Policy and the Issue of Multilateral Investment Framework, paper presented on Global Investment Forum, UNCTAD, 10 October, 1996.

Kim, J.K., S.D. Shim and J. Kim 1995 "The Role of the Government in Promoting Industrialization and Human Capital Accumulation in Korea", in Takatoshi Ito and Anne Krueger (eds) Growth Theories in Light of the East Asian Experience. Chicago: University of Chicago Press.

King, D. 1997 "The Big Polluter and the Constructing of Ok Tedi: Eco-imperialism and Underdevelopment along the Ok Tedi and Fly Rivers of Papua New Guinea", in G. Banks and C. Ballard (eds) The Ok Tedi Settlement: Issues, Outcomes and Implications. Canberra: National Centre for Development Studies, Research School of Pacific and Asian Studies, ANU and Research Management in Asia-Pacific and Asian Studies.

Kirsch, S. 1989 "The Yonggom, the Refugee Camps along the Border and the Impact of the Ok Tedi Mine", Research in Melanesia 13: 30-61.

Klavens, J and A. Zamparutti 1995 Foreign Direct Investment and Environment in Central and Eastern Europe: A Survey. Washington, D.C.: World Bank.

Kline, J.M. 1990 "A New Environment for the Code", in The CTC Reporter 29: 2-4.

Kofele-Kale, N. 1990 "Host-Nation Regulation and Incentives for Private Foreign Investment: A Comparative Analysis and Commentary", North Carolina Jounal of International Law and Commercial Regulation 15: 361-99.

Kojima, K. 1978 Direct Foreign Investment: a Japanese model of multinational business operations. London: Croom Helm.

Krueger, A.O. 1990 "Government Failures in Development". Journal of Economic Perspectives 4(3): 9-23.

Kruger, A.O. 1995 "East Asian Experience and Endogenous Growth Theory", in Takatoshi Ito and Anne Krueger (eds) Growth Theories in Light of the East Asian Experience. Chicago: University of Chicago Press.

Kumar, N. 1996 Foreign Direct Investment and Technology Transfers in Development: A Perspective on Recent Literature, UNU/INTECH, Discussion Paper No. 9606.

Lall, S. 1984 "Transnationals and the Third World: Changing Perceptions", National Westminster Bank Quarterly Review (May 1984): 2-16.

"Law Firm Cries Foul over Landowner Allegations". Post-Courier, 5 May, 1994.

Lerner, N. 1980 The United Nations Convention on the Elimination of All Forms of Racial Discrimination. Alphen Aan Den Rijn : Sijthoff & Noordhoff.

Levinson, A. 1996 "Environmental Regulation and Industry Location: International and Domestic Evidence", in J. Bhagwati and R Hudec (eds) Fair Trade and Harmonisation: Prerequisites for Free Trade? (Two Volumes) 2. Cambridge, Mass: MIT Press.

Ley, R. 1996 "Multilateral Rules to Promote the Liberalisation of Investment Regimes", in OECD Towards Multilateral Investment Rules. Paris: OECD.

Lipstein, K. 1945 "The Place of Calvo Clause in International Law", British Yearbook of International Law 22:130.

Lofland, J. 1971 Analysing Social Settings. USA: Wadsworth Pub.

Lui, Tai-Look and S.K. Chiu 1996 "Interpreting Industrial Restructuring in Hong Kong: State, Market and Institutions", in J. Lele and K, Ofori-Yeboha (eds) Unravelling the Asian Miracle: Explorations in Development Strategies, Geopolitics and Regionalism. Aldershot, UK: Dartmouth Publishing Company.

Malone, M. "Fear and Xenophobia in Silicon Valley" Wall Street Journal, 23 February 1987.

Marshall, A. 1879 The Economics of Industry. London: Macmillan.

Maskus, K.E and D.R. Eby 1993 "Developing New Rules and Disciplines on Trade Related Investment Measures", in R.M. Stein (ed) The Multilateral Trading System: Analysis and Options for Change. Ann Arbor, M.I.: University of Michigan Press.

Maun, A. 1997 "The Impact of the Ok Tedi Mine on the Yonggom People", in G. Banks and C. Ballard (eds) The Ok Tedi Settlement: Issues, Outcomes and Implications. Canberra: National Centre for Development Studies, Research School of Pacific and Asian Studies, ANU and Research Management in Asia-Pacific and Asian Studies.

McLeod, R.M. and R. Garnaut (eds) 1998 East Asia in Crisis: from Being a Miracle to Needing One. London; New York: Routledge.

Mehmet, O. 1978 Economic Planning and Social Justice in Developing Countries. London: Croom Helm.

Mehren and Kourides 1981 "International Arbitration between States and Foreign Private Parties: The Libyan Nationalization Case". American Journal of International Law 75: 476-552.

Miliband, R. 1983 Class Power and State Power. London: Verso.

Minchiello, V., Aroni, R., Timewell, E. & Alexander, R. 1990 In-Depth Interviewing: Researching People. Melbourne: Longman Cheshire.

Mo, J.S. 1996 "China, the World Trade Organization, and the Agreement on Trade-Related Investment Measures", Journal of World Trade 30: 89-113.

Morgenthau, H. 1973 Politics Among Nations: the struggle for power and peace. N.Y.: A.A. Knopf.
Muchliniski, P.T. 1995 Multinational Enterprises and the Law. Oxford: Blackwell Publishers Ltd.
Myrdal, G. 1968 Asian Drama: an Inquiry into the Poverty of Nations. New York: Pantheon.
OECD News Release, Paris, 27 May 1997.
OECD News Release, Paris, 25 March 1998.
OECD News Release, Paris, 28 April 1998.
OECD 1976 The Declaration on International Investment and Multinational Enterprises. Paris: OECD.
OECD 1987 Introduction to the OECD Codes of Liberalisation. Paris: OECD.
OECD 1989 Investment Incentives and Disincentives: Effects on International Investment. Paris: OECD.
OECD 1993 National Treatment for Foreign-Controlled Enterprises. Paris: OECD.
OECD 1994 Jobs Study. Paris: OECD.
OECD 1995 Towards Multilateral Investment Rules. Paris: OECD
OECD 1996 The MAI and the OECD Guidelines for Multinational Enterprises: Briefing Note by TUAC. Paris: OECD.
OECD 1996 Main Features of the MAI (note by the Secretariat). Paris: OECD.
OECD 1996 Multilateral Agreement on Investment: Progress Report by the MAI Negotiating Group. Paris: OECD.
OECD 1998 Commentary to the MAI Negotiating Text (24 April 1998). Paris: OECD.
OECD 1998 The MAI Negotiating Text (24 April 1998). Paris: OECD.
OECD Press Release, Paris, 6 April 2000.
Oh, C 1999 Third World NGOs against New WTO Round. Penang: Third World Network.
Parkins, D.H. 1994 "There are at Least Three Models of East Asian Development". World Development 22(4): 655-661.
Patel, S. 1996 East Asia's Explosive Development: Its Relevance to Theories and Strategies", in J. Lele and K. Ofori-Yegoah (eds) Unravelling the Asian Miracle. Aldershot, UK: Dartmouth.
Paulson, J. 1992 "ICSID's Achievements and Prospects". ICSID Review - Foreign Investment Law Journal 6: 380-99.
Pearson, C. 1976 Implications for the Trade and Investment of Developing Countries of United States Environmental Control. Geneva: United Nations.
Pearson, C. 1987 "Environmental Standards, Industrial Relocation, and Pollution Havens", in C. Pearson (ed) Multinational Corporations, Environment, and the Third World. Durham, NC: Duke University Press.
Peet, R. 1991 Global Capitalism: Theories of Social Development. London; New York : Routledge.
Picciotto, S. 1992 International Business Taxation. London: Weidenfeld and Nicolson.

Picciotto, S. 1998 "Linkages in International Investment Regulation: The Antinomies of the Draft Multilateral Agreement on Investment". University of Pennsylvania Journal of International Economic Law 9(3): 731-68.

Picciotto, S and Mayne, R (eds) 1999 Regulating International Business. Beyond Liberalization. Basingstoke: Macmillan.

Pitelis, C. 1996 "Effective Demand, Output Investment and the Transnational Corporation: an empirical investigation". Scottish Journal of Political Economy 43(2): 192-206.

Porter, M. 1990 The Competitive Advantage of Nations. New York: Macmillan.

Pruzin, D, G. Yerkey & M Felsenthal WTO Seattle Ministerial Fails: Talks to Resume at a Later Date. Available at *http://www.wtowatch.org/library/,* accessed on December 3, 1999.

Raghavan, C. 1996 "Broad Support for a revitalised UNCTAD". Third World Economics 137: 16-31.

Rasiah, R. 1995 Foreign Capital and Industrialization in Malaysia. New York: St. Martin's Press.

Rasiah, R. 1996 "Globalization and Liberalisation in East and Southeast Asia: Implications for Growth, Inequality and Poverty", in UNCTAD Globalization and Liberalization: Effects of International Economic Relations on Poverty. New York; Geneva: United Nations.

Report of the Group of Eminent Persons 1974 The Impact of Multinational Corporations on Development and on International Relations, UN Doc. E/5500/Rev. I, ST/ESA/6, at 55.

Reuber G.L. et al. 1973 Private Foreign Investment in Development. Oxford: Clarendon Press.

Revere Copper and Brass Inc. v. Overseas Private Investment Corporation, 56 I.L.R. 258, at 276.

Roberts, M.W. Export Processing Zones in Mauritius and Jamaica, 1992.

Rosenbaum, H and M. Krockenberger, The Impacts of the Ok Tedi Mine in Papua New Guinea, 1993.

Rothgeb (Jr), J.M. 1995 "Investment Dependence and Political Conflict in Developing Countries: A Comparative Regional Analysis", in S. Chan (ed) FDI in a Changing Global Political Economy. New York: St Martin's Press.

Rothgeb (Jr), J.M. 1996 Foreign Investment and Political Conflict in Developing countries. Westport, Conn.: Praeger.

Rubin, S.J. 1984 "Expropriation as an Attempt to Control Foreign Firms in LDCs: Trends from 1969-1979". International Studies Quarterly 28: 329-48.

Rubin, S.J. 1990 "Corporations, Conduct and Codes: Investment and Trade in the Uruguay Round", The CTC Reporter 29: 16-21.

Rueschemeyer D and P. Evans 1992 "The State and Economic Transformation: Towards an Analysis of the Conditions Underlying Effective Intervention", in L. Putterman and D. Rueschemeyer (eds) State and Market in Development. Boulder: Lynne Rienner Publishers.

Rueschemeyer, D. and L. Putterman 1992 "Synergy or Rivalry", in L. Putterman and D. Rueschemeyer (eds) State and Market in Development. Boulder: Lynne Rienner Publishers.

Safire, W. "Goodbye Mr. Chips". New York Times. 26 January 1987.
Schashter, Oscar 1983 "Sharing the World Resources", in Richard Falk, Friedrich Kratochwil, and Saul H. Mendlovitz (eds), International Law: a Contemporary Perspective. Boulder: Westview Press.
Schashter, Oscar 1986 "Concepts and Realities in the New Law of the Sea", in Giulio Pontecorvo (ed) The New Order of the Oceans: the Advent of a Managed Environment. New York: Columbia University Press.
Schwarzenberger, G. 1948 "The Province of Standards in International Economic law", International Law Quarterly 2: 402-420.
Schwarzenberger, G. 1969 Foreign Investment and International Law. London: Stevens.
Shihata, I. 1986 "Towards a Greater Depoliticization of Investment Disputes: The Role of ICSID and MIGA". ICSID Rev. Foreign Investment Law Journal 1: 1-25.
Shihata, I. 1991 "Promotion of Foreign Direct Investment - A General Account, with Particular Reference to the Role of the World Bank Group". ICSID Review 6: 484-509.
Shihata, I.F.I. 1992 "Guidelines on the Treatment of Foreign Direct Investment Issued by the Development Committee", ICSID Review - Foreign Investment Law Journal 7(2): 297-306.
Singh, A. 1996 "Savings, Investment and the Corporation in the East Asian Miracle", in UNCTAD, East Asian Development: Lessons for a New Global Environment. Study No. 9. Geneva: United Nations.
Singh, R.D. 1988 "The Multinationals' Economic Penetration, Growth and Industrial Output and Domestic Savings in Developing Countries: Another Look", Journal of Development Studies pp. 35-82.
Skowronkel, S. 1982 Building a New American State: the Expansion of National Administrative Capacities (1877-1920). Cambridge; New York: Cambridge University Press.
Smith, D.N. 1992 "Foreign Investment in Natural Resources: What Can Go Wrong", in H.P. Kee et al. (eds) Current Developments in International Investment Law. Singapore: Butterworths.
Smith, T. 1986 "The Underdevelopment of Development Literature", in A. Kholi (ed) The State and Development in the Third World. Princeton, N.J.: Princeton University Press.
Solomon, D and D.H. Mirsky 1990-91 "Direct Foreign Investment in the Carribean: A Legal and Policy Analysis", North-Western Journal of International Law and Business 11: 257-92.
Song, T.K. "US Action on Investment Principles Stalls APEC Progress in Jakarta". The Straits Times, 10 November 1994.
Sornarajah, M. 1986 "State Responsibility and Bilateral Investment Treaties". Journal of World Trade 20: 79-98.
Sornarajah, M. 1986 The Pursuit of Nationalised Property. Dordrecht ; Boston: Martinus Nijhoff.
Sornarajah, M. 1994 The International Law on Foreign Investment. Cambridge; New York: Cambridge University Press, Grotius Publications.

Soskice, David. 1999 "Divergent Production Regimes: Coordinated and Uncoordinated Market Economies in the 1998s and 1990s", in H. Kitschelt, et al. (eds) Continuity and Change in Contemporary Capitalism. Cambridge: Cambridge University Press.

South Centre 1997 FDI, Development and the New Global Economic Order. Geneva: South Centre.

Speech by Mr. Neil Hyden, Treasury (Australia), to the 22nd International Trade Law Conference, Canberra, 27 October 1995.

Steiner, H.J and P. Alston 1996 International Human Rights in Context. Oxford: Oxford University Press.

Stephane, A. 1978 The state and society: Peru in comparative perspective. Princeton, N.J.: Princeton University Press.

Summers, 1932-33 "The Calvo Clause", Virginia Law Review 19: 459.

Taylor, M. 1997 "Putting Ok Tedi in Perspective", in Banks, G and C. Ballard (eds) The Ok Tedi Settlement: Issues, Outcomes and Implications. Canberra: National Centre for Development Studies, Research School of Pacific and Asian Studies, ANU and Research Management in Asia-Pacific and Asian Studies.

"The Non-governmental Order: will NGOs democratise, or merely disrupt, global governance?" The Economist, December 11, 1999.

The Ok Tedi Settlement and Text of the Agreement 1997 in Banks, G and C. Ballard (eds) The Ok Tedi Settlement: Issues, Outcomes and Implications. Canberra: National Centre for Development Studies, Research School of Pacific and Asian Studies, ANU and Research Management in Asia-Pacific and Asian Studies.

The Parliament of the Commonwealth of Australia 1999 Multilateral Agreement on Investment: Final Report (Report 18). Canberra: Commonwealth of Australia.

Third World Resurgence, No. 90/91, Feb-March 1998.

Timberger, E. K. 1978 Revolution from Above. New Brunswick, N.J.: Transaction Books.

Turcon, R.J. 1993 Foreign Direct Investment in the United States. London: Sweet & Maxwell.

UN General Assembly Resolution Resolution 824 (IX) of 11 Dec. 1954, in UN Resolutions Series, Vol. 4 (1954-56).

UNCTAD 1992 The Determinants of Foreign Direct Investment: a Survey of the Evidence. Geneva: United Nations.

UNCTAD 1993 World Investment Report. New York; Geneva: United Nations.

UNCTAD 1996 World Investment Report. New York; Geneva: United Nations.

UNCTAD 1996a International Investment Instruments: a Compendium. Vol. I-III. New York; Geneva: United Nations.

UNCTAD 1997 World Investment Report. New York; Geneva: United Nations.

UNCTAD 1998 World Investment Report. New York; Geneva: United Nations.

UNCTAD 1999 World Investment Report. New York; Geneva: United Nations.

UNCTAD/ILO 1988 Economic and Social Effects of Multinational Enterprises in Export Processing Zones. Geneva: ILO.

UNCTC 1988 Bilateral Investment Treaty. London: Graham and Trotman.

Union Carbide Corporation (UCC) 1985 Bhopal Methyl Isocyanate Investigation Team Report. Danbury, Connecticut: Union Carbide.

United Nations 1995 Social Development Summit Declaration and Program of Action. New York; Geneva: United Nations.

United Nations 1996 Midrand Declaration and a Partnership for Growth and Development. TD/377, 24 May 1996. New York; Geneva: United Nations.

United Nations Centre on Transnational Corporations 1988 The United Nations Code of Conduct for Transnational Corporations. New York: United Nations.

United Nations Centre on Transnational Corporations 1992 The Determinants of Foreign Investment. New York: United Nations.

United Nations Commission on Transnational Corporations 1976 Report of the Second Session, UN Doc. E/C.10/16 annex 1-4, 1976. New York: United Nations.

United Nations Commission on Transnational Corporations 1988 Bilateral Investment Treaties, London : Published in co-operation with the United Nations Centre on Transnational Corporations by Graham & Trotman.

United Nations Environment Programme Bankers to Link Environment and Financial Performance, Press Release, New York, May 1997.

United Nations Environment Programme 1996 Financial Services Initiative. Issue 1. Geneva: UNEP.

United Nations International Law Commission 1958 Yearbook of the International Law Commission, Vol. II. New York : United Nations.

United Nations 1993 Transnational Corporations from Developing Countries. Geneva: United Nations.

United Nations 1998 Debt Situation of the Developing Countries as of Mid-1998. Report by the Secretary-General at the 53rd Session of the UN General Assembly, 11 September 1998.

USA-BIAC Committee on International Investment and Multinational Enterprises 1975 A Review of Standards and Guidelines for International Business Conduct. New York: USA-BIAC.

Vagts, D. 1990 "Protecting Foreign Investment: An International Law Perspective", in C.D. Wallace (ed) Foreign Direct Investment in the 1990s: a New Climate in the Third World. Dordrecht; Boston: Martinus Nijhoff.

Vernon, V. 1966 "International Investment and International Trade". Quarterly Journal of Economics 80(2): 190-207.

Wade, R. 1990 Governing the Market: Economic Theory and the Role of Government in East Asian Industrialization. Princeton, N.J.: Princeton University Press.

Wallace, C.D. 1983 Legal Control of Multinational Enterprises. The Hague; Boston: Martinus Nijhoff.

Wallerstein, I.M. 1974 "The Rise and Future Demise of the World Capitalist System", Comparative Studies in Society and History 16: 387-415.

Warr, P.G. 1998 "Case Studies: The Troubled Economies – Thailand", in McLeod, R.M. and R. Garnaut (eds) East Asia in Crisis: from Being a Miracle to Needing One. London; New York: Rouledge.

Warshofsky, F. 1989 The Chip War: the Battle for the World of Tomorrow. New York: Scribner.

Wegen, G. 1985 "Dispute Settlement and Arbitration", in S.J. Rubin and R.W. Nelson (eds) International Investment Disputes: Avoidance and Settlement. St Paul: West Publishing.

Wells, J. 1986 "Investment Incentives: an Unnecessary Debate". The CTC Report 22: 58-60.

Westphal, L. 1990 "Industrial Policy in an Export-Propelled Economy: Lessons from South Korea's Experience". Journal of Economic Perspectives 4(3): 41-59.

White, G., Nationalisation of Foreign Property, 1961.

Wight, M. 1978 Power Politics. Leicester: Leicester University Press.

White, G. (ed) 1988 Developmental State in East Asia. Houndmills, Basingstoke, Hampshire: Macmillan Press in association with the Institute of Development Studies, University of Sussex.

World Bank 1992 "World Bank Guidelines on the Treatment of Foreign Investment", reproduced in International Legal Materials 31: 1379-84.

World Bank 1993 The East Asian Miracle: Economic Growth and Public Policy. New York. : Oxford University Press.

World Bank 1995 World Development Report. Washington, D.C.: World Bank.

World Bank 1997 World Development Report. Washington, D.C.: World Bank.

World Wide Fund for Nature, The OECD Multilateral Agreement on Investment (MAI), Briefing, October, 1996.

World Wide Fund for Nature, The OECD Multilateral Agreement on Investment (MAI), Briefing, March 1997.

WTO 1996 Singapore Ministerial Declaration, WT/MIN(96)DEC. Geneva: WTO.

WTO 1996 Trade and Foreign Investment, Annual Report. Geneva: WTO.

WTO 1997 Working Group on the Relationship between Trade and Investment – Work Undertaken in other Intergovernmental Organisations, WT/WGTI/W/8. Geneva: WTO.

WTO 1997a Working Group on the Relationship between Trade and Investment - Submission by Hong Kong, China, WT/WGTI/W10. Geneva: WTO.

WTO 1998 General Council – Minute of Meeting Held in the Centre William Rappard on 9-11 and 18, December 1998. WT/GC/M/32. Geneva: WTO.

WTO 1998 Report of the Working Group on the Relationship between Trade and Investment to the General Council. WT/WGTI/2. Geneva: WTO.

WTO 1999 EC Approach to Trade and Investment: Communication from the European Communities. WT/GC/W/245. Geneva: WTO.

WTO, Preparation for the 1999 Ministerial Conference – Agreement on Investment – Communication from Japan, 1999a.

WTO, Press Release, 15 December 1996, Geneva.

WTO, Remarks of Ambassador Charlene Barshevsky (Closing Plenary Session), December 3, 1999a.

WTO, The WTO Trade-off, Issue No.3, December 11, 1996.

Yelpaala, K. 1985 "In Search of Effective Policies for Foreign Direct Investment: Alternatives to Tax Incentive Policies", Northwestern Journal of International Law and Business 7: 208-66.

Yue, C.S. 1986 "Direct Foreign Investment and Industrialisation Process in Singapore", in L. Chong-Yah and P.J. Lloyd (eds) Singapore: Resource and Growth. Singapore; New York: Oxford University Press.

Index

For Product Safety Concerns and Information please contact our EU representative GPSR@taylorandfrancis.com Taylor & Francis Verlag GmbH, Kaufingerstraße 24, 80331 München, Germany

Batch number: 10726009

Printed by Printforce, the Netherlands